# Baltic Ferries
Bruce Peter

Published by:
**Ferry Publications**, PO Box 33, Ramsey, Isle of Man IM99 4LP
Tel: +44 (0) 1624 898445   Fax: +44 (0) 1624 898449
E-mail: ferrypubs@manx.net   Website: www.ferrypubs.co.uk

# Introduction

In summer, Mariehamn in the Åland Islands is an idyllic little town, surrounded by coniferous forest and by inlets of clear, tranquil water. The lofty masts of the preserved full-rigger *Pommern* form an impressive backdrop to the modern harbour and remind the visitor that the town's residents have long had a close affinity with the sea. Indeed, the captain-owners of Mariehamn were amongst the last to trade out East with large cargo-carrying sailing ships. These hardy men and their equally hardy crews went to sea for months and sometimes years at a time and this tradition finally ended only in the early 1950s.

Not so many years later, the first car ferries appeared on the Baltic and, even today, many of these are registered in Mariehamn and crewed by Åland Islanders. Two of the largest Baltic cruise and ferry operators, the Viking Line and the Birka Line, have their headquarters there.

Just after noon every day, a succession of large streamlined funnels appears above the dense pine forest which reaches right to the water's edge and reflects bottle-green in the shallows around the rocky outcrops of the archipelago. As the approaching ships draw nearer, their bulky masses of superstructure loom above the surrounding land and seascape with deck upon deck of windows glinting in the early afternoon sunlight. These are the super-ferries – ships that are not only among the largest and most advanced of their kind in the world but also a socio-cultural phenomenon unto themselves, transporting many thousands of Swedes and Finns every week on escapist binges of eating, drinking, dancing, gambling and shopping.

Firstly, it is the turn of the predominately white- and blue-liveried Silja Line ferries, the *Silja Europa* and the *Galaxy*, to dock briefly. The former is arriving from Stockholm *en route* to Turku and the latter is on the same routeing, but heading in the opposite direction. They glide serenely past the coastal walkway, their white hulls reflecting in ripples as the wash from their propellers laps the shore. The *Silja Europa*, in particular, is enormous – a floating pleasure palace, twelve decks high and filled with every kind of entertainment and distraction. Around her two main saloon decks, there is a continuous expanse of tinted floor-to-ceiling glazing, through which crowds of passengers can be discerned, gazing out at the passing scene but cocooned in an environment of temperate air-conditioned comfort. The *Galaxy* is only slightly smaller and of more conventional design but, to compensate for this, her entire hull and superstructure are decorated all over with a mural by an Estonian surrealist artist, Navitrolla, depicting white clouds against a blue sky on the superstructure with animals, such as giraffes and zebras, plodding through snowfields painted on the hull topsides.

The two ships turn around nimbly, each within her own length, and they sidle up to their berths. A few cars drive off through the stern doors and, after a few minutes, a handful of passengers emerge from the terminal. The overwhelming majority of those disembarking, however, walk straight from one vessel to the other along glazed elevated walkways. They are 'day trippers' who will return whence they have come, having enjoyed a day at sea and having stocked up with large quantities of duty-free booze and tobacco. With their returning passengers swapped over, the *Silja Europa* and the *Galaxy* continue on their way to Turku and to Stockholm respectively. No sooner have they left the confines of the harbour, though, than a further pair of ferries materializes – the *Amorella* and the *Isabella*, painted in the lipstick-red livery of Viking Line, and the same procedure takes place all over again.

Once the Viking Line ships have set sail, there is an afternoon lull, broken only by the regular calls of the shuttle ferry *Rosella* to Kapellskär, the closest Swedish port to the Åland Islands. From midnight onwards, activity picks up again as first the night ferries to Helsinki and Tallinn pass through, followed by those sailing to Turku. After these have left, the ships involved in the 22-hour cruise trade from Stockholm arrive and tie up overnight – the *Cinderella*, the glitzy *Birka Paradise* and the veteran *Birger Jarl* which is the favourite of Stockholm's pensioners. Each one of these ships has her own market niche and loyal following.

For sure, the Baltic super-ferries have brought a great deal of prosperity and employment to the Åland Islands where they have become a part of the everyday scene. Although the locals may have become blasé about their presence, for shipping historians and design commentators these are significant vessels which have set important trends for developments elsewhere. For the first time, this book examines the evolution of their design, their operation and the cultural milieu from which they have emerged; it concentrates on ferry services to and from Finland and a future work will examine ferry operations in the Southern Baltic.

**BALTIC FERRIES**

# Contents

Introduction ............................................................................................. 2

Chapter 1   A History of the Baltic Ferry Scene ................................................ 6

Chapter 2   Evolution of the Baltic Super-Ferry ............................................... 35

Chapter 3   Recession, Bankruptcy and Disaster ............................................. 73

Chapter 4   The Champagne Economy and Mini-Cruise Culture .................... 86

Chapter 5   Destination Tallinn ...................................................................... 95

Bibliography ........................................................................................... 118

Produced and Designed by Lily Publications Ltd

Printed and bound by Gomer Press Ltd., Wales

© Ferry Publications 2009

All right reserved. No part of this book or any of the photographs may be reproduced or transmitted in any form or by any means, electronic or mechanical, including photocopying, recording or by any means of information storage and retrieval system without written permission from the publisher, save only for brief extracts which may be used solely for the purpose of review.

The **Finnjet** approaches Helsinki from Tallinn during icy winter weather in February 2004. *(Bruce Peter)*

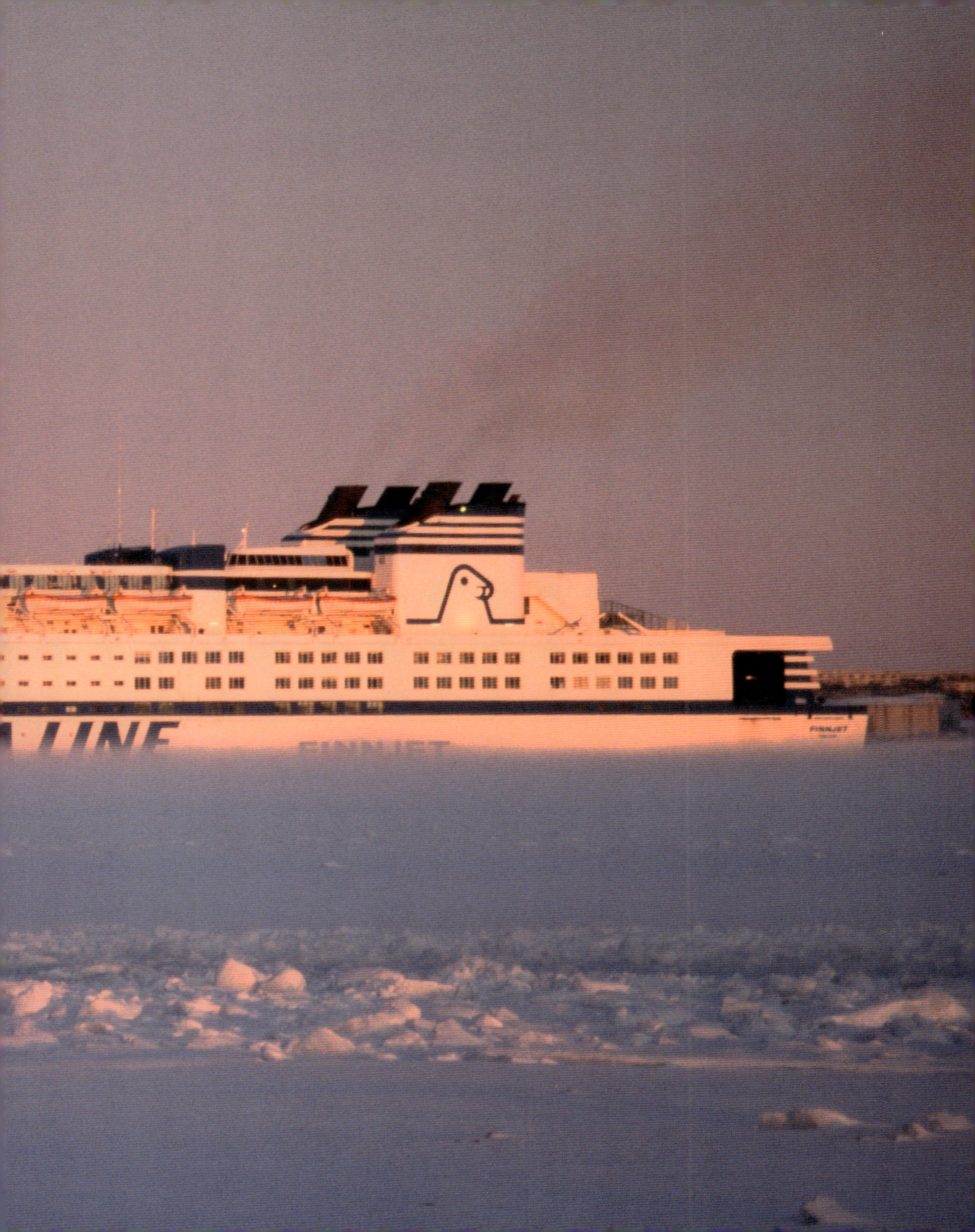
LINE

# CHAPTER ONE

# A History of the Baltic Ferry Scene

The Northern Baltic has witnessed more dramatic changes during the last forty years than any other area of ferry activity and this remarkable expansion in traffic between Finland and Sweden has centred on the roughly parallel routes linking the capital cities, Stockholm and Helsinki, plus the link from Stockholm via Mariehamn in the Åland Islands to Turku in Finland. Subsidiary routes have been run at various times from Naantali in Finland, via Mariehamn, to Kapellskär and Stockholm in Sweden. More recently, since the latter 1990s, a network of routes has been developed from Stockholm, Helsinki and Kapellskär to Tallinn in Estonia.

It was only in 1959 that serious attempts were made to establish roll on-roll off services and a further two years passed before the first purpose-built car ferries made their debut. Only three decades later, the ten largest ferries yet constructed anywhere figured prominently in this traffic. The enormous investment in new tonnage has been rewarded by ever-increasing business and, although it is estimated that more than the entire population of Finland has to make at least one crossing per year to achieve the present figures, the companies are confident that there is still potential for further growth in the ferry business – their high standard of onboard facilities providing as much a social and recreational amenity as pure transportation.

The giant ferries of today conceal a fundamental climatic problem – the sub-zero temperatures which once closed the Baltic shipping lanes for long periods of the year. The first solution in the 1900s was the steam-powered ice-breaker which kept the channels open at least for parts of the winter. Now the big, powerful ferries are sufficient in all but the worst conditions to do the job for themselves. Nevertheless, away from the moderating influence of the westerlies and the depressions they bring, the colder conditions are. Even in the middle of winter, ferries continue to plough through the ice and, despite sub-zero temperatures, the lines claim that consistently high occupancy levels are maintained. The Stockholm-Helsinki route is regarded as the flagship operation of each line – accounting for about 40% of trade. The crossing takes a leisurely 14 hours overnight. In contrast, the Stockholm-Mariehamn-Turku service is intensively operated with both day and night sailings in both directions, each ship making a complete return crossing in every 24-hour period. Sailing from Stockholm, the ferries have to thread their way through the narrow channels between the thousands of islands of the archipelago. This voyage is stunningly beautiful with pine forests growing to the water's edge. Nestling among the trees are groups of brightly painted wooden houses and small harbours. The splendour of the scenery is a big attraction for tourists but navigating a large ship through these restricted waters requires the utmost skill on the part of the helmsman. Until relatively recently, he was guided in many places only by stakes in the water which indicated sudden

Rush hour at Mariehamn: the outward-bound Silja Line ferries **Galaxy** and **Silja Europa** pass the inward-bound Viking Line vessel **Isabella** in August 2008. *(Bruce Peter)*

The FÅA steamer **Oihonna**. *(Ambrose Greenway collection)*

The famous **Ariadne** - one of the FÅA's longest-lived steamers. *(Bruce Peter collection)*

changes in the channel depth and required split-second timing of adjustments of course. This was difficult enough on a fine summer's day but much more so in an autumn gale, or in the freezing fog and ice of winter. To make matters worse, wind forces the thick ice floes together between the islands where it is trapped, creating hard pack-ice. Today, satellite navigation and Global Positioning Systems have made life easier for Baltic ferry captains. Even so, groundings still occasionally occur.

After four hours slowly cruising through the islands, two hours of fast sailing are possible across the open waters of the Åland Sea. The Baltic has relatively fresh water and, although usually placid, storms can be sudden and ferocious and even a breeze produces short, high waves. Next, Mariehamn on the Åland Islands is reached. After a twenty-minute stop, the ship sails on through another archipelago to Turku. There is less than two hours in port at either terminal.

In winter, these two main trunk routes between Stockholm and Helsinki and between Stockholm and Turku remain in operation thanks to the ice-breaking capabilities and sheer size of the ships themselves. It is only after retiring for the night in an outside cabin, once the noises of the ship and the night close in, that the differences become really noticeable. Over the sounds of the air-conditioning system, the occasional jolt is felt and the sound of scraping, as against rocks, is heard. As night passes, these noises become louder and more frequent and a glance out of the window reveals in the reflections of the ship's lights not sea and waves but brilliant white buckled ice as far as the eye can see. As the ship moves forward the great ice-floes are forced up and over so that they fall back on themselves to pile up alongside the hull. Temperatures in winter can drop as low as -20° C – a tolerable figure as long as the weather is still and dry – and are a pleasantly warm 15-25° C at the height of summer. Recent Baltic car ferries are designed with fully-enclosed decks and numerous technical adaptations to suit local geographical and climatic conditions.

**Initial Developments**

Since the early 1960s, the rival Viking Line and Silja Line co-operatives have dominated Baltic ferry traffic. More recently, in the 1990s, Tallink emerged and grew rapidly as a third serious competitor, later absorbing Silja Line in 2006.

Passenger connections between Sweden, Finland, Germany and the Baltic States have a history going back to the days of sail. The

Rederi AB Svea's steamer **Brynhild**, built in 1935 by Burmeister & Wain in Copenhagen and, from 1964, one of the first passenger ships in the Stena Line fleet. *(Bruce Peter collection)*

The FÅA steamer **Aallotar** went to the Soviet Union in 1945. *(Ambrose Greenway collection)*

The **Wellamo** survived in the FÅA's fleet until the latter 1960s. *(Ambrose Greenway collection)*

first sea links between Finland and Sweden were developed in the Medieval period, allowing the fishermen of Turku to export their catches to comparatively wealthy Sweden. Thereafter, Baltic schooners traded from port to port in summer and acted as an important lifeline to the communities scattered across the 24,000 islands of the archipelago. In winter the sea ices over and, until recently, ports in the north and eastern Baltic had to be closed between November and March.

Finland, however, sat in a dangerous position between two mighty regional powers – Sweden and Russia – and both countries had interests in Finnish territory. In 1809, Russia invaded Finland, beating the Swedes, and so Finland became an autonomous Grand Duchy within the Russian Empire. Czar Alexander made Helsinki the Finnish capital in 1812. At that time, the population was only around 3,500, but Helsinki expanded, especially once a new urban plan was drawn up by the visionary local architect Johan Albrecht Ehrenström for the first stage in the development of the modern port city Helsinki has become today. The Russian invasion was, however, the first of a number of incursions from the East to affect Finland in the modern era, but the Finns fought hard to retain their identity. As the country began to industrialize in the mid-nineteenth century, it was in a good position to trade with both its dominant neighbours.

Steamship services across the Baltic first began in 1821 when Samuel Owen introduced the paddle steamer *Stockholm* on the Stockholm-Turku route. This initiative continued for seven seasons, the ship carrying passengers, mail and general cargo between Sweden and Finland. Later, in 1835, the Åbo Ångfartygs Bolag (Turku Steamship Company) was founded in Turku, commencing operations in 1836 with the paddle steamer *Fürst Menschikoff*, an iron-hulled vessel built in Turku using machinery and paddle wheels imported from Sweden. Not only was this the first Finnish-owned steamer to operate regular services from Turku to Degerby and Stockholm, but she also marked the foundation of the modern Finnish shipbuilding industry. A second paddler, the *Storfursten*, was acquired in 1837 to open a steamer route to Helsinki, Tallinn and Kronstadt (later, St Petersburg), but this vessel was built in England. The *Finland* followed in 1842.

In 1837, a northerly steamer service began across the Gulf of Bothnia between Umeå and Vaasa, using first the *Norrland* and, later, the *Örnsköld*. Subsequently, a number of entrepreneurs attempted to run summer routes across the Northern Baltic, utilizing a variety of tonnage.

As Finland industrialized, a number of entrepreneurs began thinking seriously about opening regular steamer services to the wider world. Russia, Finland's main trading partner at that time, was viewed by many as being an uncertain market, given that commerce took place in the context of Russia's apparently vastly superior military power. To be guaranteed wealth, stability and freedom, Finland would need to fend for herself. As well as exporting agricultural and forestry products, the transportation of emigrants from both Finland and Russia to North America was also a growing trade, handled mainly by the Thingvalla Line via Sweden.

In Turku, the industrialist Carl Korsman did much to develop business as a director of a variety of firms. For example, he founded the Åbo Mekaniska Verkstad (Turku Mechanical Shipyard), later known as the Chricton-Vulcan Shipyard and, later still, as Wärtsilä. Thereafter, Korsman moved south to Hanko, a port at the entrance to the Gulf of Finland that was slightly less affected by winter ice than either Turku or Helsinki and which, furthermore, was rail-connected in 1873. In 1878, Korsman introduced a steamer service from there to Stockholm using the *Express*.

The origins of Silja Line go back to 1883 when Captain Lars Krogius founded the Finland Steamship Company (Finska

The **Bore III**, the most traditional-looking of the three Olympic ships. *(Bruce Peter collection)*

Rederi AB Svea's **Birger Jarl**. *(Bruce Peter collection)*

The FÅA's **Aallotar** at Skeppsbron Quay in Stockholm in the mid-1950s. *(Bruce Peter collection)*

The Bore steamer **Bore**. *(Ambrose Greenway collection)*

Ångfartygs Aktiebolaget, or FÅA, but known since 1976 as Effoa, the phonetic version of 'FÅA'). The Line introduced a number of services from Helsinki to other Baltic ports and to the United Kingdom. The company's first ship, the *Sirius*, began operating on the lengthy Helsinki-Turku-Hull route in 1884, followed by a sister vessel, the *Orion*. Steamer services from Helsinki were run between March and November each year. The port of Helsinki was closed during the winter months due to the Gulf of Finland being iced up.

In 1894, FÅA bought out Carl Korsman's operation from Hangö, including his ship, the *Express*. Four years later, two new steamers, the *Wellamo* and *Oihonna* which were built by Gourlay Bros & Co in Dundee, were introduced by FÅA between Hangö and Stockholm. Later, in 1898, the *Arcturus* arrived. This remarkable, sturdy vessel, initially intended for cargo and passenger services from Helsinki and Turku to Copenhagen and Hull, continued in FÅA service until 1960 when, belatedly, she was sold for scrap.

Meanwhile, in Turku, Ångfartygs AB Bore was founded in 1897, taking its name from the Nordic God of Winter, King Bore. A Turku-Stockholm service was opened in 1898, using the purpose-built steamer *Bore* which was delivered from Helsingør's Jernskibs og Maskinbyggeri in Denmark. A second steamer, the *Bore II*, arrived in 1900.

In 1904 FÅA entered into an agreement with Bore to co-operate in running steamer services across the Baltic to Sweden. Later, in 1909, the two companies briefly fell out and went into competition instead but, by 1910, they had reached a satisfactory joint agreement to work together again. The reality of running steamers in the difficult Baltic environment made collaboration their best option.

Progress was hampered by the near five-year suspension of passenger steamer services from Helsinki brought about by the First World War and by the Finnish Civil War (1914-1918). As Finland lost 34 vessels in the conflict, including three major FÅA vessels – the *Titania*, *Urania* and *Wellamo* – Rederi AB Svea of Stockholm began their own co-operation with FÅA in 1918 to reopen the Stockholm-Helsinki route. That summer, for the first time, the three companies – FÅA, Bore and Svea – began to market themselves on the Stockholm-Helsinki and Turku routes as 'De Samseglande Rederierna.' Between them, they could also provide a wide network of sailings between Sweden, Finland,

Three passenger steamers lay over at Skeppsbron in Stockholm in the early 1960s: nearest the camera is the **Bore**, with the **Svea Jarl** berthed astern and the **Birger Jarl** in the distance. Note the damaged paintwork on the ships' bows, the result of breaking ice. *(Alistair Deayton collection)*

The River Aura in Turku, with a variety of small passenger ships berthed. In the middle of this view is Silja Line's first passenger ship, the steamer **Silja** (ex **Heimdall**). (*Bruce Peter collection*)

Åland, Denmark, Germany and the UK. In 1922, the three companies jointly bought out an upstart competitor on the Stockholm-Mariehamn-Turku route, Ångfartygs AB Tor based in the Åland Islands, which operated the 1856-vintage steamer *Mailand* (ex *Gute*).

Until 1928, the Stockholm-Helsinki route had been operated entirely by FÅA and by Rederi AB Svea, with Bore steamers restricted to the Stockholm-Turku service. Not surprisingly, Bore's directors regarded this situation as being manifestly unfair as the 'capital cities' link, then as now, was the most prestigious cross-Baltic route – and the most profitable. Despite considerable reluctance on the part of FÅA and Svea, Bore were permitted to place the steamer *Bore II* (ex *Halland*) on the Stockholm-Helsinki route in 1928. Thereafter, all three partners jointly ran both main services.

As a consequence of political and economic instability following the 1929 Wall Street crash and the rise of Stalin in the Soviet Union, 'De Samseglande' used mainly pre-war and second-hand tonnage during the 1930s. Thereafter, services were again severely truncated by the Finno-Russian War and by the Second World War (1939-1945). The Russians demanded the surrender of the newest members of the FÅA and Bore fleets as compensation. Indeed, Soviet President Nikita Kruschev only formally recognized Finland as an independent nation in 1952.

**Post-War Developments**

After the Second World War, a motley collection of frail-looking and elderly steamers, mainly dating from the 1900s, reopened the Stockholm-Helsinki and Stockholm-Turku routes. The finest of these vessels was FÅA's 1914-vintage *Ariadne*, which had been ceded to the Russians but which ran aground *en route* to Leningrad and was abandoned by her new Soviet owners. Rescued by the Finns, rebuilt and lengthened by six metres, the *Ariadne* returned to FÅA service in 1948 and continued sailing until 1969.

In the early 1950s, each of the three Lines ordered a new ship, the hope being that these would enter service in time for the 1952 Helsinki Olympic Games. FÅA's *Aallotar* was built in Helsingør in Denmark, the Bore-owned *Bore III* was constructed by AB Oskarshamns Varv and Rederi AB Svea's *Birger Jarl* was delivered from the Finnboda shipyard at Nacka, both in Sweden. Alas, only the *Aallotar* was delivered in time for the Helsinki Olympics, her half-sisters not being ready until the winter of 1952-53. These new ships were small single-screw steamers of about 3,000 grt each and their traditional appearance, steam power plants and limited passenger facilities, consisting of a restaurant and smoking room in each class, only highlight how radical have been the subsequent changes in Baltic ferry design. These vessels could carry only around 230 passengers in berths with the remainder in 'Deck Class'. There was space for fifteen cars which were loaded by crane.

The 1954 Nordic Passport Union, coupled with growing prosperity and an increase in tourist traffic, brought about discussions between the directors of FÅA, Bore and Svea about the desirability of building car ferries. The three companies' directorates were, however, conservative by instinct and their powerful chairmen were all men in their fifties and sixties with strong views about how passenger ships should be designed. In particular, Bore's Chairman, Hans von Rettig, strongly believed that any vessel worthy of flying his company's houseflag had to be steam-powered and, furthermore, adorned with two traditional steamship funnels, whether or not she actually required them. So far as propulsion was concerned, von Rettig's position was not entirely illogical. Steamships may have been more complex and costly to operate, even in the 1950s, but they were near-silent and, given that the premier Stockholm-Helsinki and -Turku routes were lengthy overnight affairs, passengers would probably have objected to the throbbing sound and inevitable vibrations of diesel motors. Throughout Scandinavia, however, by the 1950s nearly every other shipowner preferred diesel power to steam – and

Silja Line's steamer **Silja** (ex **Heimdall**). (*Ambrose Greenway collection*)

passengers just had to try to sleep as best they could.

During the 1950s, the airlines began to increase their market share, but passenger volumes grew overall, meaning that the steamers remained busy during the summer season. Besides, they conveniently departed from and arrived at Skeppsbron quay in the heart of Stockholm and the Olympia Terminal in central Helsinki, whereas aircraft flew from the urban fringes. Taking the steamer across the Baltic was a costly affair, however, especially in First Class, meaning that there was less of a price advantage in sailing rather than flying than might be imagined. Meanwhile, car ownership grew exponentially, meaning that there was a requirement both for greater vehicle capacity and also for lower fares to attract tourist traffic.

In 1955 a group of Finnish business entrepreneurs announced plans to buy the 1937-vintage Norwegian car ferry *Peter Wessel* and to introduce her on a short mid-Baltic route between Sweden and Finland. This initiative caused the three companies behind 'De Samseglande', who had a monopoly, to announce their own plans for a ferry service and so the independent initiative to acquire the *Peter Wessel* was not pursued in view of the possibility of having to compete with these comparatively large, established shipping companies.

Of the three Lines, FÅA were most keen to see ships with greater car-carrying potential built as soon as practicable. In 1955 their Chairman, Birger Krogius, had a tentative design drawn up for discussion with his counterparts, Emmanuel Högberg of Rederi AB Svea and Hans von Rettig of Bore. Krogius wanted new car-carrying vessels to enter service in 1957. Von Rettig thought that tenders should be invited from possible builders to get some idea of the likely costs involved, whereas Högberg warned that the project would require a minimum of two ships to be constructed to offer an effective service; coming so soon after the 'Olympic Ships', the project was likely to place too much of a strain on the Lines' finances. Thus, the project was not taken forward and the idea was not discussed again at the top level until August 1956. Once again there was stalemate, this time because the three Chairmen could not decide what sort of ferry to build, if any at all. For example, Krogius was convinced of the need for ships with enhanced vehicle capacity, but he thought that ro-ro ferries such as the *Peter Wessel* were inherently dangerous due to their full-width car decks which could allow fire to spread quickly or flooding to bring about a rapid capsize. Instead, he thought that side-loading vessels, able to carry cars and buses in their forward holds, would be a safer solution. (This position paralleled that being taken by Denmark's DFDS at the same time and exemplified by vessels such as the 1957 *Prinsesse Margrethe* and the 1964 *England*.)

What was agreed was the need urgently to respond better to the needs of tourists and budget travellers and to prepare for a future scenario in which car ferries would be purchased. The best way to achieve these aims was jointly to form a fourth shipping line in order to market a 'budget' service distinct from the existing operations of 'De Samseglande' and, thereafter, possibly to use this new company as a means to test car ferry operations. Thus, FÅA, Rederi AB Svea and Bore formed the Silja Shipping Company in 1957. This took its name from the heroine of a book by a Finnish author called F.E. Sillanpää. The first Managing Director was Nils Wetterstein (1914-1999) who was a lawyer by training and had begun his career in shipping as a manager in FÅA before becoming the Deputy Managing Director of Bore in Turku. Between 1957 and 1974, when he retired, Wetterstein developed Silja Line into one of the Baltic's leading ferry operations.

Initially, Silja started with one vessel, the *Silja*, a veteran steamer dating from 1915 which had originally been Rederi AB Svea's *Heimdall*. This operated three round-trips per week between Stockholm and Turku in the summer season and one per week in spring and autumn, being laid up like all the other Baltic steamers through the winter months. During the first season, an average of 168 passengers and 14 cars was carried per trip. With ticket prices deliberately set lower than those of the more upmarket steamers in FÅA, Bore and Svea colours, the service nevertheless made a loss. No wonder – the old *Silja* was inefficient (cars had to be crane-loaded on board) and had very spartan accommodation. 'Deck Class' meant exactly that. The vessel was, however, merely a stop-gap measure until new car ferry tonnage could be designed, ordered, built and delivered – a process which would take some time to finance and arrange.

Notwithstanding the *Silja*'s obvious limitations, her inauguration marked the beginning of the Silja Line brand which later was applied to all of the FÅA, Svea and Bore-operated Baltic ferries. It proved to be a great success – especially once new purpose-built car ferries were introduced. Indeed, by 1962 passenger figures had trebled on the route network served by the consortium's ships.

**The Car Ferry Pioneers**

Back in the latter 1950s, the main ferry routes between Sweden and Finland were apparently so secure in the control of the FÅA, Bore and Rederi AB Svea that serious doubt might have been expressed about the judgement of anyone rash enough to try to compete. Yet, within a week at the beginning of 1959, two independent rival operations got under way. One was started by two Åland seafarers – Captain Gunnar Eklund (1916-2009) and his close friend, Captain Henning Rundberg (1919-1973). While the long-established FÅA/Bore/Svea consortium was still dithering about the future direction of its trade in the light of airline competition and increasing car ownership, Eklund and Rundberg were convinced that car ferry services on the shortest and most direct routes between ports in Stockholm's outer archipelago and Finland ought to be developed.

Rederi AB Vikinglinjen was the brainchild of Gunnar Eklund who returned home to the Åland Islands after a lengthy seafaring career in 1957 to convalesce after suffering from a lung condition. While lying in bed recovering, he hatched a plan to acquire a suitable ship to open a car ferry service from Sweden to Finland, via the Åland Islands. During his years at sea, he had been able to follow the progress of ferry operators elsewhere in the world and he became convinced that ferry services between Sweden and Finland would be successful. Besides, Eklund reasoned that the airlines could never carry cars. Car ownership in Finland and Sweden was doubling every year in the late 1950s and early 1960s and the road network was also expanding. Once fully recovered, Eklund discussed his ideas with his old seafaring acquaintance, Captain Rundberg. Back in 1937-38, the two men

Crowds look on as the **Viking** arrives at Graddö and lowers her stern door to load cars. *(Ambrose Greenway collection)*

had sailed together on board Gustaf Erikson's famous four-masted barque *Pamir*, making no less than three passages round Cape Horn. Later on, in 1942-43, they shared student lodgings while studying at the Åland Maritime College.

Rundberg was a relatively wealthy man who had already been planning to make a number of new shipping investments; he told Eklund that he too had been toying with the idea of opening a ferry route across the mid-Baltic and that he was keen to invest in such a project.

Although Eklund and Rundberg believed wholeheartedly in the project and were well aware of the risks they were taking, neither of them had any obvious business experience in short-sea shipping. The first company office was in a spare room in Eklund's home, where his wife spent many hours organizing the work that lay ahead. The first potential candidate for conversion to a ferry became known to Eklund through a contact in Brighton, England. The ship in question was the 1,765 grt *Dinard*, a 1924-vintage railway steamer. Eklund and Rundberg augmented their life savings with a loan from the Bank of Åland and she was duly purchased for £30,000 and renamed the *Viking*. The vessel was taken to Aalborg in Denmark where she was converted. On entering service for Viking Line, she had a capacity of 900 passengers and 85 cars. A speed of 19 knots could be attained. She began sailing on 1 June 1959 on the Gräddö-Mariehamn-Korpoo-Parainen route. The Swedish newspapers hailed her as being 'the largest and finest ship ever to call at the village pier in Gräddö'.

Amongst the larger investors in Rederi AB Vikinglinjen was another Åland Islands-based shipping entrepreneur, Algot Johansson (1898-1986), Chairman of Rederi AB Sally, Finland's

The **Dinard** in the Channel, off the English coast. *(John Hendy collection)*

The **Slite**, converted to carry passengers and cars. *(Micke Asklander collection)*

The converted Rederi AB Slite coaster **Boge** at Mariehamn. *(Micke Asklander collection)*

The Southern Railway's **Brittany**, later Viking Line's **Ålandsfärjan**. *(John Hendy collection)*

largest privately-owned shipping company, which was headquartered in Mariehamn. After working in a local ship repair yard during his teenage years, Johansson emigrated in 1921 to America, where he made money during the 1920s economic boom which preceded the Wall Street Crash. He then re-invested what he had earned in a number of shipping lines, returning to the Åland Islands in the early 1930s and, thereafter, founding first Rederi AB Havnia in 1935 then, in 1937, Rederi AB Sally; this took its name from the local author Sally Salminen, whose 1936 novel 'Katrina' had been critically acclaimed and whose writing Johansson also admired. Rederi AB Sally was principally an oil tanker company and it was profits from this deep-sea trade which Johansson invested in Rederi AB Vikinglinjen and its successor companies in which his Rederi AB Sally gradually gained a controlling influence.

Some years before Rederi AB Vikinglinjen had been founded, Johansson had investigated the possibility of investing in a ferry link from Sweden to Finland, which he reasoned would be bound to be lucrative. Ever since the mid-1950s he had tried to persuade Birger Krogius of FÅA to begin just such a service and to allow him to buy shares in it. Although Krogius was indeed planning to introduce ferries as part-owner of Silja Line, Johansson's offer of a cash investment in that company was not accepted and hence he backed Rederi AB Vikinglinjen instead. The largest private shareholder, however, was Captain Henning Rundberg and so, naturally, he was elected Managing Director rather than Johansson.

Only six days later another ferry pioneer, Carl Bertil Myrsten (1910-2000), who was from a prominent shipping family based at Slite on the island of Gotland, was also preparing to introduce a car ferry between Mariehamn and Simpnäs on the Swedish mainland. He too realized the risky nature of investing in ferry services but he based all his financial calculations on the hope that 40,000 passengers would use the route each season. As the Åland Islands only had about 40,000 tourists a year, many people, especially in the tourist industry, thought that he was being unduly optimistic. However, undaunted, Carl Bertil Myrsten persisted with his scheme. Rederi AB Slite, as his company was known, commenced operations on 5 June 1959. The vessel used was a diminutive motor coaster called the *Slite*. Her cargo holds were converted to carry cars by her original builder, Sölvesborgs Varv.

The service had an inauspicious start as the ship ran aground on the maiden sailing. At first, the picture was gloomy in that only 3,000 passengers travelled in the first month. Many were convinced that financial disaster would follow. By July, however, passenger figures had risen to 25,000 and the initial investment of 170,000 Swedish kronor was recovered. As an interim measure, a second coaster, the *Boge*, was similarly converted into a side-loading ferry.

Rederi AB Vikinglinjen's *Viking* had also exceeded expectations, so much so that the company had ordered a large, new ferry from Hanseatische Werft in Hamburg, West Germany, which went bankrupt when the ship was nearing completion. Vikinglinjen were told that, due to the bankruptcy, it would cost more than expected to finish the ship and, as the Line was only recently established, it

Dressed overall, the **Ålandsfärjan** steams through the archipelago in the early 1960s. *(Viking Line)*

*The somewhat basic landing craft ferry* **Panny**. *(Micke Asklander collection).*

*The* **Rospiggen** *of Eckerö Linjen arriving at Eckerö. (Anders Ahlerup)*

took time to raise the additional capital. Algot Johansson – who was, at this early stage, more of a speculator than a dedicated believer that Vikinglinjen was the only company capable of running ferries – thought that the best solution would be for FÅA to take over the contract. Consequently, once again he tried to persuade his friend Birger Krogius to seize the opportunity and also to accept an investment in the project from Rederi AB Sally, but Krogius refused as his company, as part of Silja Line, already had their own car ferry plans. Weeks later, when Vikinglinjen finally raised the necessary capital, the builder informed them that, in the meantime, the vessel had been sold elsewhere. The purchaser was Finnlines, who introduced her in 1962 as the *Hansa Express* on a new ferry route between Helsinki and Travemünde. Vikinglinjen would need to look elsewhere. To compensate for failing to secure their new flagship, they converted a cargo coaster, the *Panny*, into a third basic ferry of the same primitive type as Myrsten's *Slite* and the *Boge*.

To the North, meanwhile, another new car ferry route linking Sweden and the Åland Islands had opened between Grisslehamn and Eckerö. Even in the latter 1930s, a car ferry had been planned there, but the Second World War intervened and it was not until 1958 that Rederi AB Eckerölinjen was formed. The pioneering ferry *Rospiggen* was ordered from Åsiverken at Åmål in 1959, but the small shipyard had difficulties building the ship which was delayed considerably and, worse still, there were serious design and construction errors. For example, even when unloaded, the plimsoll mark was below the water-line, meaning that the ship had negative deadweight capacity. After only a short time in service with special dispensation from the Swedish authorities, she was sold in 1962 to Italy and replaced by a pre-war double-ended ferry from the Horten-Moss route across the Oslofjord which was refurbished as the *Alandia*. The short-lived *Rospiggen* was, however, the first purpose-built car ferry to operate regularly between a Swedish and a Finnish port.

### Silja Line responds

The long-established steamer companies – FÅA, Bore and Rederi AB Svea – were understandably taken aback by the appearance of so many upstarts with their motley collections of hastily-converted car ferries. As a first step into the car ferry era, in 1959 'De Samseglande' had investigated the possibility of buying for their Silja Line subsidiary an American Great Lakes double-ended car ferry, the *Vacationland*, which traversed the Mackinaw Sound between Lake Michigan and Lake Huron. The *Vacationland* was capacious, if a little strange-looking, but, as she had insufficient ice-breaking capacity, the idea was abandoned and, instead, in December 1959 a contract to build the first of two new car ferries was signed with the Wärtsilä shipyard in Helsinki.

The *Skandia* entered service in 1961 and introduced the capability of loading vehicles through both bow and stern doors to Baltic waters. The ship carried no less than 175 cars, or 100 cars and 20 lorries, in addition to a passenger complement of 1,200. With a grey hull and funnel and a white superstructure, she appeared crisp and purposeful-looking, albeit with rather bluff hull lines. Most significantly, the *Skandia* was a motor ship with two 9-cylinder Wärtsilä-Sulzer diesels powering twin controllable-pitch propellers and giving a respectable 18-knot service speed. This was in contrast to the stately progress made by the old single-screw steamers which continued to form the majority of the 'De Samseglande' fleet. The *Skandia*'s passenger facilities were relatively comfortable and certainly modern in style. There were lounges, a restaurant, a cafeteria, a playroom, a shop to sell tax-free liquor and cigarettes and saloons containing airliner-style reclining chairs, but a low proportion of cabin berths (only 136) as, for most of the year, the ship sailed only during day-time hours between Norrtälje, a town to the north-east of Stockholm, Mariehamn and Turku, making three return crossings per week. Only during the busy July and August holiday season were daily departures offered with day crossings in one direction and night crossings in the other. Thus, for much of the year, the inherent efficiency advantages of car ferry operation initially were under-exploited as the market had yet to catch up with the potential capacity. The 'funnel' was an unusual feature as it actually housed an observation lounge with reclining seats, all exhaust being carried away by a duct at the base of the after mast.

With her more competitive fares and modern, air-conditioned facilities, coupled with the growing attraction of tax-free shopping, the *Skandia* created her own demand and so it was fortunate that her sister ship, the *Nordia*, was already under construction and ready to enter service in May 1962. The old *Silja*, meanwhile, was shifted to Stockholm, from which she made fairly cheap day cruises to Mariehamn and back so that passengers could buy relatively inexpensive tax-free drink and tobacco.

Day trips of this kind took advantage of several local factors. Firstly, although their language and culture is Swedish, the Åland Islands are actually part of Finland; thus tax-free shopping is a big attraction as the voyage, albeit short, is international. Secondly, during the 1960s Sweden's Socialist Government imposed more

Silja Line's first purpose-built car ferry, the **Skandia**. *(Shippax archive)*

The observation lounge, amidships on the topmost deck. *(Shippax archive)*

punitive taxation on alcoholic drinks – this forced part of the country's drinks industry offshore and so ferries could easily be filled day after day with thirsty mini-cruisers. Thirdly, Mariehamn is only 90 nautical miles from Stockholm, and so the ships could cruise at half-speed and still have ample time to make a daily round-trip – thus fuel costs were minimal. Fourthly, the route through the archipelago is surely one of the most idyllic short-sea voyages anywhere in the world.

The mid-Baltic car ferry routes all linked fairly remote ports in the archipelago, accessible only by road. The overnight 'capital cities' route from central Stockholm to central Helsinki, in contrast, remained the last bastion of traditional passenger steamers and, even in the 1960s, a final generation of overnight ships of this type was commissioned. The *Bore* of 1960 had a quadruple-expansion steam engine, which allowed her to chug along at only 16 knots, while the *Svea Jarl* was only slightly more advanced mechanically, having a 6-cylinder steam engine. Externally, the two could hardly have been more different as the *Bore* had a rather quaint, but cute, twin-funnelled silhouette which could equally have belonged to a vessel built at least thirty years previously. The *Svea Jarl*, in comparison, at least looked like a passenger ship of the 1960s with her more modern, streamlined design. Both vessels were very comfortably appointed – at least for First Class passengers, while Deck Class conditions remained rather spartan. There was space for only 50 and 60 cars respectively, loaded through side hatches. FÅA's participation in the Stockholm-Helsinki passenger route was the motor ship *Ilmatar*, delivered by Wärtsilä in 1964. Although only a single-screw vessel, she was of considerably more up-to-date design than Bore and Svea's most recent contributions to 'De Samseglande.' In fact, she appeared to have much in common with the most recent Silja Line car ferries from the same shipyard. On board, she was exceptionally well appointed, with comfortable saloons and spacious cabins – and the quality of her catering also drew much favourable comment.

Silja Line's three parent companies instinctively wanted to offer their passengers an elegant and upmarket service with modern tonnage. Moreover, their lack of success in running a budget operation with the elderly steamer *Silja* may have convinced them to leave cost-cutting to others. Yet, equally, there was now a great deal of competition from numerous small companies whose older, cheaper tonnage appeared to be squeezing margins. Thus, in 1963 Rederi AB Svea, which was a well-established Stockholm company used to doing things on a grand scale, took the unusual step of trying a budget ferry and tax-free shopping route from Gräddö to Mariehamn, using a small 1936-vintage ferry, the *Marina*, which they had acquired for the purpose from Rederi AB Gotland. This vessel had begun life as the Göteborg-Frederikshavn Linjen's *Kronprinsessan Ingrid* and, subsequently, had been operated by Rederi AB Gotland from Nynäshamn and Oskarshamn to Visby as the *Christopher Polhem*. To manage the ship at arm's length, Rederi AB Svea set up a subsidiary company called Expresslinjen AB – even although the 14-knot *Marina* was anything but an 'express'. A small network of bus routes was

The **Skandia**'s 'tax-free shop' consists only of a small kiosk. *(Shippax archive)*

A corner of the attractive smoking saloon on the **Skandia**. *(Shippax archive)*

The *Ilmatar* when newly-completed by the Wärtsilä shipyard in 1964. *(Bruce Peter collection)*

established to bring tax-free shoppers to the terminal at Gräddö. The intention was quickly to replace the *Marina* in 1964 with a new ferry, the *Scania*, which was already under construction at Landskrona. This did not happen, however, as the *Scania* was redeployed elsewhere to Rederi AB Svea's Skandianvisk Linjetrafik subsidiary on the Southern Baltic, initially between Kiel in West Germany and Korsør in Denmark.

In 1964, the Gothenburg shipping entrepreneur Sten A. Olsson chartered a German passenger ship, the *Wappen von Hamburg* which had previously sailed from Hamburg to Helgoland, to introduce short tax-free shopping-orientated day cruises from Stockholm to Mariehamn. With her official name shortened to *Wappen*, she was marketed to the Swedish public as 'Jätten Finn', which translates as 'Finn the Giant', but she was known to most Stockholmers as 'Jätten Full', or 'The Drunken Giant', which hinted strongly at her true *raison d'être*.

In order to give Stena a run for their money, Rederi AB Svea transferred the *Marina* to the Stockholm-Mariehamn route in 1965, offering shopping mini-cruises in place of the old *Silja* which was laid up then sold for further service across the Northern Baltic as the *Coccolita*. When this happened, the existing Silja Line bus network was retained except that, rather than bringing passengers to Gräddö, the routes were adjusted to converge on Norrtälje where residents of Roslagen, the region to the north of Stockholm, could instead buy tax-free bargains on the *Skandia* and *Nordia*. With a more intensive timetable, daily departures

The Second Class saloon on board the *Ilmatar*. *(Bruce Peter collection)*

The *Ilmatar*'s First Class smoking saloon. *(Bruce Peter collection)*

Stena Line's **Wappen** (ex **Wappen von Hamburg**). *(Rickard Sahlsten collection)*

Stena Line's **Poseidon** at her berth in Stockholm. *(Bruce Peter collection)*

were offered from both Norrtälje and Turku, with the two ferries meeting half-way in Mariehamn. This enabled day trippers to transfer from one ferry to the other and to return whence they came, making a pleasant day trip, while topping up the ships' passenger capacity and greatly increasing onboard revenue flows.

### Car Ferries reach Stockholm

The first car ferry service from Stockholm via Mariehamn to Turku commenced in the spring of 1962 when a group of Finnish businessmen attempted to operate a rather strange former Dover Strait ferry, the *Halladale*, which they had acquired from Townsend Bros. This was a converted one-time Royal Navy frigate, whose slender hull and turbine propulsion made possible a formidable 22-knot service speed. Renamed the *Turist Expressen*, she made three return trips per week from Nybrokajen, near Stockholm's Central Railway Station, with a Sunday cruise to Mariehamn. Although the route and timetable were logical and the *Turist Expressen* had an impressive turn of speed, she was also a fuel-hungry ship with limited capacity, rather perfunctory facilities and, besides, she was elderly and difficult to maintain. Moreover, after only two weeks in service, she was blacklisted by the Finnish Seamen's Union who were concerned by the poor condition of her crew accommodation, and the authorities in Turku prevented her from sailing until improvements were made. Around 200 prospective passengers, waiting on the quayside to board, had to make alternative travel arrangements, or to go home. The resulting bad publicity must have greatly pleased Silja Line. Perhaps inevitably in these circumstances, the *Turist Expressen*'s operation lasted only for one summer season before the ship was sold to Venezuelan interests, amazingly for further service.

It was not until December 1965 that another attempt was made to run a car ferry from Stockholm. In the meantime, Silja Line had acquired an additional ferry, the *Holmia*, which had been purchased on the second-hand market in 1965 from Sweden's Lion Ferry. Built at Århus in Denmark and delivered in 1960 as the *Prins Bertil* for service across the Kattegat, she had quickly been replaced by a larger vessel bearing the same name, which gave Silja Line the opportunity to make a speedy purchase.

Initially, as with Silja Line's existing ferries, the *Holmia* sailed for Mariehamn and Turku from Norrtälje but, once a new dedicated ferry port was commissioned in Stockholm's modern Värtahamnen docks, just north of the city's main business district, the *Holmia* was switched to a Stockholm (Värtahamnen)-Långnäs-Naantali route in December 1965. At Värtahamnen, unlike the existing Skeppsbron quay, there was ample space for vehicles to muster and for passengers to check-in in an orderly and efficient manner. The demand for ro-ro services between Sweden and Finland continued to grow apace and, to meet the increasingly sophisticated expectations of this expanding market, Silja Line introduced the much larger *Fennia*, built at Landskrona in Sweden, on the Stockholm (Värtahamnen)-Mariehamn-Turku route in 1966 – arguably the first true cruise ferry on the Baltic. Meanwhile, the old *Marina* remained in Baltic service until 1969 when she was sold to Yugoslavia. Remarkably, she continued to operate there on the Dalmatian coast until 2006, after which she was converted to a floating restaurant and night club at Mali Losinj where she remains today. The idea of generating significant amounts of money through tax-free sales was firmly ensconced by the second half of the 1960s and even the overnight Stockholm-Helsinki steamers began making regular calls at Mariehamn and Långnäs in the Åland Islands to encourage this trade, as well as frequent short cruises to Mariehamn slotted between their longer sailings to and from Helsinki.

### Viking Line emerges

Encouraged by their early success, Carl Bertil Myrsten's Rederi AB Slite, meanwhile, had ordered their first purpose-built car ferry for delivery in 1964 as the *Apollo*. This little 1,291 grt ferry was built by Sölvesborgs Varv, which had previously converted the *Slite* and the *Boge*, and was painted with a bright red hull. When the Myrsten family went to Sölvesborg to discuss the ship's specifications with the builder, there was a lengthy debate about what colour the hull should be painted. One of the wives in the group solved the problem by producing her lipstick, which was a shade called 'Mexican Fire.' On each side, there was an arrow motif and the marketing name 'Ålandspilen' ('Åland Arrow') was painted in bold, white lettering.

While Myrsten's Rederi AB Slite were preparing to commission the *Apollo*, Rederi AB Vikinglinjen's founders, Eklund and Rundberg, disagreed over the future direction of their company. Eklund advocated a line with ferry services only, whereas Rundberg wanted to invest money in cargo ships and tankers as well as ferries. Fearing that Rundberg's approach would dissipate money which could be more effectively re-invested in newer, larger and

Silja Line's magnificent **Fennia** - the epitome of modern ferry design in the mid-1960s. *(Bruce Peter collection)*

more efficient ferries, Eklund stood his ground and set up a new ferry company, Rederi AB Ålandsfärjan, with investment from a successful Åland Islands shipowner, Fraenk Lundqvist, who was the owner of Rederi Alfa and Rederi Hildegaard. The first Rederi AB Ålandsfärjan ship was the 1933-built Channel steamer *Brittany*, which was acquired with help from the same shipping agent as had previously brokered the *Dinard/Viking* deal, and she entered service as the *Ålandsfärjan* on 20 June 1963 on a route between Mariehamn and Gräddö. Later, the Swedish mainland port was changed to Kapellskär as Gräddö had extremely cramped pier facilities and was linked only by a bumpy single-track road with passing places, which caused bottle-necks for disembarking ferry traffic.

With so many ferries touting for business, it quickly became apparent that, unless some co-operation took place, the smaller companies might not survive for long. Thus, in 1965, Rederi AB Vikinglinjen and Rederi AB Slite recognized the potential benefits of integrating their schedules better to compete against the large, new car ferries of Silja Line. Vikinglinjen and Slite, too, quickly were frustrated by the limitations of Gräddö as a ferry port and so they also moved to Kapellskär. Operations commenced with a joint service, run by the *Viking* and the *Apollo* from Kapellskär via Mariehamn to Parainen. Rederi AB Vikinglinjen and Rederi AB Slite split profits from the route on a 60%/40% basis as the former

The **Fennia**'s smoking saloon, complete with 'Swan' chairs. *(Bruce Peter collection)*

The **Fennia**'s restaurant. *(Bruce Peter collection)*

had a larger ship which was longer-established in the Sweden-Finland trade. Vikinglinjen also controlled the port facilities at Parainen, which gave the company extra leverage in negotiations. The following year, 1966, Gunnar Eklund's Rederi AB Ålandsfärjan belatedly were invited to join the co-operative, which was substantially reorganized through the creation of a new 'Viking Line' marketing company to co-ordinate the timetabling and joint promotion of the three shipping lines who ran the ferries. An Åland shipbroker, Stig Lundqvist (1924-2007), was appointed Managing Director of this new umbrella publicity and sales operation. Trained as a lawyer, Lundqvist had a sharp mind and, as Chairman of the Åland Shipowners' Association, he did much to encourage co-operation between owners with shared interests and efficiency of operation, which benefited the Islands' economy as a whole. It was Lundqvist who had first persuaded Vikinglinjen and Slite to work together and who subsequently argued for Eklund's company also to be included.

Under Lundqvist's management, the brand name 'Viking Line' would be used to promote all ferry services. To avoid confusion between this new brand name and the shipowner Rederi AB Vikinglinjen, the latter was re-styled Rederi AB Solstad, although this was short-lived as Algot Johansson's Rederi AB Sally bought the business from Henning Rundberg and subsequently it was fully absorbed into the Sally company. As well as the new Viking Line brand name, all ferries were henceforth to be painted in a similar colour scheme. Hitherto, Vikinglinjen's *Viking* had sailed with a blue hull and buff funnels, while the *Ålandsfärjan* was painted golden yellow and Slite's *Apollo* was, of course, lipstick red. This latter colour scheme was chosen for all of the ferries

A well-appointed cabin on board the **Fennia**. (*Bruce Peter collection*)

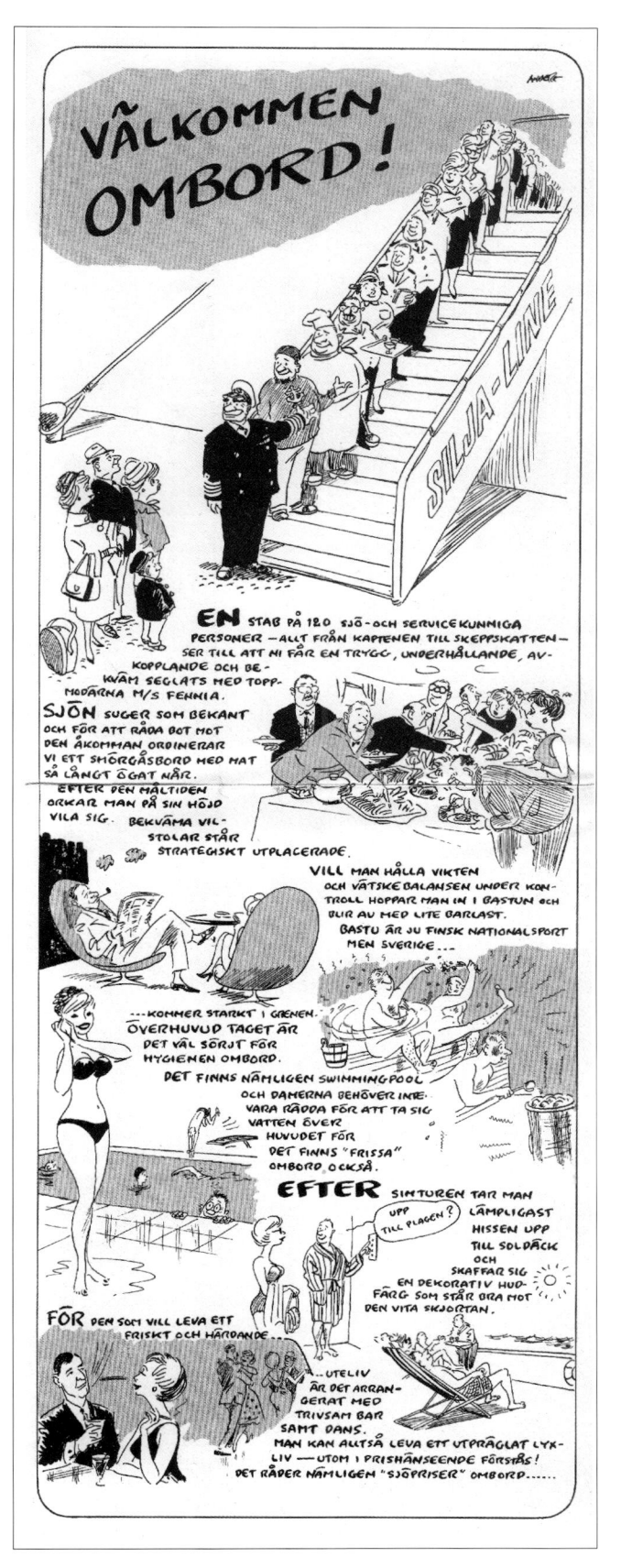

A cartoon from the **Fennia**'s inaugural brochure, showing the different attractions on board. (*Anders Bergenek collection*)

Baltic Ferries

*Later in her service for Viking Line, the **Ålandsfärjan** sports the operator's standard red-hulled livery. (Viking Line)*

involved in the new joint operation as it was thought to be the most eye-catchingly distinctive and most visible in ice.

After a year of joint running, Viking Line, which had begun only six years before, had silenced their detractors by carrying nearly 300,000 passengers, 30,000 cars and 900 lorries and coaches.

1967 was an eventful year for Viking Line. The company opened their own offices in Stockholm and Helsinki in order to promote their services as travel agents had shown very little inclination to assist. At the same time, Rederi AB Ålandsfärjan took delivery of the 3,159 grt Yugoslavian-built *Kapella*, their first purpose-built ferry for Viking Line services. Gunnar Eklund was very ingenious at finding shipyards which could construct ferries for a fraction of the cost of building similar ships in Finland or Sweden. In that regard, he was matched by Eric D. Nilsson of Rederi AB Gotland and by Sten Allan Olsson of Stena Line, each of whom subsequently ordered ferries for their respective companies from Yugoslavian yards. For Eklund, there was the further advantage that keel plates had already been assembled at the Titovo shipyard in Kraljevica for a cancelled ferry order and this meant that construction could advance quickly to his modified design specifications. In the preceding years, he had travelled widely on modern ferries throughout Scandinavia and so he combined the innovations he had observed in the *Kapella*. In the meantime, Viking Line further boosted the Kapellskär-Mariehamn-Naantali

*The **Apollo**, Rederi AB Slite's first new ferry. (Micke Asklander collection)*

*The **Viking** at Mariehamn in August 1970 at the end of her career. (Viking Line)*

The **Viking** and the **Kapella** pass each other on the Åland Sea in the latter 1960s. *(Viking Line)*

service by chartering from Rederi AB Gotland their 1964-built car ferry *Visby* for three years.

At this point, by a two-to-one majority vote, the three Viking Line partners moved their Finnish terminal from Parainen to Naantali which, like Kapellskär in Sweden, had more space and better road connections. Algot Johansson of Rederi AB Sally initially protested in forceful terms against this move as his company had inherited the port of Parainen from the original Vikinglinjen via Rederi AB Solstad and, with Viking Line moving away, he stood to lose out financially. The need for more space and better facilities won the day and Johansson eventually had to concede defeat as gracefully as possible.

Viking Line also devised a clever advertising campaign to promote their services as 'official' extensions to the road network. The E3 trunk road required sea connections over the Stockholm-Helsinki route, and so Viking Line ferries appeared for the 1968 season with luminous green panels on their sides in the style of road signs with E3 prominently displayed to attract extra traffic from the road. Along with this move came a drastic reduction in fares – partly to undercut what were seen as complacent rivals and partly to offset an unpopular 10 markka Finnish port tax, levied on departing passengers and introduced in the wake of a devaluation of the Finnish markka in October 1967. This was short-lived, however, and after a cut-throat price war with Silja Line in 1967-68 during which Viking Line introduced free travel for children, Viking emerged with an increased volume of passenger and freight traffic – but Silja also expanded, albeit at a slightly lesser rate.

Viking Line were not quite finished, however, with ageing second-hand tonnage, however. Not only did the steam-driven *Viking* and the *Ålandsfärjan* remain in service, but Rederi AB Sally made the canny purchase of a 1940-vintage ex-Danish motor ferry which had started life as Grenaa-Hundested Linien's *Marsk Stig*. After a chequered career during which the vessel had capsized twice, she was sold to Swedish breakers in damaged condition following a dry-dock accident during maintenance work. Algot Johansson had the old ferry patched up and towed to his shipyard at Mariehamn where she was fully repaired, entering Viking Line service between Mariehamn and Kapellskär as the *Viking 2* in April 1968.

Silja countered Viking Line's expansion with their *Botnia* and the *Floria*, delivered in 1967 and 1970 respectively, and from near stagnation in the 1950s the ferry industry continued to experience strong and sustained growth. The stimulus of entrepreneurial competition had quickly transformed the mid-Baltic shipping scene and, by the late 1960s, there were twelve car ferries competing for business. Although relatively small and functional by today's standards, passengers reacted favourably to these new-comers which in their day were thought revolutionary – and certainly a vast improvement over the old passenger-only steamers.

Flushed with success, in 1969 the three Viking Line partners took the major decision to order new tonnage for the 1970s and no less than six new vessels were purchased from the West German shipyard, Jos. L. Meyer Werft, at Papenburg. At first, Carl Bertil

Gunnar Eklund's first purpose-built ferry for Viking Line was the Yugoslavian-built **Kapella**. *(Viking Line)*

The **Marella**, the second new Viking Line ferry from Yugoslavia. *(Viking Line)*

*Rederi AB Sally's* **Viking 2**, *originally the Danish domestic ferry* **Marsk Stig**, *berthed ahead of the preserved full-rigger* **Pommern** *at Mariehamn. (Viking Line)*

Myrsten's Rederi AB Slite had intended to build only one ferry – a new *Apollo* to replace the existing vessel of the same name which was too small and, apparently, not particularly seaworthy; he had planned to build the ship at another West German yard, Werft Nobiskrug at Rendsburg on the River Eider, a firm already well-established as an expert builder of car ferries. However, Werft Nobiskrug were already in discussions with their most regular client, Lion Ferry, regarding a series of new orders – and so Jos. L. Meyer Werft won the Rederi AB Slite contract, based on a faster delivery time.

While Carl Bertil Myrsten was staying in Stockholm, he was visited in his hotel by Algot Johansson, Rederi AB Sally's Chairman, to whom he showed the design for his new ferry. As the Viking Line operation split profits between the three companies based on the size and capacity of their ferries, Johansson immediately decided he would order a vessel of the same design. Thereafter, Myrsten too ordered a second example and Johansson bought a further three, making a grand total of six to shuttle back and forth between Sweden and Finland. Johansson's largesse was financed entirely from profits Rederi AB Sally had earned through operating large oil tankers between the Persian Gulf, Europe and the USA. Indeed, with 35 ships, the company was Finland's largest in terms of the total deadweight capacity of the tanker fleet.

Gunnar Eklund, meanwhile, took delivery of a second car ferry from Yugoslavia, the *Marella*, which was a half-sister to his existing *Kapella*. (Incidentally, these names referenced the names of the ports, Mariehamn and Kapellskär.) At this point Eklund's company, Rederi AB Ålandsfärjan, was renamed SF Line, meaning that the three Viking Line partners were now Rederi AB Sally, SF Line and Rederi AB Slite.

The new *Apollo* was delivered to Rederi AB Slite in August 1970 – the same month that the veteran *Viking*, the pioneering Viking

*The little* **Viking 2** *at sea. (Viking Line)*

Silja Line's **Botnia** motors through the islands in the early 1970s. By this stage, Silja Line ferries had adopted the various funnel liveries of the three parent companies and so the **Botnia** sports Bore's colours. *(Robert Spark)*

Line ship, sailed to the breaker's yard. Within ten years, the three companies behind Viking Line had gone from sailing two elderly Channel packet steamers and a converted coaster to running a fleet of eight purpose-built car ferries. Meantime, Silja Line had moved from a handful of even older steamers to an equally impressive array of modern vessels.

### Ferries between Stockholm and Helsinki

Still, there was, as yet, no direct dedicated car ferry service from Stockholm to Helsinki, which remained the sole province of 'De Samseglande.' In the latter 1960s, FÅA and Rederi AB Svea each decided to order a new car ferry with substantial overnight accommodation to inaugurate a new ferry service between the capital cities. The *Aallotar* and the *Svea Regina*, each of 8,020 grt, were constructed by the Dubigeon Normandie shipyard at Nantes in France, then emerging as an accomplished builder of modern ferry tonnage, and delivered in 1972.

Between ordering these vessels and taking delivery of them, the three Silja Line parent companies, FÅA, Bore and Svea, decided to reorganize their steamer and ferry services, creating a structure more like that of their increasingly powerful rivals which operated the Viking Line partnership. Thus, Silja Line ceased to be a shipping company in its own right and, instead, became a marketing brand name, and various Silja ferries were allocated between the three shipping Lines. Thus, the *Skandia* and the newly-built *Floria* were operated by FÅA, while the *Nordia*, the *Holmia* and the *Fennia* went to Rederi AB Svea and the *Botnia* was acquired by Bore. All of these ships were partially repainted with each of the owning Lines' funnel colours being applied, but with the marketing name 'Silja Line' being painted in large letters on the hull topsides. At this point, a new logo depicting a stylized seal's head was introduced on the ships' hulls and on all publicity material.

The Silja Line brand was also extended to the passenger steamers on the Stockholm (Skeppsbron)-Helsinki route and so all

A History of the Baltic Ferry Scene

The smoking saloon on the **Floria**. *(Bruce Peter collection)*

The **Floria**'s restaurant. *(Bruce Peter collection)*

The **Floria** is photographed passing at sea in the early 1970s. Her funnel is painted in the livery of the FÅA. *(Robert Spark)*

The cafeteria on the **Floria** - note the psychedelic table tops. *(Bruce Peter)*

The **Floria**'s night club. *(Bruce Peter)*

Baltic Ferries

25

Rederi AB Sally's **Viking 1**, one of the successful 'Papenburger' ferries. *(Viking Line)*

A stern quarter view of the **Viking 1**. *(Robert Spark)*

The **Viking 4** at sea: this and subsequent members of the series had the main deck superstructure built aft to the stern. After her Baltic service, the **Viking 4** became Sealink's **Earl Granville**, sailing between Portsmouth and the Channel Islands. *(Viking Line)*

The **Viking 5** was an enlarged version of the 'Papenburger' design. *(Viking Line)*

The **Viking 6**, originally the **Stena Britannica**. *(Viking Line)*

A Viking Line brochure from 1970 - the point of transition when the old steamers were withdrawn and replaced by the new 'Papenburgers'. Note the colourful interior design of these vessels. (Bruce Peter collection)

of the FÅA, Bore and Svea vessels on the mid-Baltic routes from Sweden to the Åland Islands and Finland were marketed jointly as Silja Line for the first time.

Likewise, the new Stockholm-Helsinki car ferries *Aallotar* and *Svea Regina* entered service in the spring and early summer of 1972 with Silja Line emblazoned on their hulls, but each with different funnel colours reflecting their separate ownership. *En route* from France to the Baltic, the *Aallotar* called at London, Amsterdam and Hamburg, where she was shown off to invited guests from the tourism and travel trade in order to encourage international patronage of the new Stockholm-Helsinki route.

Each new ferry could carry 170 cars, meaning that Silja Line's Värtahamnen terminal became increasingly busy while the passenger services from Skeppsbron fell into rapid decline during the 1970s – especially after the 1973 Oil Crisis which followed Arab protests at Israel's invasion of Egyptian territory in the Yom Kippur war. Exasperated by what they saw as Egypt's plight, Arab Gulf States, which dominated OPEC, sharply increased oil prices and this situation had the immediate effect of rendering relatively fuel-hungry steamships uneconomical, at least when in liner service. Thus, the Stockholm (Skeppsbron)-Helsinki passenger route only survived for a few more years, before finally running out of steam at the end of August 1976. The car ferry services from Värtahamnen, in contrast, went from strength to strength and a succession of ever larger ships was ordered for the routes to Turku and to Helsinki.

Birka Line, founded in 1971 as the Ålandslinjen by the Åland-based shipowner Bror Husell, was another of a number of companies involved in this trade. At first, Husell bought the 1957-vintage DFDS motor ship *Prinsessen* (ex *Prinsesse Margrethe*) and commissioned her as the *Prinsessan* on short overnight tax-free shopping cruises from Stockholm to Mariehamn and back. In 1972, her erstwhile sister ship was also purchased, this time third-hand from the Hong Kong-based China Mutual Navigation Company (Swire Group) which, in turn, had bought her from DFDS to link Hong Kong with Keelung in Taiwan. Renamed the *Baronessan*, every evening she sailed in tandem with the *Prinsessan* to Mariehamn, usually filled to the last berth with shoppers and drinkers. Buoyed by their initial success with the *Prinsessan* and the *Baronessan*, in 1973 Birka Line made a bold decision to introduce a daily ferry service from Stockholm to Helsinki, marketing the route as the 'Baltic Star Line' and using a large and superbly-appointed cruise ferry called the *Freeport*. This had been delivered in 1968 for Caribbean service from Miami to Grand Bahama Island and was an outstanding ship in terms of passenger facilities with two restaurants, three lounges, a casino, a swimming pool and berths for all passengers in cabins with *en suite* facilities.

At the same time, Birka Line chartered a second ferry from Statens Järnvägar (Swedish State Railways, or SJ) to enable daily departures. The *Drottningen*, however, was most dissimilar in character from the *Freeport*, being essentially a large train ferry and with a totally different layout and range of facilities.

Unfortunately, the enterprise was a failure, partly as a result of the fuel crisis following the war between Israel and the Arab World and partly because Birka's terminals in Stockholm and Helsinki were less centrally located than those of Silja Line. Besides, paying charter fees for two ships placed an additional financial strain on the operation. Moreover, Silja's Swedish partners, Rederi AB Svea, were anxious to kill off their unwelcome competitor almost at birth and entered into negotiations with the *Freeport*'s American owner to buy the ship for service between Helsingborg and Travemünde – so Birka Line had no option but to capitulate. The *Freeport* was subsequently renamed *Svea Star* and, thereafter, had a nomadic existence with further spells of service in the Caribbean and the Baltic for a succession of owners. Birka Line survived, however, and prospered as a niche operator of short tax-free shopping cruises rather than a point-to-point ferry

Silja Line's French-built Stockholm-Helsinki ferry **Aallotar**. *(Bruce Peter collection)*

line.

By the early 1970s, the Viking Line partners Rederi AB Slite and Rederi AB Sally had each taken delivery of their new ferries from Jos. L. Meyer Werft in Papenburg. Slite's *Apollo* (1970) and *Diana* (1972) were named after Greek gods, while Sally's *Viking 1* (1970), *Viking 3* (1972), *Viking 4* (1973) and *Viking 5* (1974) repeated the name of Rederi AB Vikinglinjen's pioneering steamer. In addition to this fine new armada, in 1973 SF Line took delivery of a larger, high-capacity 'jumbo' ferry named the *Aurella* from the J.J. Sietas shipyard in Hamburg. Gunnar Eklund had correctly reasoned that it would be more profitable to order one large ferry of much greater deadweight capacity which could do the job of two examples of the 'Papenburger' type. Perhaps inevitably, his *Aurella* helped SF Line quickly to become the dominant partner on the Kapellskär-Mariehamn-Naantali route. Inadvertently, he had also begun a race to see who could build the largest ferry and this continued at an ever more frantic pace until the early 1990s.

Of more immediate concern was the fact that, with six practically identical modern 'Papenburger' ferries, plus the veteran *Viking 2*, as well as the *Kapella*, *Marella* and *Aurella*, the Viking Line partners obviously had too many ships for their existing routes. Thus, Carl Bertil Myrsten of Rederi AB Slite and Algot Johansson of Rederi AB Sally agreed that the best solution would be to establish their own Stockholm-Mariehamn-Turku and Stockholm-Helsinki services, in direct competition with Silja Line. (Hitherto, Kapellskär had become the main Swedish port for Viking Line ships, although a Stockholm-Mariehamn route was tried briefly in 1964 using a chartered steamer, the *Drotten*.) The Stockholm-

The **Aallotar**'s smoking saloon. *(Bruce Peter collection)*

The dining saloon on the **Aallotar** with Finnish designer furniture. *(Bruce Peter collection)*

Turku route began in August 1973, using SF's *Marella* plus Sally's newly-arrived *Viking 4*. When it came to launching Stockholm-Helsinki the following July, Sally were to contribute the new *Viking 5* and Slite were to provide the *Diana* but, in between agreeing in principle to begin operations and the service being advertised and launched, Carl Bertil Myrsten sold the *Diana* to Vaasa-Umeå Oy for use on their northerly route across the Gulf of Bothnia. Algot Johansson was keen to proceed anyway and so he bought yet another ferry, the *Wickersham* (ex *Stena Britannica* of 1968). This was the sister of the *Stena Germanica* and, since being sold out of the Stena fleet in nearly mint condition, she had operated in American, Canadian and Alaskan waters. The *Wickersham* was brought to the Baltic via the Panama Canal and repainted in Viking Line's livery with the name *Viking 6*. Thus, the Viking Line Stockholm-Helsinki route began in July 1974, operated entirely by Rederi AB Sally's ships. Unlike Birka Line's abortive Baltic Star Line, the Viking service was a resounding and enduring success.

### Services from Denmark and Germany

Since their foundation, FÅA had run regular services to German Baltic ports and to Copenhagen. In the 1920s and '30s, the German shipping company R.C. Griebel operated steamers from Stettin to Tallinn and Helsinki. Later, from 1935, Germany's National Socialist Government, keen to support a 'Greater Germany,' opened a route from Pillau and Zoppot in the enclave of East Prussia to Helsinki – but all of these services ended with the outbreak of the Second World War and many of the ships were lost during the conflict.

After the war, FÅA recommenced operations between Helsinki and Copenhagen using the restored *Ariadne* (dating from 1914) and the 1927-vintage steamer *Wellamo*. In anticipation of the Helsinki Olympic Games, DFDS joined the fray in 1949 with their steamer *Botnia* (ex *Aarhus*) which dated from 1912 and was amongst the oldest vessels in the company's fleet. In the latter 1950s, FÅA switched the *Wellamo* to sail between Helsinki and Travemünde. Both the *Botnia* and the *Wellamo* continued until the end of the 1966 summer season, by which time they were surrounded by modern car ferries.

By the 1960s, the West German economy was growing rapidly – and Finland was also experiencing sustained growth. It was against this background that the first car ferry service between the two countries was established between Travemünde and Helsinki. The route was a lengthy one, taking at least 40 hours. The operator was Finnlines Oy which had been created in 1947, shortly thereafter becoming the shipping arm of the Government-controlled Enso-Gutzeit forestry and paper conglomerate. This firm had its origins in the nineteenth century when W. Gutzeit (founded in 1872) and Enso AB (established in 1889) began pulping timber to make paper. Gutzeit was nationalized in 1919 and Enso was absorbed in 1927. As part of the Finnish Government's industrialization strategy, it was Finnlines' job to carry forestry exports to European and American ports, using an expanding fleet of cargo liners.

In 1962 the company spotted an opportunity to buy a partially-completed car ferry which had been ordered by Rederi AB Vikinglinjen from Hanseatische Werft in Hamburg. As the yard had suffered cash-flow problems, building costs increased and, while Vikinglinjen sought to raise more capital, Finnlines intervened. Thus, the ferry entered service in 1962 between Travemünde and Helsinki as the *Hansa Express*.

Having been intended only to make short day crossings between Kapellskär in the Swedish archipelago and Parainen in Finland,

The **Svea Regina**, Rederi AB Svea's contribution to Silja Line's 'capital cities' ferry service between Stockholm and Helsinki. *(Bruce Peter collection)*

The **Baronessan** (ex **Kong Olav V**) of Birka Line motors across the Åland Sea during one of her short cruises from Stockholm to Mariehamn. *(Ambrose Greenway)*

the *Hansa Express* was too small and had insufficient overnight accommodation for the Finnlines route. Consequently, during her first winter overhaul, she was lengthened and, soon afterwards, Finnlines ordered two much more substantial ferries from the Wärtsilä shipyard in Helsinki. Unfortunately the first of these, the *Finnhansa*, was seriously damaged by fire while fitting out, meaning that she could not enter service as planned in 1965. As a stop-gap measure, therefore, Finnlines chartered a newly-built Israeli ferry, the *Nili*, which had just been completed by Upper Clyde Shipbuilders' Govan yard for Somerfin Line's Mediterranean services from Haifa. While retaining her official name on the hull, she was marketed by Finnlines as the 'Helsinki Express.'

Finally, in 1966, both the *Finnhansa* and her near sister, the *Finnpartner*, were completed. *En route* from Travemünde to Helsinki, these large and elegant ferries called at Copenhagen and also made occasional brief stops at Rønne on Bornholm and Slite on Gotland during the summer and at Nynäshamn and Karlskrona in Sweden during the winter. During the low season, when demand for Baltic crossings was lower, Finnlines introduced a cruise programme and the ferries ventured as far as the Western

The **Drottningen** on charter from SJ to the Birka Line subsidiary Baltic Star Line passes Lidingö, outward-bound for Helsinki. *(Anders Ahlerup)*

The **Baronessan** manoeuvres in Stockholm. *(David Trevor-Jones)*

The **Freeport** is seen at Stockholm, during her brief spell on the Baltic. *(Robert Spark)*

Mediterranean.

Following the withdrawal of the elderly *Wellamo* in 1966, FÅA introduced their own large ferry, offering a similar standard of design and facilities to those of Finnlines. The *Finlandia*, also built by Wärtsilä and commissioned in 1967, was in many ways a slightly enlarged and improved version of the Finnlines ships. Capable of 22 knots, she was the largest and fastest car ferry on the Baltic – and also the best appointed. As well as the usual lounges and restaurants, she boasted a hairdressing salon, a cinema, sauna baths and a night club. It became clear, however, that running three such large passenger ships was more than the route could withstand – especially as much of Finnlines' core forestry exports were sent to Germany on sophisticated, dedicated freight ferries and so the passenger ships could not rely on year-round cargo flows to offset costs. Thus, after only four years, the *Finnpartner* was sold to Rederi AB Svea in 1970,

The **Hansa Express** (later **Finndana**), originally intended for Rederi AB Vikinglinjen and not really suitable for Finnlines' lengthy route to West Germany. *(Thomas N. Olesen collection)*

The **Nili**, operating for Finnlines as the 'Helsinki Express.' *(Ambrose Greenway collection)*

A deck scene on the **Finnpartner** - note the pod house on display. *(Ambrose Greenway)*

becoming the *Sveaborg* on the southerly Trave Line Hälsingborg-Travemünde route.

Thereafter, the *Finnhansa* and FÅA's *Finlandia* continued on the route until 1973, when Finnlines decided to try once again with two passenger ships on their own account between West Germany, Denmark and Finland. An opportunity arose to purchase a suitable ship from Stena Line, the *Stena Atlantica*. Built by Lindholmens Varv in Gothenburg in 1966 as the *Saga* for Swedish Lloyd's Gothenburg-Tilbury route across the North Sea, Stena had bought her only to add additional sailings to their Gothenburg-Kiel route during the 1972 Olympic Games in Munich. As far as Finnlines were concerned, not only did she offer excellent accommodation on a par with their existing Travemünde-Helsinki vessel but she also offered the possibility of being used during the winter season as a cruise ship. She became the second *Finnpartner* and sailed opposite the *Finnhansa* until 1975, when FÅA and Finnlines finally merged their Helsinki-Travemünde passenger services. At this point, the *Finlandia* was repainted in Finnlines' livery and the *Finnpartner* (II) was chartered out, first to Folklines, a short-lived Northern Baltic operator, then to Olau Line for service across the English Channel as the *Olau Finn*.

Finnlines replaced both the *Finnhansa* and the *Finlandia* in 1977 with the famous gas turbine-powered high-speed cruise ferry *Finnjet*.

Briefly, in 1974, Germany's TT-Linie attempted to run a cruise service from Travemünde using the 1962-vintage ferry *Gösta Berling*, formerly the first *Nils Holgersson*, which had inaugurated the Travemünde-Trelleborg route across the Southern Baltic. The ports of call were Rønne, Helsinki and Leningrad, but the initiative was unsuccessful; the ferry's car deck remained largely empty, she was not well enough appointed to justify the costs of the cruises, and so she was sold.

### Across the Gulf of Bothnia

After the Second World War, traffic across the Gulf of Bothnia reopened in 1947 when Suomi Shipping's steamer *Pörtö* was placed on the Umeå-Vaasa route. Initially, passenger and freight volumes were small due to tough customs restrictions and the *Pörtö* was offered for sale at the end of the first summer season. In May 1948 a new company, Rederi AB Vasa-Umeå, was established by Toivo Asp, the Chairman of Pälsindustri AB in Vaasa, which exported furs to Sweden. When he discovered that the *Pörtö* was for sale, he immediately made an offer to secure the ship, which was vital for his business. Renamed the *Turisten*, she made 84 return crossings during the 1948 season. As the post-war economy picked up, business grew quickly and larger ships were acquired. The *Korsholm* (ex *Tjust*) could even carry five cars, but she did not last long, being replaced in quick succession by the *Korsholm II* and *Korsholm III*. The latter steamer was rebuilt with a car deck capable of carrying 35 cars and was, therefore, arguably the first true car ferry under the Finnish flag, but even this was insufficient and so, the following year, the *Örnen* was acquired with space for 40 cars. Remarkably, after several further

The smoking saloon on-board the **Finnhansa**. *(Bruce Peter collection)*

The **Finnhansa**'s restaurant. *(Bruce Peter collection)*

The Finnlines flagships of the latter 1960s - the **Finnhansa** and the **Finnpartner** - sailing in tandem for this publicity image. Note that the two ferries are not identical. *(Bruce Peter collection)*

rebuilds and a diverse career, the former *Korsholm III* still exists as Strömma Kanalbolaget's Stockholm-Waxholm excursion vessel *Stockholm*. Today, she has both steam and diesel propulsion, although only the latter is used in everyday service.

In 1958, rumour spread that FÅA planned to introduce a steamer of their own across the Gulf of Bothnia in direct competition with Rederi AB Vasa-Umeå and so, in order to strengthen the company and to make any such would-be competitors think twice, the company entered into negotiations with Finnlines which was, of course, part of the mighty Government-controlled Enso-Gutzeit conglomerate.

With Finnlines' backing, Rederi AB Vasa-Umeå was restyled to Finnish as Vaasa-Umeå Oy and the company continued to expand quickly. In the early 1960s, tenders were sought for a new car ferry from both Sölvesborgs Varv and Valmet Oy but, instead, the opportunity arose to buy the 1955-vintage *Thjelvar* (ex *Prinsessan Margaretha* of Sessanlinjen) from Rederi AB Gotland. This entered service in 1965 as the *Wasa Express*, to be followed by three other ex-Sessan vessels, the *Botnia Express* (ex *Prinsessan Christina*), *Polar Express* (ex *Prinsessan Margaretha* (II)) and *Fenno Express* (ex *Prinsessan Desirée*). As well as the main Umeå-Vaasa route, these shared a growing network of ferry services from Vaasa to Örnsköldvik and to Jakobstad. None of the ex-Sessan ferries operated by Vaasa-Umeå Oy was ice-strengthened, however, meaning that their routes were suspended during the winter, just like in steamship days.

Vaasa-Umeå Oy also planned a ferry route from Umeå to Jakobstad, but a competitor had got there before them. Jakob Lines was actually a front for the von Rettig family's Bore Line. Indeed, Bore owned a third of the share capital with a further ten per cent belonging to Strengbergs Tobaksfabrik, a tobacco firm also owned by von Rettig. So, even though FÅA had reconsidered entering into competition with Vaasa-Umeå Oy when they were bought by Finnlines, Bore, which was the other Finnish constituent in 'De Samseglande Rederierna' on the mid-Baltic, entered the fray instead.

Jakob Lines commenced operations in 1969 with the ex-Danish car ferry *Nordek* (built in 1961 as Grenaa-Hundested Linien's *Kattegat*). In 1971 the steamer *Bore II* (formerly FÅA's *Aallotar* of 1952) was added. Thereafter, Vaasa-Umeå Oy hit back in 1972 with the *Scania Express* (ex *Scania*) – strangely enough, the first

The smoking saloon on the **Finlandia** of 1967. *(Bruce Peter collection)*

The *Finlandia*'s dining saloon, designed by Jonas Cedercreutz. *(Bruce Peter collection)*

The night club at the after end of the *Finlandia*'s superstructure. *(Bruce Peter collection)*

ice-strengthened ferry actually to serve on what was probably the iciest ferry route in the world. Built in 1964 for Rederi AB Svea, this ferry had been intended to run between Gräddö and Mariehamn in place of the *Marina* but had instead been diverted to Svea's Skandinavisk Linjetrafik subsidiary, for which she sailed in the Southern Baltic on a Germany-Denmark routeing between Kiel and Korsør and the short Sweden-Denmark Öresund link between Tuborg Havn and Landskrona. When the *Scania Express* was introduced on the Gulf of Bothnia, for the first time year-round departures could be offered.

Throughout the 1970s, Vaasa-Umeå Oy and Jakob Lines co-existed – but, following the Yom Kippur war and the ensuing Oil Crisis, both firms felt an urgent need to prune their fleets of small ferries and to replace these with larger, ice-strengthened vessels to achieve better economies of scale and to ensure year-round operation. Thereafter, all ships introduced on the Gulf of Bothnia routes were second-hand acquisitions from the mid-Baltic. Because of their association with Bore Line, Jakob Lines bought mainly ex-Silja Line tonnage, while Vaasa-Umeå Oy acquired a succession of ships from the Viking Line partners.

The boom in leisure travel begun in the 1960s was the start of a craze which was to transform ferry travel on the main Baltic routes over the ensuing decades and which gave rise to some of the most innovative and striking passenger ships the world has ever seen – the super-ferries.

The FÅA's Helsinki-Travemünde ferry *Finlandia*. *(Ambrose Greenway collection)*

CHAPTER TWO

# Evolution of the Baltic Super Ferry

In the mid-Baltic area, it was the Finnish Wärtsilä shipyards in Helsinki and Turku which made the most significant contribution to car ferry and, later on, to cruise ship design. The Helsinki yard traces its origins to 1867 when the Heitalahti Shipyard was founded. There, a dry-dock, filled and emptied using steam pumps, was completed in 1868 to enable ship repair work to be carried out, as well as the construction of new steamships. In 1939 Wärtsilä was established, incorporating numerous industrial enterprises mainly involved in shipbuilding, supply and outfitting. The Chricton-Vulcan shipyard in Turku, the origins of which are described in the first chapter, was merged with Wärtsilä in 1967. At a time when long-established British yards – which traditionally had built much of the world's passenger fleet – were struggling for survival, the Finnish upstart began its long association with passenger vessel design and construction. This happened notwithstanding an exceptionally harsh climate with temperatures often lower than -20° Celsius during the winter.

Wärtsilä's first truly modern passenger ferries were the *Skandia* and *Nordia* for Silja Line, delivered in 1961-62. These ferries were equipped with two 9-cylinder Wärtsilä-Sulzer diesels, giving a respectable 18-knot service speed, appropriate for services through the difficult waters of the Swedish and Finnish archipelago. Within compact dimensions (101.6 x 18.5 metres) they could accommodate up to 1,200 passengers, around 136 of whom were berthed, plus 175 cars on a vehicle deck with enough vertical height also to carry lorries and buses, if the hoistable mezzanine platforms were retracted. The engine casing was located towards the stern and there was a narrow centre casing, containing service uptakes, stair- and lift-shafts. Bow and stern doors were provided, meaning that, during the busy summer peak, the vessels could be turned around very quickly at each terminal port. Thus, in terms of overall layout, these ships were similar to numerous others in their size range and class then being planned for short-sea routes all over Scandinavia.

They were, however, exceptional due to the robustness of their hull construction. Wärtsilä, not surprisingly, were expert constructors of ice-breakers and, as the *Skandia* and the *Nordia* were intended for year-round service, they had ice-breaker bows which were thickly plated and cut back below the water-line to make a 'knife edge' to smash through sheet ice. They were also notable for their very bright, fresh and modern passenger

The Finnlines ferry **Finnhansa**, built by Wärtsilä and designed to operate on the long route from Helsinki to West Germany. *(Ambrose Greenway collection)*

Silja Line's **Skandia**, Wärtsilä first ro-ro car ferry. *(Bruce Peter collection)*

The **Ilmatar**, another significant 1960s Wärtsilä passenger ship. *(Bruce Peter collection)*

accommodation – an outstanding feature of which was an oval-shaped observation lounge, contained in a 'dummy funnel' amidships, giving passengers panoramic views of the passing archipelago scenery. Externally and inboard, the sleek and stylish *Skandia* and the *Nordia* were clearly ships of the 1960s and a world away from the steamers from the Edwardian era they indirectly replaced. Another major difference from the old steamers was that these were one-class vessels, the entire passenger accommodation being air-conditioned and outfitted in light, contemporary colours and with comfortable furniture in which to relax. For the first time, crossing the Baltic by sea became a guaranteed pleasure rather than, as it had sometimes been in the past, especially in Deck Class, a necessity to be endured. Eating, drinking, shopping and a visit to the sauna were welcome attractions for adults, while children could enjoy the playroom. The relatively high capacity and efficient diesel propulsion, coupled with increased onboard sales, meant that ticket prices could be reduced – and this, in turn, helped to create demand for short cruises, rather than taking the ferry only to get from A to B.

A third passenger-only ship was the *Ilmatar*, completed in 1964 for the Stockholm-Helsinki service of FÅA. Notwithstanding her sleek appearance, from a technical standpoint the *Ilmatar* was rather a primitive craft in comparison with what other designers, such as Knud E. Hansen A/S, were fashioning at the same time. She had only a single Sulzer diesel engine and, consequently, she was a single-screw ship with only one rudder. Moreover, she operated on a passenger-only service of a type fast becoming anachronistic at that time. Her great success, however, was her interior design, which was widely acclaimed for its elegance and modernity.

Both the rather yacht-like exterior silhouette and the interior design were by Jonas Cedercreutz, a distinguished Finnish modernist architect. Cedercreutz was from a famous artistic family, the son of the eminent artist and sculptor Baron Emil Cedercreutz, to house whose work Cedercreutz designed a museum in 1963. At around the same time, he worked with Alvar Aalto and other Finnish architects on a grandiose masterplan to redevelop and improve the amenity of tracts of central Helsinki – but this bold scheme remained unexecuted. Otherwise, Cedercreutz designed several public, commercial and residential buildings in Helsinki which are identifiable by their sombre understatement, horizontal façade composition and high-quality materials.

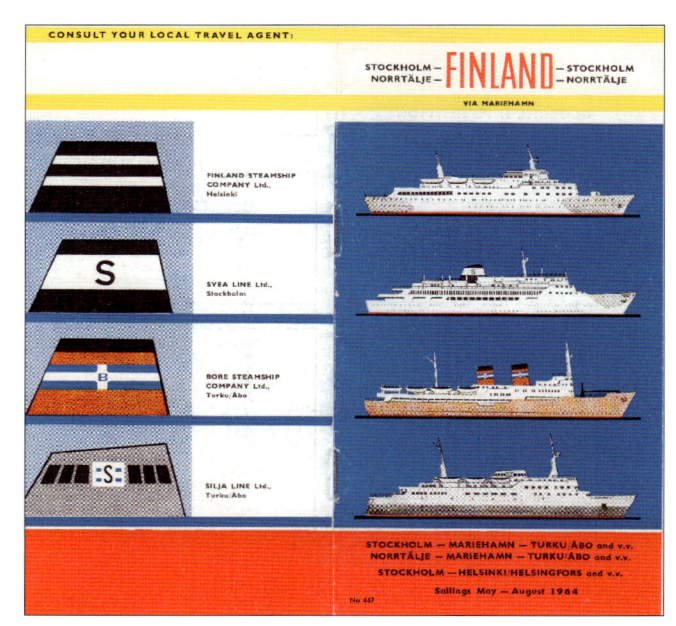

The *Ilmatar* was equally stylish, with elegant saloons, panelled in varnished wood veneer and with modern furniture in fresh colours under smooth, white ceilings. Indeed, in many respects, the standard of design was rather similar to that of the forthcoming Swedish American liner *Kungsholm*, albeit rendered on a far smaller scale. Above the bridge was an outdoor viewing platform, located in the top of the ship's dummy funnel. As well as being a popular ship for 'De Samseglande' on the Stockholm-Helsinki and Stockholm-Turku routes in the 1960s, the *Ilmatar* became a successful cruise ship during the 1970s, even venturing as far as the Western Mediterranean in the 1977-80 period. Lengthened and re-engined in 1973, she was sold to Norwegian interests in 1980, eventually ending up as a gaming cruise ship in Florida named the *Palm Beach Princess*, in which guise she continues to operate today.

Wärtsilä learned quickly about modern ferry design and, less than two years after the *Ilmatar* was completed, they delivered the first of a series of five large and well-appointed cruise ferries: the *Finnhansa*, the *Finnpartner*, the *Prins Hamlet*, the *Finlandia* and the *Bohème*. Of these, the *Prins Hamlet* was built by the Chricton-Vulcan yard in Turku but shared a similar basic design to the others.

The *Finnhansa* and the *Finnpartner* were introduced in 1966 by Oy Finnlines, a part of the Enso-Gutzeit industrial conglomerate. As these ferries were conceived to operate on the long crossing from Helsinki to Travemünde, via Copenhagen and other ports, a far higher 21-knot service speed was required, as well as a greatly increased number of cabin berths and a more extensive range of entertainment facilities. To achieve the necessary speed, two larger Sulzer diesels were specified but, as the draught and freeboard were no greater than on the *Skandia* and *Nordia*, the tops of the engines penetrated the vehicle deck, meaning that a large casing had to be built around them; this caused a blockage in the aft section around which cars, trucks and buses had to drive. Higher up in the superstructure, this had the effect of creating a Y-shaped circulation plan with a single main axial corridor in the forward two-thirds of the main cabin deck and two parallel corridors on either side of the casing towards the stern. In addition, as building innovative ships of this kind was, to an extent, a case of trial and error in the early 1960s, the trim tank arrangements were perhaps unduly complex. These issues aside, the design was commendable.

Above the vehicle deck, there was a deck entirely given over to cabins, which extended almost to the forepeak. This meant that it would not have been possible to fit a lifting bow visor and so, instead, hinged doors were developed, opening outwards and meeting at the stem. This solution also avoided the problem of upward pressure caused by wave action placing a strain on visor locking pins as, instead, waves would tend to force the doors more tightly shut. In addition, there were side doors with fold-down ramps and outer covers which closed flush with the shell plating in the starboard bow and stern quarters. These were used when the ship called at intermediate ports *en route* between Finland and Germany.

Further economy cabins were located below the vehicle deck, forward of the engine room, and on Boat Deck, above the main passenger saloons. Forward on the saloon deck, there was a large *à la carte* restaurant, giving a panoramic view ahead. Above, the smoking saloon on Boat Deck offered a similar vista. Towards the stern, there was a cafeteria and a night club. The *Finnhansa* and the *Finnpartner* had full-width public rooms, entered from hallways forward and aft of amidships. Off the aft hallway, there was a casino, a gift shop and a hairdressing salon while, towards the stern, there was a splendid indoor swimming pool beneath a Perspex roof – a miniature version of the one on the French Liner *France* and also found on the East German-built Soviet *Ivan Franko*-class liners. Below the car deck, there was a cinema.

Enso-Gutzeit were also renowned patrons of progressive design, being regular clients of the internationally-regarded Finnish modernist architect Alvar Aalto whose office designed the interiors of some Finnlines vessels. Although Aalto was not responsible for either the *Finnpartner* or the *Finnhansa*, some of his lighting and furniture designs were used on board and, when combined with light wood veneers, colourful fabrics and contemporary artworks, the effect was very stylish indeed. A design highlight was a spiral open-tread staircase linking the night club with a lounge aft on Boat Deck – the ultimate in 1960s modernist elegance.

Of the other ships of the same class, the *Prins Hamlet* and the *Bohème* were built for Swedish interests, Lion Ferry and Wallenius Lines, to operate on the North Sea between Hamburg and Harwich. In the latter 1960s, however, there was insufficient custom to justify two ferries and so the *Bohème* became a Caribbean cruise ship instead, based in Miami and run by Commodore Cruise Line. Nowadays, as the *Freewinds* and operated by the Church of Scientology, she is the last of the 'first generation' of Wärtsilä-built cruise ferries to remain in existence.

The *Finlandia*, delivered in 1967 to FÅA for their Helsinki-Travemünde route, was very much an improved version of the *Finnhansa/Finnpartner* class – indeed, the ship was regarded as the Finnish national flagship and was widely acclaimed for the beauty and flair of her exterior and for the refined ambience of the accommodation. Whereas the Finnlines sisters had two Sulzer diesels, the *Finlandia* had four smaller Sulzers, coupled in pairs to the propeller shafts and giving a higher speed of 22 knots, and a completely unobstructed vehicle deck, but also slightly poorer fuel economy. Otherwise, the general hull design was very similar to the earlier vessels – but the superstructure was somewhat differently arranged. Once again, FÅA engaged Jonas Cedercreutz both to style the exterior and to design the interiors, based on the enthusiastic acclaim of his earlier work on the *Ilmatar*.

In the mid-1960s, ferries on the Central Baltic routes remained somewhat perfunctory in terms of size and the facilities on offer. Even so, the *Skandia* and the *Nordia* compared favourably with anything sailing in British waters at that time. On the Baltic, the most outstanding ships were used on the lengthy route from Helsinki to Travemünde in West Germany.

The first vessel for Central Baltic traffic that was large enough to be compared on an equal footing with the Helsinki-Travemünde ships was the *Fennia*, built in Sweden by the Öresundsvarvet in Landskrona and delivered in 1966. The ship sailed between Stockholm, Mariehamn and Turku and immediately made a wonderful impression on account of her futuristic profile and crisp, modish interiors. Externally, she somewhat resembled Holland America Line's 1959-built *Rotterdam* with a dove grey hull and twin exhaust stacks located two-thirds aft. In order to balance the profile, an ovoid-shaped observation lounge was located amidships atop the superstructure. The design was developed from that of the smaller *Skandia* and *Nordia* by Silja Line's Technical Director, Carl-Bertel Ekström, while detailed design work was carried out by Öresundsvarvet's own design office.

The **Fennia** was the largest and most luxurious ferry linking Sweden and Finland in the latter 1960s. In this fold-out brochure, the illustrations give a sense of her impressive external appearance and attractive, modern interiors. (Anders Bergenek collection)

Being intended both for night and day crossings in the fairly sheltered waters of the archipelago, the hull was quite beamy with a pronounced knuckle joint at car deck height and a roomy superstructure. Cabins and open saloons, containing large numbers of reclining seats, were provided on the main deck of the superstructure with a saloon and restaurant deck located above. Interestingly, each superstructure deck was slightly narrower than the one below, giving a slight 'stacked' effect when viewed from close quarters. By offsetting the vertical framing, however, enhanced longitudinal rigidity was introduced, making for a more robust overall superstructure whilst saving weight at the same time. This design solution was unique to Silja Line's ferries of the latter 1960s and early 1970s and was not attempted by other shipping lines or ferry naval architects. On the mechanical side, the *Fennia* was fitted with four British-made 9-cylinder Ruston & Hornsby diesels, unique in the Silja Line fleet and rare in Scandinavian ferries in general. They did not last for long, however, being replaced by four Atlas-MaK diesels in a complex operation carried out at Helsingør between January and June 1975. The arrangement of four engines, coupled in pairs via gearboxes to two propeller shafts, allowed the car deck to remain unobstructed, save for a narrow centre casing, while still enabling a respectable 18.5-knot service speed to be maintained.

Apart from her noteworthy 6,178 grt size, which made her by far the largest ferry on the mid-Baltic routes, the most outstanding aspect of the *Fennia* was her splendid interior design, the work of the renowned Finnish architect Bengt Lundsten.

Lundsten believed that a ship's interior should act as an elegant backdrop to the passengers, whose clothes and movement provided colour. The neutral palettes of browns, blues and greys for carpets, curtains and upholstery were accented with boldly-coloured contemporary artworks and with modernist Eero Saarinen 'Tulip' and Arne Jacobsen 'Swan' and 'Ant' chairs in leather, all set against unadorned expanses of matt-varnished wood-veneered panelling. This understated approach was very different from that of subsequent Baltic ferry interior designers who invariably preferred glitz and bold ornamentation to understatement. Overall, the *Fennia* could carry 1,200 passengers in more spacious comfort than on the smaller *Skandia* and *Nordia* (there were 300 berths for night crossings, as opposed to the mere 136 of the earlier ships) and up to 225 cars. Below the vehicle deck, there were further cabins, a cinema, a swimming pool and a sauna bath and, on the topmost deck, there was an oval-shaped cocktail bar inside the dummy funnel with a 360-degree panoramic view across the beautiful archipelago scenery. Most importantly, at least from a commercial viewpoint, the *Fennia* was the first Baltic ferry to have a self-service tax-free shop, which was placed forward of amidships on the main deck. As all existing ferries sold duty-free items over-the-counter at kiosks, passengers could queue for hours before successfully making their purchases. After the *Fennia*, the self-service 'snabköp' became a standard feature of Baltic ferries and, as the ships increased in size, so too did the shopping facilities which, in time, became veritable floating supermarkets.

Sailing daily from Stockholm to Mariehamn, Turku and return, the *Fennia* set the standard for future ferries to emulate and she went on to enjoy a long and highly successful career on a number of Baltic routes. Now, nearly forty years since she was first commissioned and having been much rebuilt in the interim, she remains in the Baltic area, latterly having operated across the Gulf of Bothnia twice a day as RG Line's *Casino Express*.

After the *Fennia*, which remained a one-off design, Silja Line returned to Wärtsilä to have built two 'mini-Fennias' which combined the general arrangement and dimensions of the *Skandia* and the *Nordia* with the most successful aspects of the

The **Fennia** discharges cars in Turku in the early 1970s. *(Ambrose Greenway)*

*Fennia*'s onboard design. Although Bengt Lundsten's interior design was, once again, warmly praised, so far as size was concerned Silja Line had made the wrong decision. The *Botnia* and the *Floria*, as the ships were named upon delivery in 1967 and 1970 respectively, were too small to cope with growing demand – indeed, with space for only 1,042, their capacities were actually lower than those of the original Silja car ferries. In order to optimize fuel economy when sailing at different speeds on day and night crossings and to provide extra power for ice-breaking during the winter, an unusual engine arrangement was specified with no less than eight small diesels, four geared to each propeller shaft. As a result, the pair were also mechanically complicated and so both were sold out of the fleet in 1975 to Compania Trasmediterranea in Spain. The two remained in Spanish territorial waters until 2008 when both were withdrawn and consigned to scrap. The former had become ARMAS' *Tarrafal*, linking the Canary Islands with Morocco, and the latter ended her career as Iscomar's *Carmen Del Mar*.

The *Floria* was followed by two ro-ro ferries, the *Holmia*, delivered in 1971, and the *Silvia*, which arrived in 1972. These were built by Kristiansands Mekaniske Verksted in Norway for a Silja Line freight service from Norrtälje to Turku, but this initiative was short-lived and, after only one year, both had been sold. Quite simply, the freight market had not developed sufficiently to support dedicated ships and so, thereafter, Silja Line concentrated on expanding their passenger business. (Much later, incidentally, the *Holmia* became the Isle of Man Steam Packet Company's *Peveril*).

The **Floria**, built by Wärtsilä, photographed when new. *(Robert Spark)*

*The handsome **Bore I** in her original livery. The forward funnel is a dummy and the windows near the base show that it actually contains a conference room. (Bruce Peter collection)*

Silja attempted once again to replicate the *Fennia*'s winning formula when, in the latter 1960s, the Line began development work on two new overnight ferries to inaugurate a car ferry route from Stockholm to Helsinki. The early development work was, once more, carried out by Carl-Bertel Ekström, following capacity specifications provided by Silja's Swedish and Finnish Marketing Directors, Gösta Ryning and Kalevi Etelä, and with a great deal of design input from FÅA's newly-appointed Passenger Director, Björn-H Harms. A lawyer by training, he had joined FÅA's Legal Department in 1962, dealing with accident claims and other matters arising mainly from the company's general cargo operations, but his real desire was to be promoted to the Passenger Department. He succeeded in 1965, becoming Passenger Director only three years later when the existing incumbent, Captain Arnold Neumann, retired.

Partly because Wärtsilä's order book was already well filled with cruise ships to be delivered to Royal Caribbean and Royal Viking Line and partly because a good price was quoted, the new Stockholm-Helsinki ferries were to be constructed by the Dubigeon-Normandie shipyard at Nantes in France. Fortunately, this yard already had some car ferry design and building expertise as, in the 1968-71 period, they had designed and built two large overnight ferries for Paquet Lines and for P&O Southern Ferries – the *Massalia* and the *Eagle*. A third vessel of a broadly similar kind, the *Bolero*, had been ordered by a Norwegian consortium of Fred. Olsen Lines, Fearnley & Eger, J. Ludwig Mowinckels and Roald P. Aukner. This had been intended for a new ferry service between Travemünde in West Germany and Södertälje in Sweden. During construction, the plan was abandoned and, upon delivery in 1973, the *Bolero* was used instead by Fred. Olsen in North American waters and subsequently on the North Sea. Eventually, she did briefly appear in the Baltic in 1985 under charter to Vaasa-Umeå Oy.

These three vessels all shared a hull form and layout copied with

*The twin funnels of the **Bore I**. (Robert Spark)*

permission from the Knud E. Hansen A/S-designed *Freeport* of 1968, albeit slightly longer. Uptakes from the twin Pielstick diesels were routed through broad side casings, which also contained two decks of outside cabins. The main deck of the superstructure was filled with further cabins and, above, there was a saloon deck. More public rooms were found on Boat Deck, with the officers' accommodation one deck higher still. Twin funnels were located towards the stern whereas, on the *Freeport*, the split uptakes rejoined in the superstructure and were routed upwards through a central casing. This general layout was perpetuated in the new Silja Line Stockholm-Helsinki ferries, which also incorporated design features imported from the *Fennia* – for example, the stepping inwards of the superstructure decks – and, from FÅA's *Finlandia*, the specification of hinged bow doors rather than lifting visors.

As with the existing Silja Line ferries, the new overnight vessels were to be ice-breakers to ensure year-round operation and, once again, the interior design was largely entrusted to Bengt Lundsten, working with his assistant Annukka Mikkilä. One thousand passengers could be carried, 439 of whom were berthed in cabins, and there was space for 170 cars. Forward on the saloon deck, there was a large lounge and night club, which was outwith Bengt Lundsten's brief and instead designed by French architects. Amidships, there was a cafeteria and, towards the stern, the buffet and *à la carte* restaurants, both of which Lundsten decorated in vivid colours with fashionable Finnish glassfibre chairs. Below the car deck were economy cabins, a swimming pool, sauna baths and a disco.

The *Aallotar* and the *Svea Regina* were delivered to Silja Line in February and May 1972 respectively, perfect timing to build up spring trade before offering a summer service of daily departures in both directions. The initiative proved to be a considerable success, so much so that, after only three years, larger vessels were introduced in their place and they were switched, albeit briefly, to the Norrtälje-Turku route before being sold in 1976 when Silja Line carried out a rationalization programme. The service from Norrtälje was withdrawn at the same time as the traditional overnight passenger route from Stockholm (Skeppsbron) to Helsinki finally closed. In future, Silja Line would concentrate their resources on running fewer routes but using larger ferries to achieve effective economies of scale. The policy of reducing operations to the core Stockholm-Helsinki and Stockholm-Turku routes was devised by Harry Österberg (born 1922), who had replaced Nils Wetterstein as Silja Line's Managing Director upon the latter's retirement in 1974. From the mid-1970s until his retirement in early 1986, Österberg presided over Silja Line's most lucrative years, during which a succession of splendid ferries entered service for the operator.

The **Viking 1** battles through a choppy Åland Sea in the early 1970s. *(Ambrose Greenway)*

Österberg had risen quickly through the managerial ranks at Bore, where he had encouraged the building of new Silja Line car ferries. The most recent of these was the *Bore I*, which was intended as a fleet-mate for the *Fennia*. The 8,528 grt ferry was completed by the Wärtsilä shipyard at Turku in 1973 as Bore's new contribution to Silja Line's Stockholm-Turku service. Powered by four Wärtsilä-Sulzer diesels, she was capable of 22 knots. As with the *Fennia*, accommodation was provided for 1,200 passengers, 332 of whom were berthed in cabins on night crossings, and there was space for up to 359 cars. The general arrangement was also similar to that of the *Fennia*, although the hull lines were finer at the bow and, most notably, very large windows were installed in all of the public rooms to maximize the views to the passing archipelago.

If the *Fennia* vaguely resembled the *Rotterdam*, then the twin-funnelled *Bore I* had an affinity with the Swedish-American liners *Gripsholm* and *Kungsholm*, but with completely straight hull lines. As with these famous transAtlantic motor ships, however, the forward funnel was a dummy, placed there purely for aesthetic reasons to balance the profile because Bore Line's owner had a penchant for twin-funnelled ships. In fact, in its base, there was a small conference room. The ship's interiors were the work of an up-and-coming Finnish interior designer called Vuokko Laakso, who had a liking for the bright colours and synthetic materials typical of contemporary 1970s taste. Where the *Fennia* was sedate, the *Bore I* was psychedelic, garish even, but Laakso's design work was highly effective in creating warm and stimulating environments in which to unwind and enjoy food, drink and live music.

### Viking Line's First Generation of Purpose-built Ferries

Throughout the 1970s, Scandinavian car ferries continued to grow in size to achieve better economies of scale and to offer ever more elaborate passenger facilities to generate greater onboard revenue. During the first half of the decade, the various partners in the Silja Line and Viking Line consortia took delivery of a succession of new ferries – but Silja's were generally the larger and more impressive, while Viking Line's subsequent new-

The SF Line jumbo ferry **Aurella** - the first really large, high-capacity member of the Viking Line fleet - is obviously well loaded with cars and freight as she ploughs her way across the Baltic in this mid-1970s scene. *(Ambrose Greenway)*

buildings of the latter 1980s were bigger than those of Silja Line. Finally, in the early 1990s, Silja once again took the design lead. While Silja Line emphasized the quality and style of their ships, Viking concentrated on offering 'value for money' with cheaper fares to undercut their rivals and thereby increase their market share. Indeed, in the 1967-68 period, Silja and Viking had a price

The **Aurella** is seen off Kapellskär, towards the end of her Viking Line career. *(Risto Brzoza)*

The **Aurella**, viewed from a passing ferry in the latter 1970s. *(Bruce Peter collection)*

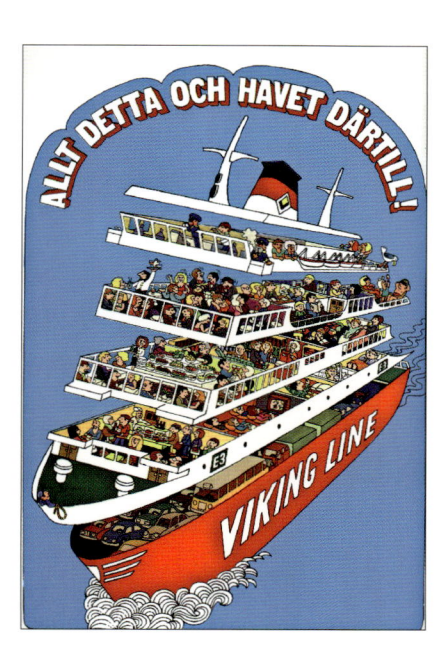

war with the latter slashing fares by half. Although Silja did not follow suit, both companies greatly increased their passenger loadings and, for the first time, tax-free sales of alcoholic drinks became the ferries' main source of income. At the same time, emigration from Finland to Sweden reached its peak with 200,000 Finns crossing the Baltic to find work. These budget-conscious travellers preferred Viking Line's lower fares and so this situation further augmented Viking Line's share of business.

Six new ferries built by Jos. L. Meyer Werft at Papenburg represented Viking Line's 'first generation' of purpose-built vessels for the 1970s. Located far inland, up the River Ems, the Jos. L. Meyer shipyard had been founded in 1795. For most of the ensuing two centuries, the yard had built small cargo vessels such as sailing barges and, subsequently, steam and motor coasters. The first significant passenger ship to be built at Papenburg was the Danish Bornholm ferry *Bornholmerpilen*, delivered to the Dampskibs-Selskab paa Bornholm af 1866 in 1963. A larger car ferry for the same operator, the *Hammershus*, followed in 1965. Due to the constricted width of the river, these ships – and all others built at Papenburg until 1990 – were launched sideways into the Ems, a spectacular and somewhat hair-raising operation. The first Viking Line ferry from Papenburg was the 4,238 grt *Apollo*, ordered by Rederi AB Slite and delivered in 1970. Although the overall dimensions of the hull (108.7 x 17.2 metres) were similar to Silja's initial ferries, the design was different. The Papenburg solution had sheer and camber – and also an ice-strengthened bulbous bow to increase buoyancy and to improve the flow of water around the hull, thereby enhancing its efficiency. There was a pronounced knuckle joint just above the water-line. Power was supplied by only two four-stroke 12-cylinder Deutz diesels, giving a service speed of approximately 19 knots and illustrating how ferry engine design had developed since the early 1960s. There were Kamewa controllable-pitch propellers and twin rudders, which made the vessel highly manoeuvrable. As with Silja Line's 'first generation' of ferries, the engine room was towards the stern, where the exhaust was routed through a vent in the base of the rear mast. To balance the profile, water tanks and the air-conditioning equipment were placed in a large dummy funnel.

The car deck had a casing located starboard of the centre-line, with three vehicle lanes to port and two to starboard. In all, 260 cars could be accommodated, also using hoistable platform decks. Twelve hundred passengers could be carried, 222 of whom were berthed in cabins, some of which were below the car deck forward of the engine room, but the majority were on the main deck above. The passenger saloons were full-width with a restaurant forward on the saloon deck, a cafeteria amidships and a lounge on Boat Deck, above. Aft of these facilities, there were saloons containing reclining chairs. Decoratively, however, the *Apollo* was typically German, with dark woodwork and sombre colours throughout - this notwithstanding the input of the well-known Swedish ship interior design specialist, Robert Tillberg, who had previously worked to considerable acclaim on Swedish American Line's famous *Kungsholm* and, thereafter, on ferries for Stena Line (the *Stena Danica* and *Stena Nordica* of 1965, followed by the *Stena Danica* of 1969) and cruise ships for Øivind Lorentzen's Flagship Cruises (the *Sea Venture* and the *Island Venture*).

Although the general arrangement of the first three of Rederi AB Sally's ferries was basically the same as that of Slite's *Apollo*, the interior design was far superior, with fresh colours and designer furniture and lighting throughout, thanks to the input of the wives of the company's directors, all of whom were enthusiastic patrons of modern Finnish design. The final vessel in the series for Sally, the *Viking 5*, was an elongated version of the previous ships, measuring 117.8 metres and powered by two 14-cylinder Smit-Bolnes diesels.

The Jos. L. Meyer Werft-built 'Papenburgers' were a conspicuous success on Viking Line's Kapellskär-Mariehamn-Naantali, Stockholm-Mariehamn-Turku and Stockholm-Helsinki routes. These vessels were all rather dwarfed by SF Line's next new contribution to Viking Line, the high-capacity jumbo ferry *Aurella*. Gunnar Eklund had learned from Viking Line's late 1960s price war with Silja that, to be successful in a future ferry market characterized by rising oil prices and increasing wages, it would be necessary to achieve unprecedented economies of scale and that the ships built for Slite and Sally by Jos. L. Meyer Werft were inefficient as the same schedule could be maintained between Kapellskär, Mariehamn and Naantali with two larger ferries, rather than four small ones. In particular, Eklund must have been aware of Stena Line's 1969-built *Stena Danica* on the Gothenburg-Frederikshavn route across the Kattegat between Sweden and Denmark. She offered two decks of high-density passenger accommodation, centred upon revenue-generating 'cruise' activities such as eating, drinking, shopping and gaming. This suggested a formula for a large, new ferry type which would be slightly longer, taller and significantly broader than their predecessors or fleet-mates. Stena had already ordered two examples of this kind of ferry from a shipyard in Yugoslavia. These were designed by the Copenhagen-based consulting naval architects Knud E. Hansen A/S who had, by this stage, practically cornered the market for ferry design in Denmark, Norway, Southern Sweden and beyond.

Viking Line's 7,210 grt *Aurella*, delivered in 1973 from the J.J.

The **Bore Star** at Stockholm, preparing to leave for Turku. *(Ambrose Greenway)*

Later in her Silja career, the same ferry became Effoa's **Silja Star**. *(Bruce Peter collection)*

Sietas shipyard at Hamburg in West Germany, was similar to the new Stena day ferries. Sailing on the Kapellskär-Mariehamn-Naantali route, the ferry had space for 1,500 passengers and no less than 420 cars. She was arguably the first 'jumbo ferry' crossing the Åland Sea and her high capacity allowed Viking Line further to reduce their fares, making ferry travel cheaper and more accessible to ever wider sections of the Swedish and Finnish populations. During 1973, Viking Line overtook Silja for the first time, transporting 1.84 million passengers as opposed to 1.78 on Silja's ferries. For Viking Line, this marked the beginning of a 20-year reign as the dominant Baltic ferry operator, at least in terms of passenger numbers.

### Silja Line's Second Generation

Only a year after having taken delivery of the *Aallotar* and the *Svea Regina*, Silja Line's three partners each placed a further order with the Dubigeon-Normandie shipyard at Nantes for a larger trio of 12,500 grt ferries. Although these had the same 1,000-passenger capacity as the existing Silja ships, a higher proportion of passengers (two-thirds) were berthed in cabins – and there was a far greater car capacity of 240. The idea was that these 'second generation' vessels would replace not only the *Aallotar* and *Svea Regina* but also the three existing passenger vessels – the *Bore*, the *Svea Jarl* and the *Ilmatar* – and would offer a high-class service with the kind of catering found in First Class on the old passenger steamers. Thus, a significant distinction began to open up between Silja Line and Viking Line ferries. Silja ships, with their slightly higher fares, emphasized comfort and style, whereas Viking Line placed emphasis on entertainment, drinking, buffet dining and tax-free shopping in the context of a more flamboyant, populist image.

The first of the new ferries, the Swedish-flagged *Svea Corona*, entered service in the funnel livery of Rederi AB Svea in May 1975. Next, FÅA's *Wellamo* arrived in September that same year, followed by Bore's *Bore Star* in December. The latter ship did not immediately enter Silja Line's cross-Baltic trades from Stockholm, however, as she was immediately chartered to Finnlines who used her on Mediterranean fly-cruises from Agadir in Morocco. She only arrived in the Baltic to take up Silja service in Bore's funnel livery in May 1976. In appearance they resembled shorter, taller versions of the North Sea vessels *Tor Britannia* and *Tor Scandinavia*, blended with Silja's existing *Aallotar* and *Svea Regina*. Given that, in 1973, the Dubigeon-Normandie shipyard had tendered unsuccessfully to build the 'Tor' sisters, it is interesting to speculate that their design and layout could very well have influenced the yard's approach to Silja's 'second generation' ferries. Furthermore, the same interior designer, Vuokko Laakso, was responsible for the 'Tor' ships as well as the new-buildings for Silja Line.

While the new Silja Line ships were essentially much larger versions of the existing Stockholm-Helsinki ferries, their internal layout marked a subtle change in planning. As before, the hull was arranged with side casings on either beam, containing circulation

The **Svea Corona**, Rederi AB Svea's latest contribution to the Silja Line fleet. *(Ambrose Greenway)*

decks, with the public rooms spread out across the remainder of these decks, aft of the cabins. The Boat Deck contained lounges, bars, a disco and a night club, while the deck below had two restaurants and a cafeteria. On Main Deck, below again, there was the reception hall, lounges with reclining seats, a large tax-free shop and a separate gift shop. The officers and crew occupied the two topmost decks of what was, for that time, a rather tall superstructure, meaning that most had outside cabins and enjoyed a very high standard of accommodation. As general wages and expectations increased in Scandinavia during the 1970s, it became difficult to recruit seafarers and hotel staff to work on ferries, especially when crew cabins on most vessels were sandwiched between the fuel tanks and the car deck, meaning that they tended to be cramped, noisy and airless. Silja Line's new ships, however, were in a different class, for passengers and crew alike. Below the car deck, there was a sauna and an indoor swimming pool, with its own poolside bar.

From a design perspective, the advantage of the 'cabins forward, public rooms aft' layout was that sleeping passengers in the forward section would be less exposed to engine noise and that it would be easier to design and operate a ship with the vertical servicing in the cabin areas – such as showers and vacuum toilets – kept separate from the hotel services of galleys, sculleries, food and bar storage rooms. Quite simply, it was Silja Line's belief that complex modern cruise ferries of this type required to be conceptualized as a series of distinct 'blocks', each with its own ambience and *raison d'etre*.

space plus a large proportion of outside cabins. In the superstructure, whereas the existing ferries had a horizontal cabin and public room layout with whole decks given over to each, the new vessels had the majority of cabins in the forward third of three

On the technical side, the new ferries each had two 12-cylinder

The **Svea Corona** manoeuvres in winter ice at Turku towards the end of her period with Silja Line. By this stage, her funnels had been repainted into Johnson Line's colours. *(Risto Brzoza)*

*The **Finnjet**, as originally envisaged by the Wärtsilä shipyard before restyling by Kimmi Kaivanto. (Shippax Archive)*

Pielstick diesels, generating 24,000 horsepower and giving a 21-knot service speed. While the hull form was basically similar to the existing vessels, one notably retrograde step was the specification of a lifting bow visor, rather than hinged doors. The visor weighed 70 tons but was held shut by only three hydraulic locking pins. During the *Wellamo*'s maiden season, as she headed out from Helsinki in stormy weather, the Captain, Holger Hermansson, noticed that the bow visor was lifting slightly each time the ship hit a wave. He immediately ordered that the ferry be turned around and sailed back to the safety of Helsinki harbour. Thereafter the bow visor was temporarily welded shut and it was only brought back into use once the locking pins had been substantially strengthened.

As ferries and cruise ships increased in size during the 1970s, their cost also grew exponentially and so banks and financiers took a greater interest in their design to ensure the maximum potential profitability – whatever this meant for their external appearance. Thus, the mid-1970s heralded further major advances in Scandinavian ferry design. As ever more capacity was required for cars and, especially, freight while foot passengers wanted to shop tax-free; there was also a need for larger ferries able to fit existing quays. The popular solution was the 'large block principle', which sought to maximize the space utilization of a ferry's hull and superstructure. If ferries could not become significantly longer, they would need to become wider and taller. Four ships developed by Stena Line for the charter market in the mid-1970s perhaps best demonstrated the new approach, being essentially shoe-box-shaped above the water-line (apart from their bows). These were the *Marine Atlantica*, *Stena Nautica*, *Stena Nordica* and *Stena Normandica*, built by Rickmers Werft in Bremerhaven, West Germany in 1974-75. While no doubt efficient, profitable and able to offer passengers a far greater range of facilities, the new generation which entered service thereafter often presented an increasingly bluff and hefty appearance.

### The Fabulous Finnjet

The three most outstanding vessels of the era – the 15,600 grt North Sea vessels *Tor Britannia* and *Tor Scandinavia* of 1975-76 and Finnlines' 24,605 grt Travemünde-Helsinki vessel *Finnjet* of 1977 – ingeniously avoided the excesses of the 'large block principle' design. Not only were all of these ships much bigger

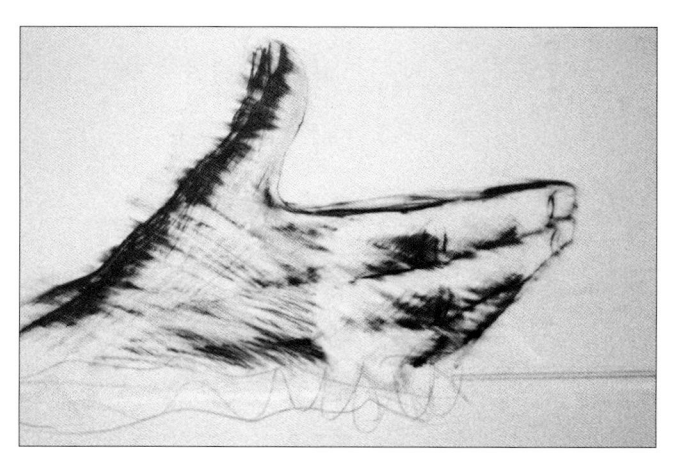

*'Hands across the sea' - one of Kimmi Kaivanto's initial sketches. (Bruce Peter)*

*The inspiration for the **Finnjet**'s funnels and hull form. (Bruce Peter)*

The **Finnjet** in her original midnight blue and white livery. The graphic design was notably successful and gave the ship a very clean, almost futuristic appearance. *(Ambrose Greenway)*

than any ferry yet seen, but they were also exceptionally fast, meaning that all had long and sleek hulls and relatively low superstructure profiles. The 'Tor' ships were slightly streamlined, each boasting an enormous funnel located two-thirds aft which usefully contained banks of exhaust silencers but also reflected their great power and speed.

The *Finnjet*, however, more closely reflected the development of 'large block principle' ferry design – albeit in elongated form. The design was produced by a team of Wärtsilä naval architects, working under the Head of the yard's Project Department, Kai Levander. The profile of the superstructure was uncompromisingly rectilinear with a flat frontal aspect, which appeared to pull the ship's dead mass along behind it, and a transom stern. Initial sketches of the vessel produced by the builder, Wärtsilä, showed a silhouette not dissimilar to Silja Line's most recent French newbuildings – in particular, it resembled the 1975 *Wellamo* of Silja Line in her subsequent lengthened form as Fjord Line's *Jupiter*. Finnlines, however, employed the artist Kimmo Kaivanto to improve the silhouette and so a series of sketches was produced, suggesting that the vessel should be styled to resemble 'hands across the sea'. The bow above the water was to be shaped like cupped hands with the funnels in the form of upturned thumbs. The demarcation of the midnight-blue hull and the white superstructure was derived from the proportions of traditional Finnish fishing craft. An unusually robust bow door arrangement was fitted with a narrow two-piece folding visor set well forward of the watertight inner door-cum-vehicle ramp. Jetting along at over 30 knots in open water, the *Finnjet*'s bow needed to be strong but, as we shall see, subsequent Baltic ferries of the 1980s were less securely designed and, eventually, this deficiency had tragic

The **Finnjet** in winter ice in the latter 1970s. *(Burkhard Schütt collection)*

The main stairwell and entrance hallway on the **Finnjet**. *(Philip Dawson)*

The **Finnjet**'s observation lounge, located on the topmost deck. *(Philip Dawson)*

The **Finnjet**'s elegant à la carte restaurant. *(Shippax archive)*

Part of the **Finnjet**'s orange, black and white cafeteria. *(Bruce Peter collection)*

The **Finnjet**'s night club, with its distinctive waffle-plate ceiling. *(Philip Dawson)*

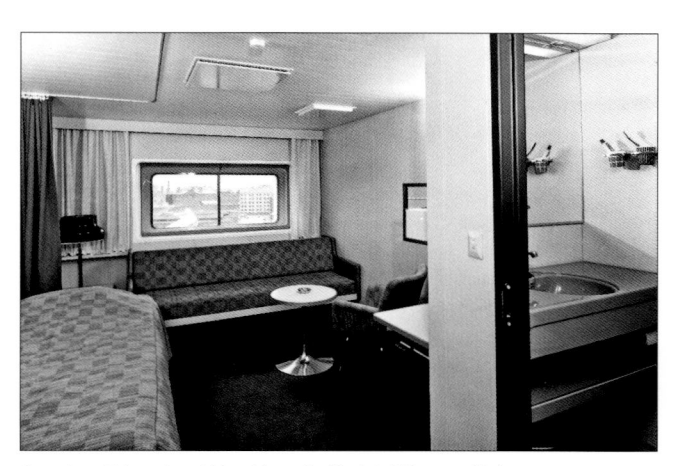

A spacious high-grade outside cabin on the **Finnjet**. *(Shippax archive)*

The walk-in tax-free supermarket on board the **Finnjet**. *(Shippax archive)*

consequences.

Appearances aside, the most significant aspects of the 'Tor' ships and of the *Finnjet* were their power plants and their passenger facilities. While the former were propelled at over 26 knots by a mighty line-up of four Pielstick PC3 diesels, the *Finnjet* could attain an amazing 30.5 knots, thanks to two Pratt & Whitney gas turbines. In the long run, these proved not to be fuel-efficient – especially when the ship was lightly loaded in the winter months – and so twin 18-cylinder Wärtsilä-Vaasa diesels were added during a 1981 refit, enabling a more economical 18.5-knot speed as a slower alternative. These were installed in casings on either side of the vehicle deck towards the stern and provided power via electric transmission to the existing propeller shafts. While the *Finnjet*'s vehicle capacity was slightly reduced due to this installation, the ferry did become profitable, at least for a time.

The high speed potential of the three ships, achieved as it was by a variety of means, considerably reduced sailing times and brought the lengths of the passages from Felixstowe to Gothenburg and from Travemünde to Helsinki down to within 24 hours. The *Finnjet* could carry 1,800 passengers, 1,532 of whom were berthed in cabins, and 380 cars.

Vuokko Laakso was involved in designing aspects of each of the ships' interiors – in the case of the 'Tor' sisters, working alongside the Danish architect Kay Kørbing on the entertainment facilities. On the *Finnjet*, Laakso conceived the dance saloon, pub and grill restaurant. Quite spectacular these spaces were too, making extensive use of her favoured glassfibre, moulded plastic and other light and fresh materials. Other spaces were designed by Studio Nurmesniemi and Sistem Oy. Because the *Finnjet*'s gas turbine power plant was inevitably noisy, the cabins were located in the forward half of the superstructure with public rooms spread over three decks aft. (The 'Tor' ships shared a similar arrangement.) Later, in the 1980s, several German-designed overnight ferries – for example the *Viking Sally*, the *Olau Britannia*, the *Olau Hollandia*, the *Peter Pan*, the *Nils Holgersson* and the *Koningin Beatrix* – also adopted this type of layout. It was seldom repeated on succeeding Baltic ferries, however, as a horizontal layering of the cabin accommodation and public rooms came to be preferred from a commercial standpoint to enable entire decks to be given over to more extensive leisure and entertainment facilities, lessening the temptation of passengers to go back to their cabins instead of spending money in the public spaces. In addition, there was a 'sky bar' on the topmost deck and a sauna and swimming complex beneath the car deck, where some budget cabins were also located.

Because the ship's necessarily broad gas turbine exhaust casings required to be routed upwards inboard of the shell and because there was a desire to make the hull as slender as possible, there were only narrow passages on either beam linking the main public rooms, rather than the wide arcades found on many another ferry of the period – not least the 'Tor' ships. The restaurant filled the entire width of Deck 4 amidships, with a galley to the rear. Above, on Deck 5, there was a grill room amidships to port, with the duty-free shop to starboard and a show lounge aft of the machinery space. (With its layered waffle-plate ceiling, this somewhat

The artwork for a large photo-mural in the **Finnjet**'s main stairwell. *(Shippax archive)*

*The view towards the **Finnjet**'s bow as she crunches through a rough Baltic Sea. (Ambrose Greenway)*

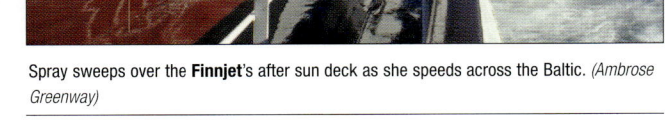

*Spray sweeps over the **Finnjet**'s after sun deck as she speeds across the Baltic. (Ambrose Greenway)*

resembled the Queen's Lounge on Cunard's *Queen Elizabeth 2*.) On Deck 6, there was a night club, snack bar and conference suite (the central space of which could also be used by passengers as a cinema).

Undoubtedly, the *Finnjet* was the outstanding ferry of her generation and she set many of the trends for future Baltic ferry design.

### Viking Line's Second Generation

Already when the *Finnjet* entered service, both the members of the Viking Line and Silja Line partnerships were in discussions with Wärtsilä about the design of their next generation of vessels. In the interim, the Viking Line partner Rederi AB Slite took delivery of the 11,671 grt *Diana II*, which appeared in June 1979 from Jos. L. Meyer Werft at Papenburg in West Germany. Previously, Meyer Werft had built Viking Line's six ferries of the early 1970s, which then remained the backbone of the consortium's expanding fleet. The *Diana II* was, essentially, a much enlarged version of these vessels with bigger dimensions, a more fulsome profile, straight hull lines and an extra deck of cabins.

In the 1979-80 period, another Viking partner, SF Line, received two 10,757 grt vessels – the *Turella* and the *Rosella* – from

*The **Viking Song** and **Viking Saga** were bulky, but hardly beautiful, ships. After only five years, they had been displaced from the Stockholm-Helsinki route by larger tonnage. (Viking Line)*

Framed by reeds and pine trees, the **Rosella** approaches Mariehamn on a blustery afternoon in August 2008. *(Bruce Peter)*

Wärtsilä. According to the Swedish ferry industry historian Klas Brogren, SF's Managing Director, Gunnar Eklund, whose company had previously built their ferries in Yugoslavia, had a keen eye for a bargain and had planned to build the ships in Japan. The Finnish bank providing the mortgage, however, baulked at the thought of such a large sum of Finnish markka going to the Far East and so the two were built in Finland, costing both owner and bank 40% more than the Japanese quotation. Because much of the conceptual design work had been carried out by SF's Technical Inspector, Kaj Jansson, based upon an enlargement of the company's existing *Aurella*, the design was atypical of the output of Wärtsilä's own drawing office. As they were intended for the Kapellskär-Mariehamn-Naantali and Stockholm-Mariehamn-Turku routes, the sisters had a high capacity of 1,700 passengers each, but with berths for only 740 in cabins located above and in the forward section below the main saloon deck. Forward, there was a cafeteria with a buffet restaurant above, just as on the *Aurella*, and there was a large bar and night club at the after end. These were linked by two parallel midships arcades, awkwardly split along the centre-line by the engine casing and, consequently, leaving room only for smaller public rooms on either side.

No less than 535 cars could be carried, the aft two-thirds of Main Deck being given over to an extra upper car deck, as on the *Aurella*. Four Wärtsilä-Pielstick diesels gave a 21.5-knot service speed. Although practical, rather than inspiring, ferries, the *Turella* and the *Rosella* proved to be extremely useful in everyday service; indeed the *Rosella* remains a front-line member of the Viking Line fleet, currently operating between Kapellskär and Mariehamn. Viking's next acquisitions were to be larger again, however – in fact, they shared many of the layout characteristics of the *Finnjet*, albeit in a shorter, broader hull and superstructure envelope – and with conventional motor propulsion.

In the wider Scandinavian region, a succession of 'large block principle' ferries, each of around 15,000 grt, was ordered for delivery in the early 1980s, mainly for Swedish operators. The Sessanlinjen-owned *Kronprinsessan Victoria* and *Prinsessan Birgitta*, as well as Rederi AB Gotland's *Visby* and *Wasa Star*, were all Danish-designed and Swedish-built for relatively short high-density crossings, offering expanded passenger entertainment and shopping facilities as well as significant cabin accommodation. The former pair were designed by Aalborg

Viking Line's **Turella** leaves Mariehamn. *(Viking Line)*

The **Diana II** navigates through winter ice among the islands of the Turku archipelago in this winter scene, taken in the mid-1980s. *(Bruce Peter collection)*

Værft, using their experience gained from the 1978 *Dana Anglia* and the anticipated 1982 Caribbean cruise ship *Tropicale*. As with this innovative vessel, the new Sessan ferries had terraced show lounges, ingeniously located above the ramps accessing the upper vehicle deck – but, having conceived them, Aalborg failed to secure the order to build them when the Swedish authorities helped Gothenburg Arendal Shipyard to place a lower (and ultimately successful) bid.

The *Visby* and the *Wasa Star* (which should have entered service as the *Gotland* but was instead chartered out to Vaasa-Umeå Oy) were designed by Knud E. Hansen A/S, the Copenhagen-based consulting naval architects, along similar lines to the Sessan sisters, with cabins forward and two decks of public rooms aft. These vessels were built with the aid of a generous Swedish Government subsidy to save the Öresundsvarvet at Landskrona from closure – but their owner, Rederi AB Gotland, did not think that there would be sufficient traffic for two 14,932 grt vessels, each carrying 2,072 passengers and 515 cars, on their domestic routes to the island of Gotland. Consequently, the second sister first entered service for Vaasa-Umeå Oy, crossing the Gulf of Bothnia in the Northern Baltic between Sundsvall, Umeå and Vaasa. Here too, she was too big for the traffic at that time and, moreover, did not have sufficient ice-breaking capacity to withstand winter service; consequently, after a short and unsuccessful Mediterranean sub-charter, she ended up sailing between Larvik and Frederikshavn as the *Peter Wessel*. The *Visby* is now Polferries' *Scandinavia*, while the Sessan sisters were absorbed early on into the Stena fleet.

Meanwhile, designs for a new generation of ferries of similar concept were developed for the Central Baltic routes. The 13,878 grt *Viking Song* and *Viking Saga* were ordered from Wärtsilä by Rederi AB Sally for delivery during the summer of 1980. Although not much larger in terms of tonnage than Silja's mid-1970s vessels, the *Wellamo*, the *Svea Corona* and the *Bore Star*, the use of a 'large block principle' design, with the superstructure extending all the way to the stern, significantly increased inboard deck space. Furthermore – and, at that time, uniquely – the lifeboats were nested in recesses built into the topsides of the hull. Thus, each of the new 'Vikings' could accommodate no less than 2,000 passengers, 1,250 of whom were berthed, as well as 462 cars, with nightly departures on the Stockholm-Helsinki route.

The brand-new **Viking Sally**, photographed from a pilot launch. *(Ambrose Greenway)*

The bar on the **Viking Sally**, finished in dark imitation woodwork. *(Bruce Peter collection)*

The **Viking Sally**'s restaurant, furnished in rich orange tones. *(Bruce Peter collection)*

On board, the new sisters arguably marked the beginning of the 1980s so-called 'champagne economy' in Scandinavia in that they felt more like floating hotels than conventional ships. As with the UK, there was a major expansion of the service industries, in particular the financial services sector, leading to a large number of city workers having a great deal of disposable income to spend in their leisure time. Of course, work and pleasure could also be mixed at business conferences and corporate events, and so both Viking Line and Silja Line placed an increasing emphasis on attracting business customers by providing ferries designed to be more like hotel resorts. On board the *Viking Song* and *Viking Saga*, there were various restaurants, night clubs, an octagonal-shaped disco located aft on the topmost deck and a large sauna and swimming pool complex. In common with the most recent SF Line ferries, the *Turella* and the *Rosella*, power was provided by four Wärtsilä diesels, coupled in pairs via gearboxes to each propeller shaft. This arrangement became standard practice on nearly all subsequent Baltic ferries.

As a result of their new-building programme, Sally reinforced their position as the dominant partner in the Viking Line consortium; indeed, they expanded widely (and, with hindsight, unwisely) on many fronts – in the international bulk shipping trades, in US-based cruise ships and in a ferry service across the English Channel from Ramsgate to Dunkerque, which was marketed as Sally Viking Line. One reason for this approach was that the company's magisterial Chairman, Algot Johansson, had retired in 1976, and subsequently the firm apparently lacked a pragmatic sense of direction.

Back on their 'home territory' in the Baltic, Sally took over an order which had been placed by Rederi AB Slite for a third large ferry from Meyer Werft at Papenburg. This was also to be delivered in 1980. The 15,556 grt ship was named the *Viking Sally* and was intended for the Stockholm-Mariehamn-Turku route. Akin to the Finnish-built *Finnjet*, the *Viking Song* and the *Viking Saga*, the *Viking Sally* had a cabins forward, public rooms aft layout. In silhouette, the vessel had a fulsome profile with a highly flared bow and a tall, flat-fronted superstructure. That the *Viking Sally* had been designed and built first and foremost to sail on a relatively sheltered route, mainly through the archipelago, was very apparent from her somewhat unwieldy appearance. Unlike the high-speed *Finnjet*, the *Viking Sally* was fitted with a lifting visor and, tragically, much later in the ship's career, the arrangement came in for severe criticism when she sank in a storm when sailing between Tallinn and Stockholm as the *Estonia* (see below). That, however, was far into the future and, in the early 1980s, there was tremendous confidence in the expansion of the Baltic ferry industry. Swedish and Finnish banks were only too pleased to extend loans to the shipping lines to purchase a succession of ever larger vessels.

When the *Diana II*, the *Viking Song*, the *Viking Saga* and the *Viking Sally* were introduced, Viking Line's 'first generation' of ferries was displaced. The *Marella* and the *Kapella* were sold to Greece, while the *Viking 1* and the *Diana* were transferred to Vaasa-Umeå Oy for service across the Gulf of Bothnia as the *Wasa Express* and the *Botnia Express*. The *Apollo*, the *Viking 4* and the *Viking 5* moved to British waters as the *Olau Kent*, the *Earl Granville* and *The Viking* respectively, although the latter quickly returned to the

The **Viking Sally** speeds towards Kapellskär. *(Anders Ahlerup)*

The newly-completed **Finlandia**. *(Ambrose Greenway collection)*

The **Silvia Regina** with Rederi AB Svea's funnel livery. *(Bruce Peter collection)*

The **Finlandia** is seen off Turku when on builder's trials, shortly before being delivered to Silja Line. *(Shippax archive)*

The **Finlandia** is seen in evening light after major surgery on her bow. *(William Mayes)*

The **Finlandia** manoeuvres in Helsinki. *(Ambrose Greenway)*

The 'Maxim Terrass' buffet restaurant on the **Finlandia**. *(Ambrose Greenway collection)*

The **Finlandia**'s 'Maxim' à la carte restaurant, below. *(Ambrose Greenway collection)*

Baltic in 1983 as the *Sally Express* of Vaasa-Umeå Oy. The reason was that Enso-Gutzeit had sold Vaasa-Umeå Oy to Rederi AB Sally, who decided that the ice-strengthened ferry would be better employed in the Northern Baltic, replacing a large chartered jumbo ferry, the *Wasa Star*.

### Silja Line's Third Generation

Silja, meanwhile, had developed a slightly upmarket reputation with their all-white fleet and higher fares and they sought to outdo Viking Line decisively with two superior overnight vessels for the Stockholm-Helsinki route which were to be the biggest ferries yet seen anywhere in the world. One ship was ordered each by Rederi AB Svea and by Effoa (formerly FÅA) from Wärtsilä for delivery in 1981. Bore's Chairman, Gilbert von Rettig, declined to order a similar ferry, arguing that such a vessel would be a poor investment for his company. Although the Baltic ferry industry was about to enter its most lucrative decade ever, in the longer term von Rettig's assessment was probably correct. Therefore, Bore withdrew from the Silja Line consortium in 1980 and their passenger ships, the *Bore I* and the *Bore Star*, were transferred to Effoa, becoming the *Skandia* and the *Silja Star* respectively.

The 25,905 grt *Finlandia* was the first to appear in March 1981 and, as befitted Finland's new national flagship, she was named in Helsinki by its First Lady, Tellervo Koivisto. Rederi AB Svea's *Silvia Regina* followed that June, having been launched at the shipyard by Sweden's Drottning Silvia.

In appearance, the new ships were typical of the 'large block principle' tonnage of the period – their all-white liveries only serving to emphasize their four-square external appearance which dominated Stockholm and Helsinki harbours in a way that no ferries had done before. In particular, the first of the new sisters to enter service, the *Finlandia*, provided a dramatic contrast with Silja's comparatively elegant previous generation of French-built ferries, dating from the mid-1970s.

The style and scale of the main public rooms was, however, the compelling feature of the sisters. Forward, they boasted restaurants on two levels with a huge window giving spectacular views of the Baltic scenery. Adjacent there were orchestra stands and marble dance floors. On the lower level was the 'Maxim à la Carte' – a gourmet restaurant fronting the dance floor. Tiffany lamps, walls featuring the signs of the zodiac in cut glass, illuminated stained glass panels, mirrored mosaic reliefs and subdued lighting mimicked the style of a cabaret club. The plan was that passengers should be able to enjoy dining, followed by a live cabaret show, with lounge dancing thereafter in a night club ambience. Such venues are highly popular on *terra firma*, both in Sweden and Finland. Above was the 'Maxim Terrass Buffet' – a self-service restaurant with 'smorgasbord' dining. This was a

The wide arcade on the **Finlandia**'s saloon deck. *(Ambrose Greenway collection)*

A superior outside cabin on the **Finlandia**. *(Ambrose Greenway collection)*

*Silja Line's **Svea** glides through a mirror-calm archipelago, shortly after being introduced on the Stockholm-Mariehamn-Turku route in 1985. (Risto Brzoza)*

marble-floored space with columns adorned by lacquered metal branches with leaves, potted plants and fresh green tones. Double-curved staircases on either side of the dance floor linked the two levels. These spaces had a warm and congenial appearance, which is what their designer, Vuokko Laakso, had intended. The other public rooms, which admittedly were less impressive, were connected by an airy arcade on the starboard side, designed by Carita Holthoer who also drew up the cabin designs. Every cabin had *en suite* facilities and some even had private jacuzzis, waterbeds and satellite television (a real innovation in 1981). Certain cabins were designed with disabled facilities, while others were trimmed in non-allergic materials. The Finnish interior designer Ilmo Issakainen was responsible for the design of the large swimming, sauna and fitness complex on the lowest passenger deck, as well as the conference suite and children's play area, both of which were higher up in the superstructure. Indeed, such was the demand for conferences at sea that, after only a couple of years in service, Silja Line had large prefabricated modules, containing theatre auditoria, added to the superstructure amidships in a space adjacent to the existing conference facilities.

A containerized system for loading supplies and unloading waste was devised so that the pair could be serviced and restocked with relative ease during their daily layovers in Stockholm and Helsinki. Silja extended their 'cruise service' policy to staff uniforms, crew training and every aspect of onboard service. They also made

*The **Wellamo** is seen near Furusund. (Anders Ahlerup)*

*A stern-quarter view of the **Wellamo** when newly introduced. (Bruce Peter collection)*

'La Coupole', the à la carte restaurant on the **Wellamo**. *(William Mayes)*

The **Wellamo**'s 'Club Fontana' in typical 1980s style. *(William Mayes)*

strenuous efforts to attract business travellers and, to that end, the ships were each fitted with 450-seat conference auditoria during their first refits. The Line claimed that conference traffic accounted for 9% of trade in 1984. Fares for return cruises began at £20 in 1981 and passenger figures rose sharply from 1,100,000 to over the 2 million mark. Cruise trips accounted for 35% of journeys.

This careful attention to detail set these sisters apart from the competition and helped to capture the public's imagination. Perhaps inevitably, such advanced ships were not without their teething problems. They acquitted themselves well in the ice of a first winter, but the *Finlandia* and the *Silvia Regina* slammed, rolled and corkscrewed alarmingly in the autumn gales due to the pronounced knuckle joints in their bow configuration immediately above the water-line, which caught every wave. The reason for this somewhat risky design solution was a desire on the part of the owners to maximize the vehicle deck area – but this was certainly at the expense of comfort and, possibly, safety as well. A precedent for this design solution was the then recently-delivered Wärtsilä-built jumbo ferry *Travemünde* for GT Linien's Gedser-Travemünde crossing of the Southern Baltic between Denmark and Germany. This is a short and sheltered route whereas the Stockholm-Helsinki service is relatively long and sails through open water for two-thirds of its duration. Consequently, extensive surgery was carried out on the bows of the *Finlandia* and the *Silvia Regina* during their first refits. The work improved their motion but they now looked as if giant slices of hull had been chiselled away – which, of course, is essentially what had happened.

Once the Stockholm-Helsinki ships were successfully settled in service, Silja set about providing similar new vessels for the Turku route. As these would sail on 24-hour round-trips, they needed to have seating for large numbers of passengers on day crossings and a night club ambience for evening departures. Wärtsilä's designers, meanwhile, made strenuous attempts to improve the external appearance of these sisters. After all, sailing during the day, they would be seen in passing by countless potential passengers. Moreover, the designers of super-ferries were coming to realize that, just as with cruise ships, the silhouette and livery of a ship are her best advertisement and that it is important for passengers to feel positive about the vessel on which they are going to sail. In terms of exterior aesthetics, the *Viking Saga*, *Viking Song*, *Finlandia* and *Silvia Regina* arguably represented a

The **Svea**'s 'Fun Fun Disco', located beneath the vehicle deck. *(Shippax archive)*

FINLAND/SWEDEN CRUISES ON THE WHITE SHIPS: A WHOLE NEW EXPERIENCE

SILJA LINE

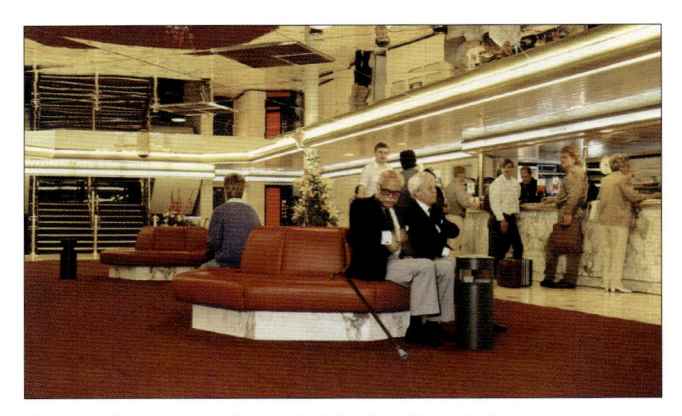

The marble-lined entrance hall on the **Mariella**. *(Bruce Peter collection)*

The **Mariella**'s 'Carl Michael Bellman' gourmet restaurant. *(Bruce Peter collection)*

The impressive-looking **Mariella** at sea: when first introduced, the ferry caused a sensation due to her remarkable size and showy interiors. Even after nearly a quarter of a century in service, she remains a very successful and popular vessel. *(Viking Line)*

The **Mariella**'s 'Cape Horn Club' steakhouse. *(Bruce Peter collection)*

The **Olympia**, the **Mariella**'s Swedish-flagged sister ship. *(William Mayes)*

The **Mariella** glides past Oxdjupet in warm late-summer evening light in August 2008. Note that she has been retro-fitted with a duck-tail at the stern. (Bruce Peter)

low point for ferry design and, thereafter, Baltic super-ferries became progressively more shapely once again.

Silja Line began this trend with the *Svea* and the *Wellamo*, which were delivered by Wärtsilä in 1985 and 1986. Whereas the *Finlandia* and the *Silvia Regina* had flat-fronted superstructures, their new fleet-mates were angled back with a gently curved frontal aspect, matching the rake of the mast and funnel. Furthermore, dark blue stripes were painted around the superstructure on three levels to break up the vertical bulk into smaller volumes, while emphasizing the ships' length. (This tactic had previously been tried on the *Finlandia* and the *Silvia Regina*, but with less success.) A further refinement was the fitting of clam-shell bow doors rather than lifting visors as, even then, there was mounting evidence that visors were prone to break open during winter storms. The clam-shell design was thought to be a safer and more robust option as waves would tend to force the doors more tightly shut, rather than imposing upward pressure on the locking pins.

Internally, the *Svea* and the *Wellamo* were similar in style to Silja's Stockholm-Helsinki sisters, but with a wider range of public rooms. Whereas Vuokko Laakso had designed the restaurants on the earlier ships, this time the task was carried out by a Stockholm architect, Lennart Janson, whose style was somewhat more clinical than the vibrant approach favoured by Laakso. There was also an attempt to attract a broader age demographic than had hitherto been associated with Silja's relatively genteel image and, to that end, a discotheque was located below the car deck, sufficiently remote as not to disturb sleeping passengers. Another,

more superficial, change was that, from the outset, the *Svea* wore the funnel livery of Sweden's Johnson Line rather than that of Rederi AB Svea, as Johnson had taken over Svea's operations in the Silja consortium in the autumn of 1981.

Although the *Svea* and the *Wellamo* were built to approximately the same dimensions as the *Finlandia* and the *Silvia Regina*, their tonnage of around 33,800 gt was somewhat greater as, in the interim, the measurement rules had been changed to include semi-enclosed spaces in the volumetric calculations. Thus, all ferries delivered after 1984, on paper at least, appeared to be somewhat larger than their predecessors. (In this book, ships measured under pre-1984 rules have their tonnages marked in 'grt', or gross registered tons, whereas those delivered post-1984, or re-measured under post-1984 rules, are marked in 'gt', or gross tonnes.)

Only five months after taking delivery of the *Wellamo*, Effoa took the opportunity to buy the gas turbine Helsinki-Travemünde ferry *Finnjet* from Enso-Gutzeit, whose Finnlines subsidiary was struggling to make this, their sole passenger ship, pay. Integrating the *Finnjet* into Silja Line's well-developed brand seemed like a sensible solution, allowing Finnlines to concentrate on their core freight business. After a major internal refurbishment, including the installation of extra cabins and conference rooms on the topmost deck, the *Finnjet* was painted in Silja Line colours for the 1987 season.

With a very superior (and largely uniform) fleet consisting of the world's four largest and best-appointed ferries, Silja appeared to be in a strong position by the mid-1980s, but their Viking Line

The **Birka Princess** approaches Stockholm Harbour in July 1993. *(Bruce Peter)*

The **Birka Princess** departs Visby on the island of Gotland in 2002. *(Bruce Peter)*

rivals were already plotting a counter-attack.

Rederi AB Sally, hitherto the dominant and most spendthrift partner, had borrowed too much money to expand in a number of areas and so did not feel able to invest in further new ferries for the Central Baltic routes. Consequently, it was left to the other partners, SF Line and Rederi AB Slite, to order anew. Between them, during the latter half of the decade, these relatively small, family-run businesses commissioned no less than seven ferries, every one of which was in the 33,000-46,000 gt range.

In 1987, Rederi AB Sally's major creditor, Föreningsbanken, persuaded Silja Line's parent companies, Effoa and Johnson Line, to buy two-thirds of the Sally shares. This deal gave Silja's owners control of Sally's Northern Baltic and English Channel ferry services and American cruise operations – but, not surprisingly, Effoa and Johnson Line were kept off Viking Line's Board, as SF and Slite split Sally's shares in the company between them. In 1990, the remaining third of Sally's shares was bought through a newly-formed joint Effoa-Johnson subsidiary called Effjohn and the Umeå-Vaasa route was subsequently fully integrated into Silja Line's operations.

The new ships for Viking Line's Stockholm-Helsinki route were designed with the express intention of trumping Silja's *Finlandia* and *Silvia Regina*. At just under 37,7800 gt, the *Mariella* and the *Olympia* were to be the world's largest ferries and, once again,

Wärtsilä was to be the builder, completing the ships concurrently with Silja's *Svea* and *Wellamo*. A team of Wärtsilä naval architects and ship designers led by SF's Technical Inspector Kaj Jansson and by Ulf Jernström of Wärtsilä, developed the concept for the ships. The *Mariella* was ordered by SF Line for delivery in 1985, with Slite taking the near-identical *Olympia* the following spring. Both the *Viking Saga* and the *Viking Song* were displaced at this point; the latter was sold to Fred. Olsen for North Sea operation as the *Braemar*, while the *Viking Saga* was retained by Rederi AB Sally to sail on Baltic mini-cruises as the *Sally Albatross*. After fire damage in 1990, this vessel was drastically rebuilt from the water-line up, meaning that she did not resemble her original design in any respect. Subsequently, she operated as a cruise ship in the Caribbean and in the Far East, known variously as the *Leeward* and the *Superstar Taurus*, before returning to the Baltic in May 2002 as the *Silja Opera*, making short cruises from Stockholm and Helsinki to Visby, Tallinn, Riga and, occasionally, St Petersburg.

Just as the *Silvia Regina* and the *Finlandia*, the new Viking Line flagships had the majority of their public rooms on a single deck, with all facilities and the lobbies accessed off a wide arcade to starboard. Unlike the Silja ships, however, dining and entertainment options were segregated. The reason was that Viking believed the cabaret concept on the *Finlandia* and the *Silvia*

The **Amorella** approaches Oxdjupet in August 2008. *(Bruce Peter)*

Moments later, the **Amorella** sails through the narrows. *(Bruce Peter)*

The arcade lounge on the **Amorella** was bright and airy. *(Bruce Peter collection)*

The Gustavian 'Bellevue' à la carte restaurant on the **Amorella**. *(Bruce Peter collection)*

A daily mid-day ritual at Mariehamn since the early-1990s: the **Amorella** (left) and the **Isabella** (right) motor serenely towards the harbour, coming from Turku and Stockholm respectively. Note that the **Isabella** was fitted with an extra panorama lounge ahead of her funnel in 1991 and is also distinguished by a red stripe along her superstructure. *(Viking Line)*

The 'Isolobella' à la carte restaurant on the **Isabella**. *(Bruce Peter collection)*

The spa complex, near the **Amorella**'s bow on the main deck. *(Bruce Peter)*

Baltic Ferries

The brand-new **Athena** on display in Slite in April 1989. *(Shippax archive)*

The 'Himmel & Hav' restaurant on the **Athena**. *(Bruce Peter collection)*

Viewed from another ferry, the **Athena** makes a splendid sight as she passes by on one of her regular 22-hour short cruises from Stockholm to Mariehamn and back. Note how the windows of the 'Blue Heaven' night club over hang the superstructure's after end. *(William Mayes)*

The **Athena**'s main hallway was light and spacious. *(Shippax archive)*

The **Athena**'s restaurants shared a vast forward-facing window. *(Shippax archive)*

A suite on the **Athena** with an angled window. *(Shippax archive)*

The **Athena**'s cocktail bar, adjacent to the à la carte restaurant. *(Bruce Peter collection)*

*Regina* had been only a limited success because passengers who chose not to dine in either the 'Maxim à la Carte' or buffet restaurants were effectively excluded. On the *Mariella* and the *Olympia*, therefore, a large buffet restaurant was located forward with the galley to port amidships, and a series of speciality restaurants and a pub were accessed from a wide starboard arcade. The ship's night club was aft, where there was slightly more vibration from the engines and propellers. One deck below was a spectacular marble-lined entrance hall with a three-level atrium punching upwards through the forward lobby on the saloon deck. Adjacent to the entrance hall, there was a coffee shop with a shopping arcade immediately aft. The remainder of the superstructure was given over to deck after deck of cabins, all with *en suite* facilities.

This layout proved to be highly satisfactory – but a mere description of where everything was located does little to communicate the stunning visual effect of the interior design. To decorate the *Mariella* and the *Olympia*, the Swedish interior designer Robert Tillberg was again hired. Tillberg evidently learned a great deal from his experiences designing for the American cruise industry as, by the 1980s, he had abandoned his earlier understatement in favour of American swagger. This meant the extensive usage of polished lacquered metal, brass, marble, moulded and cut glass combined with showy carpets and bright upholstery. It was this aesthetic which Tillberg brought to the Baltic ferry scene, giving Viking Line's ships, in particular, their distinctive onboard ambience. The entrance hallways of the *Mariella* and the *Olympia* were the earliest and most dramatic manifestations of this phenomenon, with expanses of veined pink marble, red carpet, mirrored ceilings and polished brass details. For middle-class Swedes and Finns, this represented the last word in transAtlantic modernity – as reflected in the shoulder-padded excess of Dallas, Dynasty and a thousand Hilton and Radisson hotels all over the world. It was the perfect atmosphere for escapism and over-indulgence because, although it looked luxurious at a glance, it was also extremely robust, as it needed to be. Baltic super-ferries must withstand punishing usage every night, almost 365 days a year. The *à la carte* restaurants were equally impressive, being split into four sections, each with its own decorative theme. Easily the most distinctive of these was the Gustavian-style 'Carl Michael Bellman' restaurant on the *Mariella*, complete with rococo wallpaper framed behind glass panels, reproduction Chippendale furniture and chandeliers. The flashy interiors of Viking Line's new flagships were subsequently used by Wärtsilä as references when designing cruise ships for the US market – commencing with Norwegian Caribbean Line's *Seaward*, which was delivered in 1987.

Although somewhat smaller in gross tonnage than Viking and Silja's latest ferries, the 21,484 gt Birka Line cruise ship *Birka Princess* was another significant vessel from the same era.

The **Athena**'s 'Blue Heaven' night club. *(Shippax archive)*

'Röda Lund' - the **Athena**'s indoor amusement park. *(Shippax archive)*

Rederi AB Slite's impressive cruise-ferry **Athena** glides through the archipelago. *(Bruce Peter)*

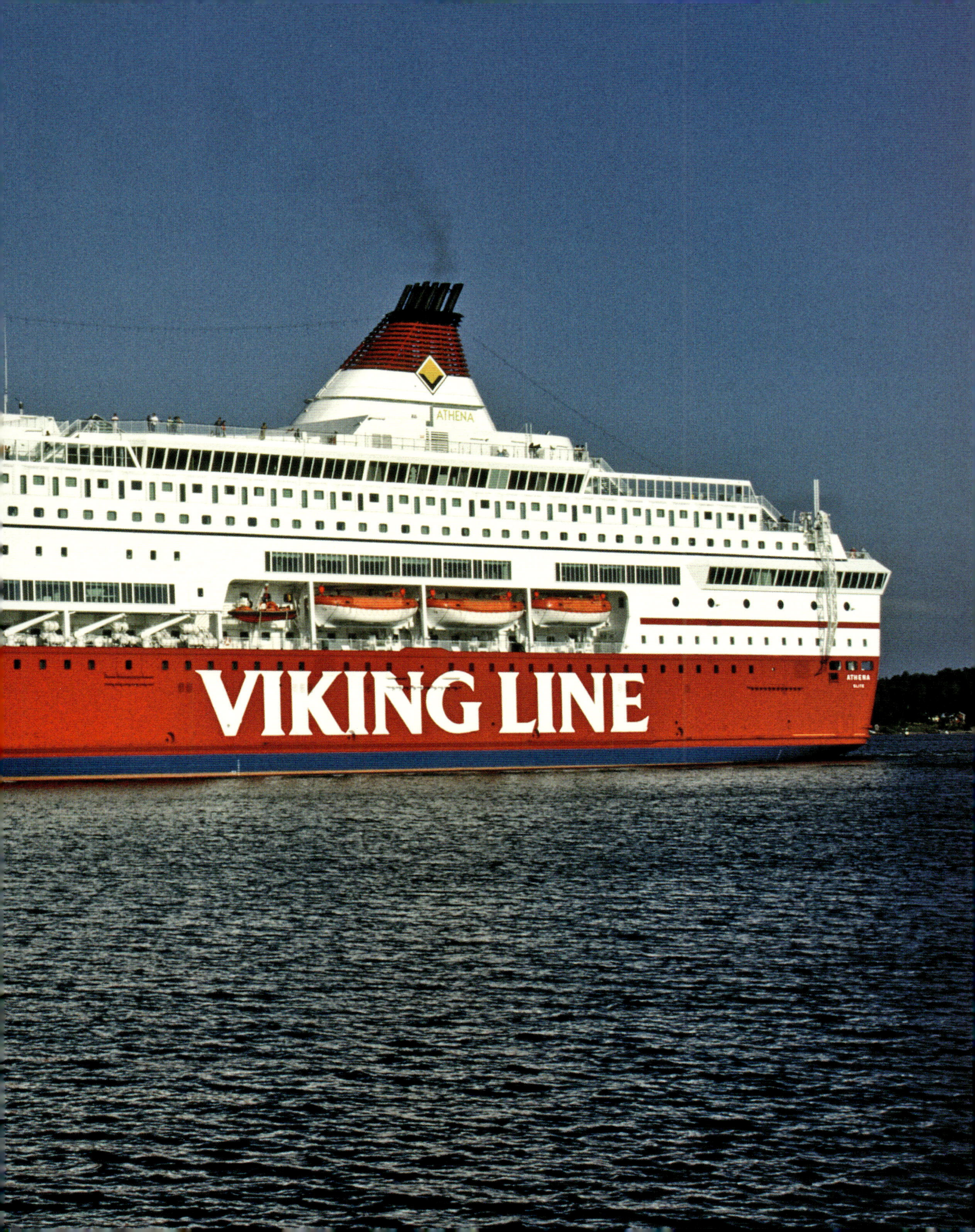
ATHENA
VIKING LINE

Rederi AB Slite's vintage cruise vessel **Apollo III**. *(Mick Lindsay collection)*

Delivered by the Valmet shipyard in Helsinki in 1986, this ship was intended solely to make tax-free shopping mini-cruises from Stockholm to Mariehamn and elsewhere. Only a small side-loading car deck with space for 80 vehicles was provided to allow passengers to park on board. Ever since the early 1970s, Birka Line had been a peripheral force in the Baltic cruise and ferry industry, building up their own loyal niche market of mainly cost-conscious older people by offering what was advertised as 'Silja luxury at Viking prices' and by refusing to serve drink to anybody under 21 years of age.

By the end of the decade, a number of cruise/ferry hybrids were in operation on the Stockholm-Mariehamn route and on short cruises from Helsinki, but the *Birka Princess* remained the most enduringly successful. At various times, Birka Line attempted to operate two ships; in 1990, they ordered a new cruise ship from Kværner Masa (formerly Wärtsilä – see below) which was to have been named the *Birka Queen*, but she was sold prior to delivery and entered service as the American-based cruise ship *Royal Majesty*. Subsequently operated by Norwegian Cruise Line as the *Norwegian Majesty*, she has recently been sold to Louis Cruise Lines. Later, during the summer of 1992, Birka instead tried to operate the former *Royal Viking Sky* as the *Birka Queen* on cruises from Stockholm to St Petersburg, but this was not successful and the ship was first chartered out, then sold altogether. While Silja and Viking expanded rapidly during the 1980s, Birka Line remained successful only as a one-ship operation.

Even before the *Mariella* and the *Olympia* were completed, however, both Viking Line partners, SF and Slite, announced further orders for two ships each. The SF new-buildings were to come from a traditional source, but one not patronized by the company for quite some time – the State-owned shipyards of Yugoslavia. Previously, in 1967 and 1970, SF had received two ferries from the Brodogradiliste Titovo yard at Kraljevica, the *Kapella* and the *Marella*, but this time an order was placed in 1986 with the Brodogradevna Industrija shipyard at Split. Although the Yugoslavs had built a number of ferries for Swedish owners such as Stena and Rederi AB Gotland in the interim, this would be their first attempt to build super-ferries. The attraction for Scandinavian shipowners was that in Yugoslavia, with its command economy and low labour costs, it was still possible to realize a huge cost saving over ordering from Wärtsilä or one of the other Scandinavian or German yards. SF had gained considerable design expertise by this point and so much of the development work on the ships was carried out in-house by the company's Technical Inspector Kaj Jansson and his colleagues, while the ships' hull configurations were developed in conjunction with the Finnish naval architects Elomatic Oy. The general layout and styling of the upperworks, meanwhile, was devised by the interior specialists Tillberg Design, while the detailed design took place in Yugoslavia. There, the shipyard was characterized by the dedication and pride of its workforce, meaning that the ferries were very precisely constructed and outstandingly well finished.

The new SF vessels were named the *Amorella* and the *Isabella* and delivered in 1988 and 1989. Each was of about 34,380 gt and had a very striking appearance with a sharply-slanted forward superstructure and the funnel casing curved to match, but with a reverse rake to the main mast atop the superstructure and to the radar mast, mounted on the bow. The hull had relatively fine lines for a super-ferry of this type and clam-shell bow doors were fitted, as per Silja's recent *Svea* and *Wellamo*. The two Yugoslavian-built ships were not identical sisters, however, as the *Amorella* had more vehicle capacity in her upper car deck for the Stockholm-Turku route (2,420 passengers and 550 cars) whereas the *Isabella* was fitted with extra cabins in the same space better suited for her Stockholm-Naantali service (2,200 passengers but only 410 cars). In terms of layout and interior design, the *Amorella* and the *Isabella* were similar to the *Mariella* and the *Olympia* and, once again, Tillberg was retained to design all of the public rooms and cabins. Perhaps reflecting the fact that they were to be used on shorter crossings, making return sailings every 24 hours and thus attracting a younger clientele because of lower fares, the *Amorella* and the *Isabella* were fitted with double-level discotheques above their main night clubs aft. Located in special rotundas with domed roofs rising to cupolas and adjacent to their sun decks, well away from the cabin areas, these had exciting light displays and sound systems. As with the *Mariella* and the *Olympia*, there were Gustavian-style restaurants amidships on the saloon deck, buffet restaurants forward and shopping arcades amidships on the deck below. The *Amorella* was delivered in September 1988, with the *Isabella* following in June 1989.

While the *Amorella* and the *Isabella* were taking shape in Yugoslavia, Rederi AB Slite meanwhile had ordered two new ferries of their own from Wärtsilä in Helsinki. The first of these 40,000 gt giants, also due for delivery in 1989 and to be named the *Athena*, was intended to be used as a cruise ship, replacing the steamer *Apollo III* (ex *Svea Jarl*) on the Stockholm-Mariehamn 24-hour cruise service. The sister ship *Kalypso* was to be used on the Stockholm-Mariehamn-Turku route, opposite SF Line's *Amorella*.

When the *Athena* was delivered as planned in April 1989, celebration was in order. As with all new Slite ships, the giant was sent on a gala cruise to the Myrsten family's home port of Slite on the island of Gotland where, dressed overall, she was opened to an admiring public. Rederi AB Slite even chartered the motor coaster *Tella*, formerly their pioneering ferry the *Slite*, especially for the occasion so that she could be compared with the new flagship.

The **Cinderella** at Mariehamn in July 1993. *(Bruce Peter)*

The multi-tiered 'Rainbow Club' on the **Cinderella**. *(Bruce Peter collection)*

Models pose in 'La Belle Epoque', the **Cinderella**'s flamboyant Art Nouveau-style à la carte restaurant. This was one of Tillberg's most extravagant creations on board a Viking Line ship. *(Bruce Peter collection)*

Finnish tango in the Garden Café on the **Cinderella**. *(Bruce Peter collection)*

The **Cinderella**'s indoor swimming pool. *(Bruce Peter collection)*

The **Ålandsfärjan** - Viking Line's smallest, oldest ferry, served on the Kapellskär-Mariehamn route from 1987 until 2008. The ferry was particularly well cared for by her crew and was in such excellent condition at the end of her long and busy career with Viking Line that she was sold for conversion into an adventure cruise ship. *(Viking Line)*

In terms of layout, the vessel represented a further step forward. The overall concept was developed by Rederi AB Slite's Technical Director Gustav Myrsten (Carl Bertil Myrsten's son) and Bo Franzén. They worked closely with the architect Per Dockson of PM Arkitekter, who previously had been involved in passenger ship design as an assistant of Robert Tillberg. Dockson devised the overall silhouette, working alongside Wärtsilä's project team, headed by Ray Essem. Dockson gave the ship a streamlined frontal aspect and funnel with the bridge much lower in the superstructure than on most recent passenger tonnage at that time. To ease orientation and to make evacuation simpler in the event of an emergency the lifeboats and inflatable rafts were nested in recesses on either beam in similar fashion to recent cruise ships. The reception hall, forward of amidships, featured an atrium with a moulded glass sculpture suspended in the void. As before, a glittering array of passenger facilities was provided, spread over two decks of public rooms and, more than on any ferry yet seen, there were huge expanses of floor-to-ceiling windows to let daylight flood in from every direction. Forward, behind a slanted double-height spread of windows almost spanning the entire width of the ship, there was an *à la carte* restaurant called the 'Smaragd', designed by Tillberg, with the 'Himmel & Hav' buffet restaurant on the deck below and an open void space between the two. Amidships on the upper saloon deck, there was a further buffet dining facility called the 'Äpplet'.

As the *Apollo III*, which the *Athena* was replacing, had been a favourite ship with Stockholm's pensioners, for whom eating was as important an aspect of the cruise experience as shopping and drinking, the ship was particularly well supplied with dining options, but to fill a 40,000 tonne ferry day after day it would be necessary for Viking Line to attract a wide demographic and so a range of technically sophisticated entertainment facilities was included in the design as well. Most remarkable was the 'Blue Heaven' night club and show lounge, filling the entire width of the aft superstructure on the upper saloon deck; the floor-to-ceiling glazed side walls were angled outwards and slightly cantilevered over the ship's sides. Below this, there was a very commodious tax-free supermarket of pretty much the same dimensions – but only a small discotheque was provided, accessed off the main hallway. The *Athena* had great expanses of marble-slabbed flooring, mirrored ceilings and festoon blinds over the windows. On the topmost deck, there was a conference suite – the most comprehensive of any Baltic passenger vessel to date – and the top-of-the-range cabins on the deck immediately below had windows angled forward and aft to give panoramic views over the archipelago. Yet that was not all.

As the *Athena* would be making cruises from Stockholm, rather than the ferry crossings of the remainder of the Viking Line fleet, her car deck was not likely to see much use and so only part of it was kept clear for cruise passengers to park their cars while they sailed. (Unlike typical ro-ro ferries with vehicles arranged in end-to-end lanes, on the *Athena* cars were parked in echelon fashion, much like in a car park on *terra firma*.) The remainder was fitted out as an amusement park with gaming arcades, fairground rides and even an aircraft flight simulator. Initially, this remarkable facility was known as 'Röda Lund', a play on 'Gröna Lund', the name of Stockholm's famous and long-established amusement park. Its owners objected, however, to Viking Line's use of a similar name and so the *Athena*'s facility was eventually renamed. Below the car deck and 'Röda Lund', there was a swimming pool and sauna complex – making the *Athena* truly a multi-level floating pleasure palace.

From the outset, the *Athena* was a big success – which was just as well as Rederi AB Slite had large mortgage repayments to make. The sister ship *Kalypso* was broadly similar, but with unobstructed vehicle lanes rather than 'Röda Lund' on the car deck.

Completing Viking Line's set of new ships was SF Line's 46,398 gt *Cinderella*, delivered in November 1989 and introduced as a third ship on the Stockholm-Helsinki route in support of Slite's *Olympia*. For SF Line, the *Cinderella* was, to an extent, a speculative venture, the result of an American company, Admiral Cruises, cancelling an order and Wärtsilä consequently having a spare slot in their building schedule, meaning that SF Line were able to negotiate a favourable price.

Upon delivery in 1989, the *Cinderella* briefly took the title of being the world's largest ferry and she too provided a vast array of entertainments. As on other super-ferries, the *Cinderella* had an asymmetrical layout, but this was more apparent from the outside than on her immediate predecessors as her entrance lobby was opened up to the exterior on the starboard side with a three-storey expanse of tinted glazing. (As the administration offices, tax-free supermarket, galley and a discotheque were to port, there were only small windows on that side.) Immediately behind the glazing, there was a series of open-tread spiral staircases rising through the main passenger decks with a winter garden lounge at the topmost level. The entrance lobby and stairwells were swathed in veined white marble and mirrors with a light sculpture plunging through a void in the centre. All of this created a multiplicity of highlights and reflections, which were intended to have a similar effect on passengers as the hallways of Las Vegas casinos. The idea was slightly to disorientate the viewers in order to encourage them to relax and to 'let their hair down', while raising anticipation for the fun and entertainment provided on the crossing.

In the same way as the *Athena* and the *Kalypso*, the majority of public rooms were arranged on two decks but, as with previous SF and Silja super-ferries, the boat deck was above these, rather than to the sides as on the latest ships for Slite. To take the lower deck first, there was a cafeteria and a steak house forward, with a rather kitsch English pub called 'The Admiral Hornblower' to starboard off a central arcade. The tax-free supermarket was off the entrance lobby to port and, adjacent to this on either beam, there were two discotheques with suitably robust 'industrial' décor. Cabins were located aft, on two decks above the main saloon decks and on a further two decks below.

The upper saloon deck, sandwiched in between, was similar in arrangement to those of the *Mariella* and the *Olympia*, with a buffet restaurant forward and an extraordinary Art Nouveau-styled *à la carte* restaurant called 'La Belle Epoque' on the port side amidships. This was one of Robert Tillberg's most spectacular creations on any Baltic ferry with its ornate columns, window hangings, chandeliers and chairs with swan-neck arms. One galley served both the buffet and *à la carte* restaurants – and also a small French-style speciality restaurant accessed directly from the starboard arcade.

At the stern, there was a vast three-storey night club called 'The Rainbow Club', designed by the Norwegian architect Njål R. Eide, with a capacity for 1,150 passengers on the main floor and on two broad curving balconies which snaked around three sides. The space had both what were claimed to be the largest dance floor and longest bar on a Baltic ferry. (Actually it contained no less than four bars – with names such as 'Gates of Heaven' and 'Amor'.) Eide, incidentally, specialized in the interior design of Caribbean cruise ships – including Royal Caribbean's *Sovereign of the Seas*, which was then the world's largest passenger ship.

The conference facilities were amidships on the boat deck level, with the most opulent cabins located forward. Some of the multi-room suites were decorated in the Gustavian manner and others even had their own private sauna baths. Altogether, the *Cinderella* could accommodate an unprecedented 2,700 passengers, all of whom were berthed in cabins, and 480 cars. She represented the high point for Viking Line's prodigious expansion drive and, having been used at different times on a variety of routes, today she remains the company's flagship.

Shortly after the *Cinderella* was delivered, in January 1990, Gunnar Eklund retired as CEO of Viking Line, his place being taken by his son, Nils-Erik. Later , in November the same year, Carl Bertil Myrsten was replaced at Rederi Ab Slite by his son, Gustav.

While Viking Line's armada of newly-built super-ferries dominated the Sweden-Finland ferry trade from the mid-1980s onwards, the company's short summer crossing from Kapellskär to Mariehamn had been maintained by a succession of chartered ferries. The route's last permanent ship, Rederi AB Sally's *Viking 2*, had been destroyed by a fire in February 1978 and, thereafter, SF Line had brought in vessels from DFDS and Fred. Olsen, amongst others, to cover the route. In 1987, however, a dedicated vessel was purchased – the Townsend Thoresen Dover Strait ferry *nf Tiger*, which had begun life in 1972 as the Danish *Kattegat*. Unlike Viking Line's other ferries, this second-hand acquisition, which was renamed the *Ålandsfärjan*, measured only 3,960 grt and had only a rudimentary ice-breaking capability. Nonetheless, she became very popular and was to remain in the fleet for over twenty years.

So great was the magnitude of the expansion of the Baltic ferry industry between 1985 and 1989 that Silja Line, which had had the world's largest ferries in the mid-1980s, now had the smallest on the principal Central Baltic routes. Although some refurbishment had been carried out in the interim in an attempt to keep the *Finlandia* and the *Silvia Regina* up to date, and the Silja partners had even toyed with the idea of having them lengthened, it was clear that to regain the initiative Silja really would require to build anew.

Amid great secrecy, development work began in the drawing office of the Wärtsilä shipyard in Helsinki, where Kai Levander and Silja Line's Managing Director Harri Kulovaara - a naval architect by training - led the design team.  At 58,000gt, the new ships were to be significantly larger than their predecessors. The starting point of the design brief was the belief that a broad range of people travel who reflect different age groups and tastes. To respond to this perceived need, it was decided to emulate the diversity of a modern shopping mall or urban high street. Thus,

The promenade on board the **Silja Symphony**. *(Bruce Peter)*

One of the **Silja Serenade**'s luxury cabins. *(Bruce Peter collection)*

The **Silja Serenade** leaves Helsinki, passing Suomenlinna Island, in July 1997. The streamlining of the superstructure, plus the ingenious application of the blue and white livery, help to break up the ferry's great bulk. *(Bruce Peter)*

'Happy Lobster', the seafood restaurant on the **Silja Symphony**. *(Bruce Peter)*

The **Silja Symphony**'s 'Bon Vivant' gourmet restaurant. *(Bruce Peter)*

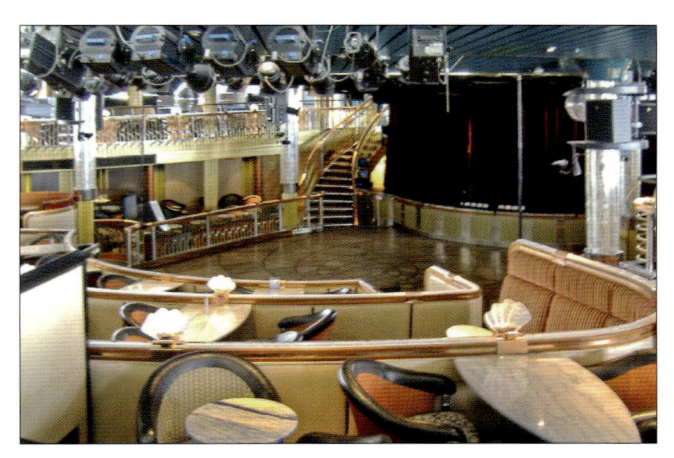

*The **Silja Symphony**'s 'Atlantis Palace' show lounge. (Bruce Peter)*

*The **Silja Serenade**'s shopping arcade. (Bruce Peter collection)*

the most startling feature of the new ships was a six-deck-high promenade filling their entire length and height from the main deck upwards, with cupolas overhead and glass lifts on either side. Right aft, there were to be large picture windows offering fine views of the sea and islands beyond. On either side, there was to be a wide range of restaurants, shops and bars, just like on a high street, with hanging banners and lighting effects to add diversity and atmosphere. While passenger liners of the 1930s – such as the French *l'Atlantique* and *Normandie* – had had split uptakes in order to open up grand vistas amidships, nothing remotely like this had ever been seen on any kind of ship in the past – let alone a Baltic ferry. The promenades were to be the 'hearts' of these ships and so all the public rooms were to be located around them. Above the restaurants, shops and bars, there were to be five decks of cabins on either side, either with windows facing outwards to sea or facing inwards onto the 'high street' below. In section, the cabins were planned logically with corridors running the length of the blocks between those facing inwards and those looking out. Stair and lift lobbies were to be located at each end, giving direct access to the 'high street' from all levels and so making passenger orientation very easy, even in such large vessels. More cabins were to be located on either side of the car deck and so the vast majority had either windows or portholes – certainly the new Silja Line vessels were to have a greater proportion of 'outside' cabins and suites than on any ferries yet seen.

To provide a variety of experiences and styles to suit a broad spectrum of tastes and moods, Silja assembled a number of Scandinavian designers, each to produce a specific part of the overall scheme. They were Rupert Gardner Design AB, FFNS Arkitekter, Studio Tomevsk, Lerber Plan Oy, Yran & Storbraaten and Vuokko Laakso. The majority had previous experience of working in the retail and hospitality industries, while Yran & Storbraaten and Laakso were both well known for their shipboard design work – indeed, the former were commissioned to design a range of *de luxe* cabins as a result of their work on the very exclusive 'Sea Goddess' yacht cruise ships, completed by Wärtsilä some years before. Of the firms who were new to designing super-ferry interiors, many certainly brought a fresher approach which was to make the new Silja vessels very distinct both from their predecessors and from the ships sailing in Viking Line colours. For example, natural finishes – such as hardwood flooring – were to be used in abundance to give an aura of quality and a distinctly Scandinavian ambience.

On either side of the 'high street', a wide range of drinking, dining and retail facilities was devised – a seafood restaurant called 'Happy Lobster', an Italian trattoria with seating and tables spilling out onto the 'street', a gourmet restaurant and a Tex-Mex grill. There was also a wine bar, a pub and a whole gamut of shops selling clothes, perfumes, electrical goods, souvenirs and stationery. While each had its own particular style and ambience, the 'high street' in between enabled them to cohere as a rich and fairly refined entity. As with the *Athena* and the *Kalypso*, the lifeboats were located at this 'main deck' level and so the 'high street' was continued out of doors, forming a teak-planked promenade deck fully encircling the ship with a sheltered observation space at the bow.

One deck below the 'high street', the new sisters resembled more conventional ferries with a tax-free supermarket amidships (complete with shopping trolleys), a 500-capacity buffet restaurant aft and a French-style *à la carte* restaurant forward. The conference facilities were built into the ships' bows above the car deck doors, giving rise to several intriguingly-shaped meeting rooms. High above, at the base of the funnel, there was a spa and swimming complex with a night club above – just like the 'Viking Crown' lounges on Royal Caribbean cruise ships, or the 'sky bar' on the *Royal Princess*.

*'Club Bali', the **Silja Symphony**'s disco, located below the funnel. (Bruce Peter)*

The **Silja Serenade** approaches Furusund in late-evening light in August 2008. *(Bruce Peter)*

In terms of technical sophistication, the new Silja ships were equally awe-inspiring and, as well as a bewildering array of the latest navigation and engine control equipment, they also incorporated special features to protect the environment. For example, they had twin-skeg stern arrangements to increase their efficiency and reduce cavitation and wash. Previously, large car ferries had been criticized for their tendency to suck water out of island bays in the archipelago, sending it back as a tidal wave after they had passed. Extra plating was fitted around the fuel tanks to prevent pollution in the event of grounding. Furthermore, they carried facilities to recycle rubbish and to purify water. The four Wärtsilä diesel engines powering each ship were designed to run on low sulphur fuel, said to cut toxic emissions by up to 70%, and, when in port, they could be 'plugged in' to the mains electricity supply to avoid air pollution in the centres of Stockholm and Helsinki.

It was announced that the ships were to be named the *Silja Serenade* and the *Silja Symphony* and the first was to be delivered in November 1990 with the second following in May 1991. Each could transport 2,626 passengers, all berthed, and 450 cars – about the same as the smaller *Cinderella*. The void space running down the middle of the ships probably accounted largely for their greater tonnages. The *Silja Serenade* and the *Silja Symphony*'s superb facilities and design captured the public's imagination and they became an instant and enduring success.

1991 was the peak year for Baltic ferry traffic. That year, over 10 million passengers travelled on the ferries between Sweden and Finland with a further 1.5 million making short cruises to Mariehamn. The presence of the *Silja Serenade* and the *Silja Symphony* seems greatly to have boosted demand as Silja's annual passenger figure grew from approximately 1.8 million per annum in the latter 1980s to almost 2.5 million in 1991.

The revolutionary design of these two vessels has influenced the planning of a whole generation of mass-market cruise ships, sailing mainly from Miami on circuits of the Caribbean. Both inside and out, Royal Caribbean's 'Voyager' class ships, built in Turku in the 2000-2007 period, resemble 'blown up' versions of the *Silja Serenade* and *Silja Symphony*. This was perhaps an inevitable development, given that Harri Kulovaara moved to the company from Silja Line in 1995. On the 'Voyager' class, however, the 'promenade' concept has been taken to a new level of complexity in terms of design detailing and in the facilities on offer.

Silja Line have claimed that their flagship ferries on the Stockholm-Helsinki route are truly indistinguishable from cruise vessels – and, in much of the layout and detailing at least, this is certainly the case. However, can an overnight ferry crossing ever truly replicate the atmosphere of a cruise? Arguably, the two genres are often close and, at times, inseparable. Yet a car ferry, no matter how luxurious and capacious, will always have her own kind of atmosphere and distinct *raison d'être*. On an overnight trip, passengers will typically behave with more abandon than on a longer voyage – and there will always be greater pressure to explore and use as many facilities as possible in the short time-span available, rather than to relax and pace oneself. This notwithstanding, the Baltic region continues to offer passengers memorable shipboard experiences on board a bewildering range of ferries that are undoubtedly amongst the finest of their type anywhere in the world.

## CHAPTER THREE

# Recession, Bankruptcy and Disaster

Before the new Silja Serenade and Silja Symphony could be completed, to the horror of shipowners who had placed orders there, Wärtsilä's Shipbuilding Division suddenly went bankrupt in November 1989. (The Marine Engine Building Division was, however, unaffected and continued to trade as normal.) The shipyards' bankruptcy was completely unexpected because the company was regarded as being the jewel in the crown of Finland's manufacturing base and, indeed, during the mid-1980s had become the first Finnish industrial conglomerate to be quoted on the London Stock Exchange. Furthermore, the Finnish Government was represented on Wärtsilä's Board of Directors – so what could possibly go wrong?

Wärtsilä's downfall had been brought about in no small measure by the company's rapid expansion. To secure so many cruise ship and ferry orders in such a short space of time, the builder had priced contracts too keenly while simultaneously investing heavily in new infrastructure and expensive inventory to construct the ships. This caused cash-flow problems, particularly in relation to the importation from the USA of fixtures and fittings for cruise ships.

Hitherto, ordering a ship from Wärtsilä was regarded as being a safe bet and so, out of the many famous shipowners who had vessels under construction there in the latter 1980s – Effoa, Johnson Line, Rederi AB Slite, SF Line and Carnival – only SF had a contract for their vessel (the *Cinderella*) which offered the owner protection from changes in the builder's financial circumstances. Thus, notwithstanding Wärtsilä's woes, SF took delivery of the *Cinderella* – which was approaching completion anyway when the crisis struck – much as planned. In contrast, the cost of Rederi AB Slite's *Kalypso* and the new Silja Line sisters *Silja Serenade* and *Silja Symphony* increased by nearly a third. For example, each new Silja ferry had been budgeted to cost 700 million Finnish markka (approximately the price of the *Svea* and the *Wellamo* together) but, to ensure completion, Silja's parent companies Effoa and Johnson Line had to pay one billion markka per ship. Similarly, the cost of building Rederi AB Slite's *Kalypso* increased by 200 million Swedish kronor and so Slite borrowed this extra money from the Swedish State-owned Nordbanken, with whom the company's existing ship mortgages were secured.

In order to protect their investments, the 'least worst' option for the shipping lines with vessels under construction there was to rescue the company – and so a new owner called Masa was formed, with investment from Effoa, Johnson Line, Rederi AB Slite and from Florida's Carnival Cruise Line, which was also having a series of ships built at Helsinki at that time. The 'Masa' name was an abbreviation of Martin Saarikangas, a shipyard executive who engineered the company's rescue. Another possible meaning, according to Nils-Gustav Palmgren who was a senior director of Effoa in the 1980s and '90s and who later became Silja Line's Managing Director between 2000 and 2003, was 'Most Acceptable Solution Available' – a designation hinting strongly at the desperation of the situation.

Later, of course, Masa Yards was sold on to the Norwegian industrial, engineering and construction conglomerate Kværner and, thereafter, it continued to expand as a successful builder of passenger ships. For Effoa, Johnson Line and Rederi AB Slite, however, the unexpected increase in their debt placed all three owners under financial duress. As we shall see, once the 1980s economic boom was superseded by the deep recession of the early 1990s, this situation precipitated ruinous consequences for the latter company.

**The Europa** is seen in Viking Line's livery at Meyer Werft. *(Andreas Wörteler)*

Only days later, she was repainted in Silja Line's livery. *(Andreas Wörteler)*

The **Silja Europa** at Stockholm, berthed adjacent to Silja Line's Ariadne Hotel in July 1997. *(Bruce Peter)*

In order to streamline their finances and the operation of their ferries, Effoa and Johnson Line merged their passenger shipping activities in 1992 under the name of their existing joint subsidiary, Effjohn, which had been created two years previously to buy the remaining shares in Rederi AB Sally. Thus, from the outset, the *Silja Serenade* and the *Silja Symphony* carried Silja Line's stylized 'seal' logo on their funnels, rather than the individual shipping line's colours. A new Effjohn logo, displayed on the superstructure, was the only other external evidence of this corporate amalgamation.

When the *Silja Serenade* and the *Silja Symphony* were ordered, however, the Viking Line consortium had understandably felt obliged to outdo their rivals by ordering an even bigger ship. It was Rederi AB Slite which did the honours. The company's C.E.O, Gustaf Myrsten, was so pleased with the success of the existing fleet, which appeared to be making more than sufficient profits to

The **Silja Europa**'s 'Bon Vivant' gourmet restaurant. *(Bruce Peter)*

The 'Neon' disco, amidships on the **Silja Europa**. *(Bruce Peter)*

pay off the company's debt, that he began work with Wärtsilä on a further super-ferry for the Stockholm-Helsinki route to replace the *Olympia*. The new Slite ship, to be named the *Europa*, was to be 59,912 gt.

Rather than building in Finland, an agreement was reached instead with Meyer Werft at Papenburg in Germany, which had previously delivered Slite's *Diana II* back in 1979. Unfortunately, by the early 1990s, Sweden – and indeed much of Western Europe – was gripped by recession. The country as a whole had borrowed prodigiously during the 1980s and had a national debt arguably out of all proportion to its size and population. Moreover, several Swedish banks had lent too generously - and now were faced with the threat of mass default. Norbanken, with which Slite's mortgages were secured, was particularly badly hit. This notwithstanding, the bank agreed to buy the *Diana II* from Slite in order to provide some of the necessary liquidity to pay for the new flagship.

Meanwhile, as the recession spread throughout Europe, the independent German Bundesbank elected to maintain the value of the deutschmark by increasing German interest rates, making exports more expensive. For Rederi AB Slite, this also made the *Europa* dearer by no less than 300 million kronor and, when combined with the extra loan to pay for the increased price of building the *Kalypso* at Wärtsilä, Rederi AB Slite now owed Nordbanken 500 million kronor over and above what had already been budgeted for these projects.

To make matters worse, as Europe's weaker economies were plunged into recession, pressure increased on the European Exchange Rate Mechanism (ERM), whose aim was to maintain parity between the values of currencies within the European Union. This situation, in turn, gave financial speculators a chance to earn money at the expense of the central banks as they sought to shore up their own currency values. Events came to a head in September 1992 when the Swedish Government gave in to the inevitable and devalued the kronor by 10%. (In Britain, 16 September has passed into history as 'Black Wednesday' – the day the Conservative Chancellor of the Exchequer, Norman Lamont, was forced to concede defeat against the speculators and withdraw the pound from the ERM.)

For Rederi AB Slite, the devaluation of the Swedish kronor simply meant that the *Europa* had ceased to be affordable, and so Slite's technical staff were instructed to leave the nearly-completed ferry to return home to Sweden. In January 1993, SF Line's Managing Director Nils-Erik Eklund was invited to Papenburg by Meyer Werft's Chairman, Bernard Meyer, and offered the Europa for 1.6 billion deutschmarks - which Eklund thought a gross overestimate of the ship's value. An aternative solution was for German banks to fund the completion of the ship, which would then be chartered from a subsidiary company established by the builder called the Papenburger Fährschiffs-reederei GmbH. Most unfortunately for Viking Line, Silja Line's parent company, Effjohn, quickly moved in and signed an agreement to charter the ship instead, buying 17% of shares in this owning company. To some industry observers, the situation appeared to be decidedly dubious, especially as Nordbanken had one director who also sat on the board of Effjohn.

Unable to finance the completion of their intended new flagship,

A view looking down the **Silja Europa**'s six-deck-high atrium, which features glass lifts. *(Bruce Peter)*

Rederi AB Slite were instead forced by Nordbanken to declare bankruptcy. Consequently, their splendid ships were withdrawn and sold abroad. Firstly, the *Olympia*, by then on charter to P&O for service between Portsmouth, Bilbao and Le Havre, was sold to Irish Ferries. Shortly afterwards, the *Athena* and the *Kalypso* went to Star Cruises, an Isle of Man-registered company backed by the Malaysian Lim casino dynasty, to continue cruising, but from Hong Kong and Singapore – both areas of strong and

The 'Food Market' restaurant on the **Silja Europa**. *(Bruce Peter)*

Following the bankruptcy of Rederi AB Slite, the **Athena** and the **Kalypso** were sold to the Malaysian Star Cruises for service from Singapore and Hong Kong. Here, the **Star Pisces** (ex **Kalypso**) is seen at the Kowloon passenger terminal in Hong Kong Bay. The **Wasa Queen**, originally Silja Line's **Bore Star**, is in the background. (*Bruce Peter*)

sustained economic growth with largely finance-orientated white-collar economies. Having met with his workforce to apologize in person for Rederi AB Slite's demise, Carl Bertil Myrsten withdrew from the shipping trade.

In order to make a case for liquidation, Nordbanken had commissioned a shipbroker to write a very negative report about Rederi AB Slite, valuing the *Athena* and *Kalypso* at only 350 million kronor each. The two ships were, in fact, sold to the Malaysians for 650 million kronor per ship. Ten years later, DFDS bought the former *Athena* for use on their Copenhagen-Oslo route as the *Pearl of Scandinavia*, paying even more for the by then middle-aged vessel. In April 2006 a Swedish business historian, Hans-Göran Björk, published a book entitled 'Den Ene Den Var Vit…' about the circumstances surrounding the *Europa* affair and Rederi AB Slite's liquidation. After painstaking research, Björk provided strong evidence alleging that Nordbanken had deliberately sought Rederi AB Slite's bankruptcy rather than assisting the company through their short-term financial difficulties.

SF Line were offered the first opportunity to buy Slite's ships and so they made a conservative offer for the *Athena* and the *Kalypso*, which was refused by Slite's liquidator. Rather than increasing their own debt, SF's directors decided instead to concentrate on paying off the loans on the company's existing tonnage. Besides, whereas Silja Line's combined parent company, Effjohn, was backed by large institutional shareholders, SF remained a locally-owned business, based on the Åland Islands. There must have been very mixed feelings amongst the SF directorate about the fate of Rederi AB Slite. On the one hand, a long-time partner had been forced out of business in unfortunate circumstances but, on the other, Viking Line was now under the sole control of SF, even though the operation now lacked three of its most prestigious ships – the *Athena*, the *Kalypso* and the *Europa*.

The remaining vessels were reorganized as well as possible to fill in the gaps, but the cruise operation to Mariehamn was temporarily axed, as was the service to Naantali. Viking, which had dominated the Baltic scene for the greater part of the 1980s, could only watch as their arch rivals Silja Line claimed 60% of the market share on Central Baltic routes by 1993, although overall passenger figures were actually down by 21 %. Thereafter, in 1995, SF Line renamed themselves Viking Line and so what had for so long been a marketing brand became the official name of the ships' owner.

The new giant from Meyer Werft, meanwhile, was renamed the *Silja Europa*, repainted in blue and white and introduced on the Stockholm-Helsinki route in the spring of 1993, temporarily displacing the *Silja Serenade* to the Stockholm-Mariehamn-Turku service. Silja could now boast the three newest, largest, most advanced ferries the world had ever seen. Although, in terms of layout and interior design the *Silja Europa* was hardly the equal of the *Silja Serenade* and the *Silja Symphony* – she was more a glorified version of the *Athena* and the *Kalypso* – her sheer size and her ability to accommodate all 3,123 passengers in *en suite* cabins were impressive. Of course, the *Silja Europa* lacked the grand promenades of her running mates and the décor was mainly in the brash style favoured by Viking Line.

The entrance hall was teak-floored and rose from Deck 6 to Deck 14 where there were two glass cupolas. Her most interesting feature was a tiered 800-seat cabaret theatre at the stern of the ship called the Moulin Rouge. Two decks above, the 'Ocean Club' was a vast lounge and bar complex, which took the title of having the longest bar and the largest dance floor of any Baltic ferry from the *Silja Europa*'s intended fleet-mate, the *Cinderella*. Further aft, a series of lounges on three levels gave panoramic views over the stern, with abstract void spaces cut into the decks between the various levels. There was a wide choice of dining alternatives – from a burger bar, initially operated as a McDonald's franchise, through the Seaside Café, a German-style food market and a Scandinavian 'smorgasbord' buffet restaurant to a series of comparatively opulent Gustavian-style *à la carte* options, located amidships. Equally, the ship had a large number of bars – including Joe's Place – fitted out in a manner vaguely resembling a Wild West barn. Towards the stern, there was what was claimed to be the biggest tax-free supermarket on any passenger ship, with an arcade of gift and perfume shops adjacent. As with the *Athena* and the *Kalypso*, outstanding features of the *Silja Europa* were her lofty deck heights and her enormous expanses of floor-to-ceiling windows, which wrapped right around the superstructure on the two passenger decks. These were the work of Per Dockson, whose ingenious styling of the ship's exterior demonstrated conclusively that super-ferries need not be ugly boxes. The *Silja Europa*'s overall profile was certainly bulky, but it was also highly curvaceous and with many attractively-resolved details. On the topmost deck, there was a conference suite with a special VIP room punching through the deckhead immediately forward of the funnel. Further aft was the Sauna Beach, a leisure and fitness complex, which had water flumes, swimming pools, saunas and jacuzzis.

So happy were Silja Line's directors at having snatched the *Silja Europa* from Viking Line that their publicity boasted 'Now the Age of the Vikings is Over!' – a somewhat tasteless slogan for which Silja subsequently apologized. In 1994, over 4.5 million passengers travelled on Silja's ferries – or just over half the total number of passengers crossing that year between Sweden and Finland.

Externally of commanding appearance and undeniably well-constructed, the *Silja Europa* unfortunately seemed to lack an obvious sense of internal co-ordination and style. Clearly, Silja were vindicated in producing such a radical and imposing design for their own *Silja Serenade* and *Silja Symphony*. Nonetheless, the ship did find her niche when switched from the Stockholm-Helsinki to the Stockholm-Mariehamn-Turku route in 1994.

The delivery of the *Silja Europa* was the last grand gesture in the 1980s phase of Baltic super-ferry development. The bankruptcy of Rederi AB Slite and the sluggishness of the European economy in the early 1990s had tempered the optimism of the previous decade. Even so, all of the ships were reasonably well loaded throughout the year as Swedes and Finns attempted temporarily to escape harsh liquor laws and an even harsher economic climate on *terra firma*.

While the *Silja Serenade*, the *Silja Symphony* and the *Silja Europa* were being introduced on the main Central Baltic routes, a whole new dimension in ferry travel was emerging in the region. Following the end of the Cold War, the Baltic States of Estonia, Latvia and Lithuania were anxious to open up long-abandoned trade routes to the West. Swedish and Finnish operators, sensing a new and untapped market, were only too happy to assist. Thus Effjohn combined with the Russian Baltic Shipping Company to form Baltic Line with a service from Nynäshamn to St Petersburg using a former Viking Line ferry, the *Viking Song*, as the *Anna Karenina*.

Meanwhile, Hans Laidwa, an Estonian émigré who had previously worked as a manager in Silja Line, was persuaded by the established Stockholm shipowners Nordström & Thulin to enter a joint arrangement with the Estonian shipping line ESCO to open a direct ferry route from Stockholm to Tallinn, marketed at Estline. Originally, they had planned to use the former North Sea ferry *Olau Britannia* on the route but, instead, N&T resold her for a profit to Fred. Olsen Lines and instead set their sights on the former DFDS Copenhagen-Oslo ferry *Dana Regina*. Between N&T first

The **Estonia** passes Skarpö, only two months before her sinking. *(Anders Ahlerup)*

A stern-quarter view of the tragic **Estonia**. *(Søren Lund Hviid)*

In evening sunlight, the **Silja Festival** (ex **Wellamo**) approaches Stockholm on a daytime crossing from Turku and Mariehamn in the summer of 2002. *(Bruce Peter)*

inspecting the ship and making an offer, however, she was sold to a company set up by DFDS' former Finance Director, Niels Erik Lund, and the Amercian package tour entrepreneur Fred Kassner, who intended to convert her for Caribbean cruise service. Consequently, N&T made an improved offer which persuaded the new owner to resell for a 5 million dollar profit.

Thus, the former *Dana Regina* was refurbished and entered Baltic service on 17 June 1990 as the *Nord Estonia* – precisely 50 years after the Soviet occupation of Estonia began. Notwithstanding the great uncertainty caused by the disintegration of the USSR and the progressive shifting of power from Moscow to Tallinn, thanks to Soviet President Gorbachev's new policies of 'Glasnost' and 'Perestroika' the route was a success. Following Estonia's gaining of full independence, Estline very soon required larger tonnage. Thus, the former *Viking Sally* was acquired in 1993, repainted in Estline colours and placed in service as the *Estonia*. Largely Swedish-owned, but Estonian-flagged, she was effectively the Estonian national flagship and a source of much pride and affection in the fledgling nation. She represented an important link with the outside world and brought shiploads of comparatively wealthy Swedish tourists with kronor to spend in the shops, bars and restaurants of Tallinn. Several of the officers were former employees of the bankrupt Rederi AB Slite, while the mainly Estonian crew were proud to work on such a prestigious vessel and they gained a reputation for being eager to please their customers. The *Estonia* became a popular and relatively cheap alternative to the established Viking and Silja Line services. Remembering Baltic ferry passengers' craving for novelty, it was no surprise that the *Estonia*'s sailings every second day to Tallinn were usually fully booked with 'cruisers'. The first year of the service was a tremendous success and the ship even carried the Olympic teams from the Baltic States to the Lillehammer Games – a publicity coup for Estline.

Then, during a stormy – but otherwise routine – crossing, disaster struck. On the evening of 28 September 1994, the *Estonia* set sail from Tallinn bound for Stockholm with 989 passengers and crew on board and encountered severe gales and a rough Baltic Sea. In particular, the vessel's port bow quarter took the full force of the waves, repeatedly battering the bow visor and straining the locking pins. It is believed that in the first few hours of the voyage, during which the ship was running at about 16 knots, the locking pins suffered metal fatigue and failed sequentially. Consequently, the bow visor came loose and began to move from side to side. On the *Estonia*, and indeed other Baltic super-ferries of the early 1980s, the watertight inner bow door, which doubled as a car loading ramp, protruded into a housing at the top of the bow visor. According to the official accident investigation, the failure of the locking pins and consequent movement of the visor caused the bow ramp to be levered open, slowly at first but faster with every wave. This damage would not have been detected immediately and so the ship continued on her heading and speed, passing close to the *Mariella* which was also bound for Stockholm but at

The **Silja Scandinavia** (ex **Frans Suell**) on the Stockholm-Turku route. *(David Parsons)*

The pub on board the **Gabriella**. *(Bruce Peter)*

The **Gabriella**, previously the **Silja Scandinavia**, passes Oxdjupet in August 2008. For Viking Line, the acquisition of this ferry was a coup which provided some compensation for the loss of the **Europa** to Silja Line. *(Bruce Peter)*

The **Gabriella**'s 'Food Garden' restaurant. *(Bruce Peter)*

The combined café and disco on the **Gabriella**. *(Bruce Peter)*

The **Gabriella** approaches Helsinki on a freezing cold morning in February 2004. *(Bruce Peter)*

a reduced rate, significantly slower than that of the *Estonia*. Not long after this, the *Estonia*'s bow visor was ripped off. This in itself did not cause the ship to sink. The close proximity of the watertight door/ramp to the visor, and the fact that the visor enclosed the top of the ramp when shut, led to the upper part of the ramp being pulled open as the visor was ripped off. This left the ship at the mercy of the elements, the Master and crew helplessly unable to save her. The car deck began to flood with water and, as more waves battered the bow ramp open, the ingress grew stronger.

All of this time, the passengers were enjoying their trip. According to survivors, a band was playing in the lounge and people were dancing, or drinking at the bar. No one knew that the ship was flooding and had become dangerously unstable. Once the officers on the bridge became aware of what was happening, however, there was little they could do other than send out a frantic 'Mayday' call for assistance. Only minutes later, other ferries in the vicinity picked up a final distress call from the *Estonia*'s agitated and frightened Third Mate: 'Really bad, it looks really bad here now', he reported – then there was no further contact from the ship.

Both the *Mariella* and the *Silja Europa* raced to the *Estonia*'s last known position – indeed the former got there within twenty minutes, but both were too late. In the interim, suddenly and without warning, the *Estonia* had capsized – taking 851 passengers and crew with her and drowning them in the perishing cold Baltic. Survivors later told of losing family members, loved ones, children and friends in the panic to evacuate the ship in the few minutes she took to sink entirely. The jovial atmosphere in the lounges, it was said, turned instantly to 'a living hell' as many people were paralysed by fear, while others scrambled to escape. There was not even enough time to launch the lifeboats and only 138 jumped clear of the doomed ferry in time. Passengers disembarking at Stockholm when the *Mariella* arrived some twelve hours late described how they had joined forces with the crew to search for survivors, taking up positions on the ship's deck and peering into the darkness for signs of life.

Estonia, Sweden and Finland were numbed by the accident. In countries with such relatively small populations, many people were either related to, or knew of, a victim. Nobody had ever seriously questioned the integrity of the Baltic ferry scene – neither the ships nor their operators. It was assumed that this being Scandinavia, everything would be done to the highest possible standards. Consequently, the Swedish and Finnish tabloid press were merciless in their criticism of the industry. For a start, there were no complete passenger lists of who was on board the ship – so nobody knew for certain who was alive or dead, all of which added to the anguish of relatives. Next, it was revealed that on the same night as the *Estonia* capsized, the *Silja Europa*, the world's newest and largest ferry, had also suffered damage to her bow doors; admittedly these were of a completely different design and the ship was in no danger. Interestingly, one of the *Silja Europa*'s passengers on that particular crossing was Carl Bertil Myrsten, the former C.E.O. of Rederi AB Slite which had ordered both the *Viking Sally* and the *Silja Europa* from Meyer Werft but which had not taken delivery of either ship. One of Slite's former Captains, Johan Kull who, in the early 1960s, had commanded the company's first purpose-built ferry, the *Apollo*, had expressed worry to Myrsten about the seaworthiness of the pioneering ferry's bow visor and Myrsten, according to Kull, was at that time rather dismissive of his Captain's concern. After the *Estonia* tragedy, however, Kull reminded a badly-shaken Myrsten of his earlier apparent lack of concern regarding ferry bow door safety.

It was subsequently revealed that there had been five incidences of Baltic ferries' bow doors breaking open since 1974. Not surprisingly, public confidence in the glossy industry was shattered. Instructions were given to ferry companies owning Swedish-flag vessels for the bow visors to be welded shut, otherwise the ships could not sail in seas with waves higher than three metres. The Finnish Government followed suit with similar guidelines.

In terms of accidental deaths, the Baltic routes hitherto had had an exemplary record with no previous fatalities – the last deaths recorded were due to mines and bombardment during the Second World War. In a wider context, ferries were viewed as being worryingly disaster-prone. The horrific loss of the *Herald of Free Enterprise* off Zeebrugge in 1987 was still fresh in everybody's mind and, before that, the sinking of the *European Gateway* off Felixstowe in 1982. In each case when a total loss occurred due to flooding, the accident happened so quickly that the ship's life-saving equipment was of little use. The *Estonia* vanished in twelve minutes from the first 'Mayday' call; the *Herald of Free Enterprise* capsized in 2 minutes 35 seconds and the *European Gateway* in seven minutes after a side collision with another ferry. Such sudden losses prevented many hundreds of passengers from being saved. Arguably, the *Herald of Free Enterprise* was lost as the result of gross human error. Leaving a ship's bow doors open as she put to sea appeared sheer stupidity and downright dangerous to industry observers. The *European Gateway*'s sinking after a severe collision, on the other hand, was viewed at the time as a dramatic but freak accident; in any case, the ship was a cargo ferry and so only a small number of crew members were at risk.

From the outset, the loss of the *Estonia* was perceived differently. This was a large modern passenger ferry of a fairly standard type within Scandinavia. The enquiry into the loss acknowledged that the vessel put to sea in the accepted manner – apparently, all doors were closed properly, the ship was correctly trimmed to sit evenly in the water and there were no prior warning signs that something might go wrong. Although some surprise was expressed that the *Estonia* was sailing as fast as 16 knots in such stormy conditions, the vessel should have been strong enough to travel at nearly full speed in far worse weather, any reduction being mainly for the comfort of passengers. Surely there was a fundamental design fault in this type of ferry?

It should be remembered that most Scandinavian ferries built since the 1970s have highly-pronounced bow flares to maximize the deck area of the hull and superstructure. On ferries with lifting bow visors, such as the *Estonia*, the repeated upward pounding can cause metal fatigue in the locking pins that hold the doors shut. In the case of the *Estonia*, this led to fatal consequences. Other ferries, such as the *Amorella*, the *Isabella*, the *Silja Serenade*, the *Silja Symphony* and the *Silja Europa*, have so-called clam-type doors which open outwards and to the sides,

The **Superseacat Three** departs Helsinki during the Sea Containers era. *(Bruce Peter)*

The **Wasa Queen** during her spell on the Gulf of Bothnia. *(Bruce Peter collection)*

similar to the passenger doors of aircraft. Because they close by plugging into the front of the hull, the upward force of the waves tends to close them tighter and so they are perhaps less accident-prone.

The issue of sudden loss of stability is rather more complex. Anybody who has carried a full watering can will know that even a small amount of water is extremely heavy – and very mobile. Tests have shown that only half-a-centimetre of water spread evenly across the car deck of a ferry has the potential to cause an instant loss of stability. During the last 30 years, as we have seen, certain design trends have enhanced the profitability and serviceability of ro-ro ferries. Firstly, ferries have become much bigger overall. Generally, the proportion of car deck space has grown faster than the ships themselves. Secondly, as the leisure and cruise element of ferry travel has grown in importance, successive ships have had ever larger superstructures with consequently more topweight. The distance from the water to the car deck, or freeboard, has remained constant at about two metres. When set against the 11- to 14-deck height of these ships, that figure is insignificant. As a vessel turns to port or starboard, she naturally heels over slightly. On modern ferries, where extra topweight is compensated by wider hulls, the effect is exaggerated. To maintain stability (i.e. a dry car deck) at large heeling angles the car deck must be fully enclosed and remain watertight.

So what happens when water gets onto a car deck? The balance and flotation of any ship is the result of an equilibrium between two forces: weight (pushing downwards) and buoyancy (pushing upwards). The centre of gravity (the point around which the hull pitches and rolls) remains fixed under normal conditions at a given point 6-10 metres above the water-line. The centre of buoyancy is a moving point about three metres below the water-line around which the ship floats. As the ship rolls or leans when turning, the centre of buoyancy swings from side to side. As the hull heels, the centre of buoyancy shifts past the point where the maximum weight of the hull is exerted (a vertical line perpendicularly

The **Finnjet** is seen in the livery of Silja Line during the latter 1980s. The ferry became a headache for Sea Containers, who first refurbished her then decided that she could have no future in the Silja fleet. *(Bruce Peter collection)*

bisecting the water-line from the centre of gravity). The centre of buoyancy passes through a new point above the centre of gravity, known as the 'metacentre'. Between these two lines, a positive 'righting lever' of excess buoyancy, known as the G-Z line, is created. Under normal circumstances (i.e. a dry car deck) this buoyancy will cause the ship to roll back to a perfectly upright position.

When there is water on the car deck, a very different chain of events occurs. On modern ferries with fully-enclosed car decks, there is no way for the water to run off, and so it swills from side to side – a phenomenon known as 'free surface effect'. As more water floods in, it accumulates on one side and causes the ship to list. The increased weight on one side of the hull makes the centre of gravity move. There is more weight than buoyancy and the point of weight moves perpendicularly to the water-line, creating a negative G-Z space; this is effectively a capsize lever as the ship will keep heeling over at rapidly steeper angles until she flips over entirely from the 12 o'clock (upright) to the 6 o'clock (capsize) position. Of course, as a ferry tips over, cars and lorries will shift and exacerbate the problems, creating an even quicker capsize situation.

Unlike other dedicated ships, designed with one specific transportation role in mind (oil tanker, bulk carrier, container ship), ro-ro ferries are hybrid designs capable of carrying out several functions at once, each as efficiently as possible. This is particularly true of the Baltic super-ferry which is essentially a cargo vessel, a car carrier, a cruise liner and an ice-breaker all rolled into one. It is not too fanciful to suggest that the design of such vessels developed as a compromise between the passenger 'hotel' elements, where human lives have to be protected, and the commercial cargo operation, where economy, punctuality and speed of loading are the dominant factors in the ship's viability.

The loss of the *Estonia* brought about a significant decline of business for all of the Baltic ferry operators and, pending the imposition of new design and operational regulations to improve ferry safety, no further vessels were ordered between the *Silja Europa* in 1993 and the *Romantika* in 2002. In the interim, a great deal of research work was undertaken and pressure was placed upon the maritime safety authorities to produce a new set of rules better to govern ferry safety.

Shortly after the *Estonia* disaster, the International Maritime Organisation (IMO) convened a panel of experts to develop new global safety rules for ro-ro ferries, and the European Union responded with its own initiative to develop new regulations for all vessels sailing to and from EU ports. For the seven countries around the Baltic and North Sea, however, this was not enough – especially as Southern European nations, such as Greece, argued that ships sailing in Mediterranean waters should be exempted due to the more temperate weather there. (The subsequent loss of the *Express Samina* off Paros in September 2000, however, showed this posture to be folly.)

Consequently, the seven Northern countries held a summit in Stockholm in 1996 at which an agreement to insist on additional stability rules for all ferries operating in the Baltic and North Sea regions was ratified. This was the so-called 'Stockholm Agreement' which was later adopted by all seafaring EU countries. As a result, all existing ferries were individually assessed for their damage survivability and, during the ensuing five years, each was retro-fitted either with external sponsons or with flood control doors across the car decks. These alterations were intended to provide extra buoyancy or to prevent floodwater spreading and causing free surface effect. In addition, all ferries were fitted with a third inner watertight door behind their existing ramps and visors.

In the Baltic, where ferries have ice-breaking capabilities, the favoured solution was to fit flood control doors across the car decks and duck-tail sponsons to add extra buoyancy at the stern. (Often, this latter measure also had a positive effect on fuel economy as it had the potential to improve the flow of water aft of the propellers.) Side sponsons were favoured on ferries sailing from British ports, where there was no need to maintain an ice-breaking hull configuration at and below the water-line.

In addition to these physical alterations, much thought was given to improving crew training and operational systems, known as the 'International Safety Management Code' or ISM. Since the *Estonia* disaster, the ferry industry in Northern Europe has been transformed for the better. Overall, ferry companies have become much more professional with crew emergency training and vessel maintenance being taken very seriously indeed. During the past fifteen years, many millions of passengers have travelled on ferries to and from Finland with no maritime safety-related fatalities whatsoever.

In the meantime, the only new addition to the ferries traversing the Central Baltic routes was the *Silja Scandinavia*, which appeared on the Stockholm-Mariehamn-Turku service in 1994. This vessel had been built in Croatia in 1992 at the *Frans Suell*, essentially to the same design as Viking Line's *Amorella* and *Isabella* but with an increased number of passenger cabins. The idea had been to operate a new route between Copenhagen, Malmö and Travemünde in competition with the established TT Line service between Travemünde and Trelleborg. The timing, however, could not have been worse as the recession significantly curtailed both passenger numbers and the movement of freight. Even Silja Line's involvement to market the route from 1993 onwards and the introduction of the *Silja Festival* as a second ship could not improve matters. (The *Frans Suell*'s intended sister, to have been named the *Thomas Mann*, had been delayed by the Balkans war.) Silja abandoned the route in 1994 and moved the *Frans Suell* to the Central Baltic, operating her for two seasons as the *Silja Scandinavia* before she was sold on to Viking Line, becoming their *Gabriella* in April 1997. Since then, she has sailed on the Stockholm-Helsinki route alongside the *Mariella*. For Viking Line, this was some compensation for the earlier loss of the *Europa* to Silja.

The incomplete *Thomas Mann*, meanwhile, was taken to Italy and auctioned. The winning bid came from DFDS and so, since 1994, she has sailed with great success between Copenhagen and Oslo as the *Crown of Scandinavia*.

Since the early 1990s Silja Line's parent company, Effjohn, had progressively sold off the majority of their American cruise operations. In 1995, Effjohn was renamed Silja Oy AB with Jukka Suominen as Managing Director. Later, in 1997, the Sally Line English Channel ferry operation between Ramsgate and Dunkerque was closed down, unable to compete with the

The **Sally Albatross** in Helsinki in the mid-1980s. *(Bruce Peter collection)*

The burned-out remains of the **Sally Albatross** in the spring of 1990. *(Anders Ahlerup)*

In 1989, the **Sally Albatross** is seen at Helsinki in her second incarnation. The superstructure was streamlined to try to make the ferry look more like a cruise ship. Unfortunately, during a refit shortly thereafter at the Finnboda shipyard in Stockholm, she caught fire and burned out. *(William Mayes)*

After rebuilding, the **Sally Albatross** is seen in the early 1990s. *(Bruce Peter collection)*

The **Silja Opera** in Helsinki on a winter's night in February 2002. *(Bruce Peter)*

Channel Tunnel. By then, the firm's shipping interests were reduced to only the Silja Line Baltic routes and the parent company was again renamed, this time to Neptune Marine. As profit margins were squeezed by a combination of recession and the ongoing after-effects of the *Estonia* disaster, institutional investors decided to sell. The largest shareholders were the Swedish NCC construction company with 40% of the total share stock, the Finnish Stora Enso forestry and paper group, UPM-Kymmene, Rauma, Pohjola and the Industriförsäkring insurance group. Shortly thereafter, in 1999, the London-based transport conglomerate Sea Containers bought 50% of the share capital in Neptune Marine and, by August 2002, Sea Containers owned 92% of the company which, by then, had been renamed yet again as Silja Oy AB.

Sea Containers had been founded in 1965 by the American entrepreneur James Sherwood. Initially, the firm had operated successfully in the container chartering business but, by the 1990s, Sea Containers had become a sprawling empire, consisting of transport and logistics companies, hotels, the Venice-Simplon Orient Express luxury train and numerous other businesses, few of which had any relationship to the others. While this diverse portfolio made James Sherwood personally wealthy, for shareholders Sea Containers proved increasingly frustrating as it was difficult to see how synergies and economies could be achieved. For the buccaneering Sherwood, though, Silja Line appeared to be another lucrative business to swallow up, especially as trade with the Baltic States and Russia looked likely to increase in future. Sherwood, however, failed to grasp the complexities of the Baltic ferry business and, moreover, he was not a man who could easily be advised. Sherwood wanted Silja to move further upmarket, believing that enough passengers would be found who would be willing to pay far higher prices for a more upscale experience, but Silja's own directors argued that, in order to ensure future profitability, the Silja Line ferries should aim to attract five million guests per annum, or 15,000 every day, and that this meant being populist, filling the ships by all possible means and generating further profits from large numbers of passengers spending on board. Sherwood also wanted Silja Line to expand in Russia with a service to St Petersburg but, although the company did try to operate cruises there using the *Silja Opera*, previously the *Sally Albatross*, they were frustrated by Russian bureaucracy (all passengers required to buy visas) and by the high port taxes levied to dock there. Sherwood allegedly failed to listen to Silja's Managing Director, Jukka Suominen, who left the company in 2000 to be replaced for three years by the long-serving director Nils-Gustaf Palmgren.

Sea Containers had acquired a majority interest in Silja Line in order to cream off profits from their lucrative Stockholm-Helsinki and Stockholm-Turku routes. The abolition of duty-free sales within the European Union and rising fuel and labour costs made Silja's other routes – such as their northerly service across the Gulf of Bothnia and their operations from Helsinki to Tallinn, Rostock and Travemünde using the ageing *Finnjet* – quickly become loss-makers. The Sundsvall-Vaasa route had closed down in 1996 and the Umeå-Vaasa service was abandoned in September 1999. Latterly, the operation had been run using chartered tonnage – for example, the *Moby Vincent*, the *Sally Star* and the *Stena Invicta*, all of which sailed on charter to Silja Line with 'Wasa'-prefixed marketing names (*Wasa Sun*, *Wasa Star* and *Wasa Jubilee*). When Silja withdrew, however, a Finnish fast food tycoon called Rabbe Grönblom, who operated a chain of pizza parlours called 'Kotti Pizza', announced that he would reopen the service. He bought from Silja Line the aged and very run-down *Fennia* which, after a quick lick of paint, was placed in service between Umeå and Vaasa as the *Casino Express*. Grönblom thought that, without the lure of tax-free shopping, passengers might instead be attracted by a ferry with a large casino on board. When this initiative failed, Grönblom instead sought a subsidy from the European Union with which he introduced a ro-ro freight service instead, using the drearily-named *RG 1* (ex *Kahleberg*).

In order to boost Silja Line, meanwhile, Sea Containers cascaded monohull fast ferries from British waters to the Helsinki-Tallinn run, but with limited success.

Silja, which at the millennium had by far the largest fleet in terms of tonnage, withdrew the *Finnjet* and the cruise ship *Silja Opera* in 2006. The former was initially chartered out as a hotel ship in New Orleans to accommodate students in the wake of Hurricane Katrina. After some months laid up at Freeport in the Bahamas, she was sold to Club Cruise, a cruise ship chartering company based in The Netherlands, for conversion to a cruise ship and towed to Genoa. When this proved too costly and complicated for her new owners, however, she was resold instead for scrap in India. The *Finnjet* was an unlucky victim of circumstances as global steel prices were at a record high at that point and her owner quickly needed to raise money. Although a consortium of Finnish businessmen tried to save the ship, which they hoped might become a floating youth hostel with student accommodation in Turku, it was too little, too late and, instead, the ferry was beached at Alang and broken up, years before her time.

The *Silja Opera*, meanwhile, was laid up at Tilbury on the River Thames until 2007, when she was sold to Louis Cruise Lines as a replacement for the *Sea Diamond* (ex *Birka Princess*) which had sunk at Santorini only a few months previously. Renamed the *Cristal*, she is now a popular cruise ship, sailing mainly from Piraeus.

With stalemate in the boardroom and no apparent agreeable strategy, Sea Containers allegedly had begun to think of selling Silja Line as early as 2004. Only two years later, Sea Containers themselves declared bankruptcy, victims of their own scatter-gun approach to business acquisition and their inability either to understand or to reinvest significantly in the markets in which they operated. Once again, Silja Line was offered for sale.

## CHAPTER FOUR

# The Champagne Economy and Mini-Cruise Culture

Since the early 1980s and the advent of the Viking Song, the Viking Saga, the Finlandia and the Silvia Regina, Baltic ferries have increasingly become leisure and entertainment destinations in themselves, rather than mere means of transportation from A to B. In Sweden, as in most of Western Europe and the USA, the service sector grew exponentially during the 1980s and, when coupled with international market deregulation and an entrepreneurial culture, many people had more disposable income to spend on leisure pursuits. In Britain, a so-called 'yuppie culture' emerged, particularly in London and the Home Counties, as city workers, entrepreneurs and speculators quickly grew wealthy. In Sweden, the same phenomenon was more elegantly named the 'champagne economy' – perhaps because, there, the negative social consequences of rapid change were less keenly felt than in Britain's northerly industrial regions. Indeed, the Scandinavian countries appeared to prosper as a whole and in a more cohesive way than in Britain or the USA, where prosperity in one region often was offset by terrible stagnation in another.

Although the Nordic lands have entrenched social hierarchies, the majority of Swedes and Finns prefer to dwell on their countries' egalitarian and social-democratic ideals. Consequently, even mentioning class issues is regarded as being at best impolite and at worst decidedly non-politically-correct. This notwithstanding, the aspirational design language of Baltic super-ferries cannot be understood without examining *bourgeois* culture and its aestheticization in the wider retail, leisure and hospitality industries in Northern Europe and beyond.

The origin of the design aesthetic found on super-ferries (and indeed on cruise ships and mass-market leisure destinations on *terra firma*, such as casinos, shopping malls and theme parks) can arguably be traced back to the latter half of the nineteenth century. The department stores of Paris – such as Bon Marché, Au Boucheron and Galleries Lafayette, constructed in the wake of Baron Haussmann's radical replanning of the city along modern lines – arguably represent the starting point of the consumerist society. Their imposing, palatial edifices, spectacularly floodlit at night, contained hitherto unimaginable displays of commodities, all seductively presented in theatrical interiors with grand stairways and atria with open galleries, cutting through many levels. These department stores transformed the shopping experience into an urban spectacle, complete with live music, fine dining and electric lighting used on a larger scale than anywhere else. Most significantly, as with latter-day phenomena such as the casino resorts of Las Vegas and indeed many large ferries and cruise ships, the department stores were hermetic and with an inward design focus around internal atria so that, once inside, consumers were subsumed in the retail environment. On Baltic ferries, the natural splendour of the passing archipelago scenery provides an additional attraction during daylight hours. As viewed from inboard, however, the experience is cinematic as the ship's windows frame one unfolding vista after another.

Since the latter nineteenth century, entertainment and leisure environments, aiming to attract the upwardly mobile, have sold themselves on the promise of luxury and escapism in exchange for money. In order to attract a wide diversity of consumers, design in leisure and retail environments had to embody an equally wide range of cultural and stylistic references. After all, younger or older generations prefer a complexity of different (but often related) types of music, dancing, entertainment, food, drink, clothes, furniture and so on.

Two constant features of contemporary mass leisure

**Music and dancing in the Finlandia's 'Maxim' restaurant.** *(Bruce Peter collection)*

**Piled high with bargains, the Amorella's tax-free shop.** *(Bruce Peter)*

Baltic ferries offer entertainment, shopping and dining - but an alternative is to sit on deck and enjoy the passing scenery. Here, two passengers relax on board the **Silja Symphony**, with the **Silja Festival** following astern. *(Bruce Peter)*

A floating 'pleasure palace' - the **Silja Europa** departs from Mariehamn, bound for Turku, in August 2008. The windowless area, aft of the lifeboats, contains a vast tax-free supermarket, complete with shopping trolleys and more than a dozen check-outs. *(Bruce Peter)*

environments are, firstly, that they tend to be self-contained, and secondly that they are filled with conglomerations of wildly diverse imagery, often far removed from their historical contexts. These exist solely to distract the viewer as a kind of theme-park spectacle, providing an inconsequential 'fantasy' backdrop for their leisure activities. Opulent decoration and eclectic ornamentation create a feast – or in the case of Baltic super-ferries, perhaps a smorgasbord – for the eyes. Because of the juxtaposition of a variety of styles and references, any meaning will be blurred or contradictory – but, just as with pornography, the viewer will be stimulated to want more. When promotional literature is produced to sell such environments to consumers, it is usual to find them described with vague, but suitably aspirational, terminology – 'classic', 'contemporary', 'traditional', 'modern' and 'luxurious' being the words most commonly used, sometimes in combination with one another. The idea is to be all things to all people – or, at least, to attract a broad cross-section of consumers. A mid-1980s Viking Line brochure, describing the then-new *Mariella*'s entrance lobby, suggested that its combination of red carpeting, marble, brass and mirrors was 'reminiscent of a first-class hotel in Manhattan' while, amongst the three *à la carte* restaurants, the Carl Michael Bellman Room provided 'an authentic 18$^{th}$ century Stockholm milieu… Its elegant Gustavian evocation is far away from the daily grind.' Adjacent, the Cape Horn Club evoked 'the old days of sail' in a 'dark mahogany and polished brass atmosphere' while the Pub Pamir had 'a British milieu', this notwithstanding its being named after a famous Finnish sailing ship. Thus, a super-ferry is a heterotopia – a complex environment containing many contrasting experiences, atmospheres and stylistic nuances in very close proximity.

The hermetic qualities of post-modern space are intended completely to immerse consumers in the retail or leisure experience and to make them relax as they lose track of the passage of time. Another reason why casinos, night clubs, resorts – and super-ferries – are designed in this way is to allow activity such as gambling, drinking, dancing, kissing, cuddling, screaming and love-making to take place concealed from the repressive gaze of the moralistic. In such a context, a large passenger ship is the perfect vehicle for escapism; America may have imposed prohibition in the 1920s, but Cunard offered cheap cruises from New York to outside the twelve-mile limit, serving up bathtub gin by the gallon to the thirsty, depression-struck multitudes. Such has been a key role of the cruise ship – and, later, the super-ferry – ever since. Once the ship disappears over the horizon, the normal boundaries governing what is socially acceptable may be temporarily suspended. Thus, the ship becomes a mechanism for social release from industry and commerce.

Scandinavia, however, has its own highly-developed leisure and entertainment culture which is reflected in the design and decoration of Baltic super-ferries. The world's first urban amusement park was Tivoli in central Copenhagen, opened in 1843. Stockholm's Gröna Lund, located on an island opposite the city's old town, dates from 1883, while Liseberg in Gothenburg appeared in 1923. Later, in 1930, the Stockholm Exhibition followed suit and, alongside the educational exhibits, its site contained 12 catering outlets, an amusement park, a cinema and two bandstands. More generally, both Stockholm and Helsinki have their many bars and restaurants, their cinemas and variety theatres and – especially – their dining and cabaret clubs. The idea of dining, followed by a cabaret show with dancing thereafter, has been a Swedish and Finnish tradition since the 1930s and its first shipboard manifestation was on Silja Line's *Finlandia* and *Silvia Regina* in 1981.

The cultural context in which the Baltic super-ferry operates is, of course, a reflection of wider social patterns since the onset of industrialization. In Sweden, there was an industrial revolution of sorts – but this was nowhere nearly as comprehensive as in Britain and, whereas here the displacement of population created a new and often rootless working class through immigration from Ireland and Continental Europe, overall migration in Sweden was outward mainly to the USA. Even so, as elsewhere, there were significant internal population shifts and a rapid progress of urbanization was experienced. In Scandinavia as a whole, rural society stayed largely agrarian and so there was less social disruption to the *status quo* in terms of culture and ethnicity. For better or for worse, the Scandinavian countries remained more uniform and cohesive than Britain or the USA but, as elsewhere in the Western World, while economic prosperity grew in fits and starts during the twentieth century, it was the middle classes who benefited the most. In addition, Sweden did not fight two debilitating and destructive world wars and so, in the post-World War 2 era, it was able to benefit from the consumer boom without first having to rebuild neglected or damaged infrastructure. Thus, in Sweden, prosperity increased rapidly during the 1950s and the growing spending power of consumers there was reflected both in expanding car ownership and in a desire to holiday abroad. Both of these factors undoubtedly benefited the Scandinavian ferry industry during the ensuing decades. In Finland, life had generally been harsher than in Sweden but, there too, increasing political stability and wealth encouraged larger numbers of Finns to travel abroad for the first time. Furthermore, during the 1960s, Finland emerged as a leading shipbuilding nation – and the many innovative vessels built there during the decades that followed were symbols of the country's industrial prowess and economic independence.

As we have seen in previous chapters, Baltic ferries built by the

The 'Club Seven' disco on the **Mariella** can be hosed clean. *(Bruce Peter)*

Wärtsilä shipyard during the 1980s often acted as design references for later vessels for the Caribbean cruise industry. The latter draws from a vast international audience – although most guests are American. In comparison, the populations of Sweden and Finland, from which Baltic ferries attract the bulk of their passengers, are relatively small. Even so, there is evidently an aesthetic and cultural relationship between the two passenger shipping phenomena. In Miami, practically every day of the week, at least one giant red and white Carnival cruise liner leaves port, followed by an equally capacious blue and white Royal Caribbean vessel. The Carnival ships, with their emphasis on partying and their modern baroque interiors, are perhaps analogous to Viking Line's Baltic vessels (*Cinderella* and *Carnival Miracle* are both names with 'fairytale' connotations). Both inside and out, the latest Royal Caribbean 'Voyager' class ships resemble inflated versions of the *Silja Serenade* and *Silja Symphony* – and these too have a similar nomenclature (*Serenade of the Seas*, for example). Tallink's ferries, meanwhile, have names comparable with those of Celebrity Cruises' ships (*Galaxy* and *Galaxy*), or with those of Princess Cruises (*Baltic Princess*). Such culturally non-specific post-modern titles are vaguely suggestive of escapism, aspiration and romance – as well as being reflective of a desire on the part of Baltic ferry operators to reach out to a wider international audience. During the summer months, ferries on the Stockholm-Helsinki route, in particular, attract a great many tourists from all over the world and so, during this 'peak season', the atmosphere onboard is far more cosmopolitan than through the winter months, when Swedes and Finns form the dominant clientele.

Of course, a ferry, unlike a cruise ship, is principally a means of transport from A to B and so, on any given crossing, there will always be an extremely wide variety of passengers. For the vast majority, a trip on a Baltic ferry provides a brief diversion from the everyday in a leisure environment that not only has a touch of populist glamour, but also is reassuringly familiar. The fact that a voyage across the Baltic lasts for one night only means that ferries are also among the most transient of environments, with new passengers boarding, sometimes several times a day. This situation also makes super-ferries potentially hedonistic as, to paraphrase a well-known observation about Las Vegas, what happens on board usually stays on board. Once passengers disembark the next morning, it is the cleaners and maintenance crews who remove all evidence left from 'the night before.' Baltic ferries experience punishing use due to the often excessive consumption of alcohol on board. Indeed, since the early-1990s recession, as the ships themselves have aged and some of their 'newness' has inevitably worn off, there has been a steady shift from the idea of taking a Baltic super-ferry primarily for a luxurious but affordable escape from the everyday to the belief that some of these ships are merely vehicles for mass consumption.

As a result, some passengers inevitably demonstrate ambivalent feelings about the shipboard environment which, on the one hand, is designed for their pleasure but, on the other, exists largely to part them from their money in exchange for short-lived intoxication or 'retail therapy'. A super-ferry may be advertised as being a luxury cruise ship for the masses but, ultimately, it is merely a large ferry with all of the physical and temporal limitations that categorization implies. (Perversely, for a small number of passengers, nihilism and purging may even form an integral part of their shipboard pleasure experience.)

In both Sweden and Finland, the sale of alcohol has long been regulated, in part due to a widespread fear of drunkenness and disorder. Indeed, Finland voted for total prohibition in 1919 and, later, in 1922 Sweden had a referendum on prohibition with a small majority voting in the negative. Finnish prohibition was repealed in 1932 but, in both countries, strict controls remained. For instance, alcohol could only be purchased in State-owned shops called 'Systembolaget' in Sweden and 'Alko' in Finland – the latter being a particularly unappealing name. During and after the Second World War, the amount one could buy was rationed and, thereafter, 'black lists' were kept of suspected alcoholics who were not allowed to buy any drink whatsoever. (These lists were abolished in 1971 in Finland and in 1977 in Sweden.) Even so, in order to control alcohol abuse, both the Swedish and Finnish Governments operated aggressive taxation policies towards the drinks industry and these, effectively, pushed quite a high proportion of alcohol sales and consumption 'offshore'. For Baltic ferry operators, this provided a wonderful business opportunity.

Since the 1960s, tax-free drink sales (and the sales of tobacco products and 'luxury' goods, such as perfumes and designer clothing) have made the Baltic cruise and ferry operators significant retailers of tax-free goods. Indeed, by the mid-1990s, Silja Line could claim to be the world's second largest seller of tax-free goods after the British Airports Authority. All of the Baltic ferries have large supermarkets with rows of check-outs and drink stacked by the crateful, just like a discount warehouse on *terra firma*. Typically, passengers arrive at the ferry terminals equipped with very large empty suitcases and luggage trolleys which they will later use to bring their tax-free drinks purchases home.

In 1999 the European Union voted by a majority to end what was seen as an anomaly in the taxation system by abolishing the sale of duty-free goods on journeys between EU Member States. For the wider North European ferry industry, this was a most unwelcome development, but for Baltic operators there was an ingenious solution. Although the Åland Islands are part of Finland, they opted out of all aspects of the EU's monetary policy and so, as long as ferries called there *en route* from Sweden to Finland or vice versa, tax-free sales could continue on board. Thus, since 1999, all cross-Baltic ferries have made a 20-minute stop either at Mariehamn or at Långnäs, another port in the Åland Islands, while *en route*. During the early afternoon, the four Stockholm-Turku ships call at Mariehamn as usual. At around midnight, however, there is a second 'rush hour' as the Stockholm-Helsinki and Stockholm-Tallinn ships dock, followed by the 22-hour cruise vessels from Stockholm which lie there overnight.

The vintage cruise vessel **Birger Jarl** was built for the Stockholm-Helsinki service in the early 1950s. Today, she is operated by Ånedin-Linjen on 22-hour cruises to Mariehamn and she has a niche following of pensioners who appear to appreciate her rather intimate atmosphere. Here, she is seen passing Furusund in August 2008. *(Bruce Peter)*

Old attitudes to drinking remain, however, as these are deeply ingrained in Swedish and Finnish culture. Because drink prices traditionally have been relatively high on *terra firma* due to high taxation, typically Swedes and Finns would buy a 'carry out' of drink from the local Systembolaget or Alko store and drink it at home before going out for entertainment in dance halls or night clubs. That way, they could enjoy the sensation of intoxication without the need to run up expensive bills at the bar. Notwithstanding the relatively inexpensive prices at the bars on board the Baltic super-ferries, some passengers still prefer to buy crates of tax-free beer or vodka in the shop on board and to drink in their cabins before going to the ship's night club later in the evening. Consequently, when one walks along a cabin corridor in the lower decks of a Baltic ferry during the mid-evening, one often finds one open door after another with each cabin filled with groups of Swedes and Finns. Perched on the edges of the bunks with a crate on the floor between them, they smoke and down drinks with studied determination. Until the early 1990s, both Viking and Silja Line attempted to prevent passengers from collecting their tax-free drinks purchases until the next morning, but drinkers inevitably found ways to get around this restriction. Lately, the Baltic ferry companies have tried to clamp down on cabin drinking with regular security patrols and the installation of CCTV in cabin corridors. (On British-based ferries, one rarely if ever sees passengers drinking in their cabins; perhaps this is because the 'go-getting' mentality of Thatcherism has created a culture in which upwardly-mobile Britons flaunt their money at the bar in a way that many Swedes and Finns would find embarrassing.)

This Scandinavian reticence is, of course, arguably one reason why super-ferries have become such a central part of Swedish and Finnish leisure and entertainment culture. Maybe this is because many people live in close-knit communities without the anonymity possible in a large metropolis? Certainly, a significant percentage of Baltic ferry passengers are brought to Stockholm, Helsinki and Turku by networks of bus routes operated by the shipping lines and covering the major parts of each country. Once on board, passengers are free from the repressive gaze of their families and local communities back home. Even so, a certain reticence remains ingrained in the Swedish and Finnish psyche – which drinking can perhaps help to assuage.

According to one female passenger, interviewed on a mini-cruise from Helsinki to Tallinn, 'the problem with Finnish men is that they are so shy and timid. Only after several drinks, when they are almost drunk, will they go and talk to a woman'. This means, presumably, that it is women who often make the first move and, according to the interviewee, 'catching' a male Finn between lost inhibition and drunken stupor is 'an art form'. Leaving nothing to chance, Silja Line decided that this situation could best be alleviated in the more liberal atmosphere on board one of their vessels. Thus, Silja attempted to operate what they called 'traffic light cruises' for singles on the *Silja Opera* from Helsinki to Tallinn. Each passenger was given three badges – red, amber and green – to signify to other passengers whether they were 'looking for company or not', as Silja Line's publicity material delicately put it. The theory was that, as the evening progressed, more red badges would be replaced by amber and green, making the *Silja Opera* the perfect vehicle for romance to blossom.

To promote the cruises, two young people were invited on board every Thursday to take part in a fly-on-the-wall 'reality' TV documentary, aired on Finnish television the following Saturday. As the cruises gained notoriety, however, the TV franchise was dropped after prime-time scenes of wild parties in cabins, 'skinny dipping' in the pool and rampaging teenagers. The fear was that this might deter the company's older passengers from making the more sedate cruises offered on other days of the week. Even so, Viking Line have since been willing hosts to a reality TV series called 'Färjan', this time for Swedish television and recorded on board the *Cinderella* which makes 22-hour cruises to Mariehamn. Although considerably more demure than the Finnish version, reference is still made to the passengers' drunken antics and to the security staff's attempts to calm down altercations. Reality TV has given the *Cinderella*'s short cruises a very high media profile and has made stars of members of the crew – particularly the jovial bartender Håkan and the long-suffering security guard Anita. Indeed, 'Färjan' may well have attracted a more boisterous clientele to the *Cinderella*'s weekend cruises. To counter this, Viking Line has recently increased the minimum age limit to 23 specifically to exclude groups of drunken and aggressive youths. Mid-week, an older generation of passengers is attracted by more traditional onboard entertainment than at weekends – such as Swedish dance bands playing country and western music, or rock and roll hits from the 1950s and '60s. On Tuesdays, for example, a popular Swedish talk show hosted by Ulf Elfving (Sweden's answer to Michael Parkinson) takes place in front of a live audience in the *Cinderella*'s night club.

The most extreme usage of Baltic super-ferries is an annual charter of an entire vessel for a week to the Finnish students' association, Goom, to undertake a week of student 'jamboree' party cruises. In Finland as elsewhere, the expansion of higher education in the latter twentieth century led to the creation of universities specializing in technical subjects and, reflecting this, traditional Finnish student party wear is a coloured boiler suit, combined with a construction worker's hard hat to protect the skull in case of falling over. Given the ferocity with which Finnish undergraduates 'party', this type of outfit is entirely practical!

When the *Cinderella* was switched from the Stockholm-Mariehamn-Turku route to the Helsinki-Tallinn 24-hour cruise circuit in the latter 1990s, she became the first ship of choice for 'Goom' jamboree cruises as her three-deck-high 'Rainbow Club' discotheque made the perfect venue for rock music concerts and for party games – usually involving drinking and often stripping naked. These cruises have since become a much-anticipated annual fixture in the Finnish student calendar with a number of fan web-sites and photo-galleries on the internet, recording the shipboard high jinks in all their gory detail. In more recent years, Viking Line have sought to distance themselves from this type of activity and so, instead, the *Romantika*, the *Silja Festival* (formerly the *Wellamo*) and, most recently, the *Silja Europa* have been chartered for 'Goom' cruises.

To an extent, these types of trip have made the shipping lines realize that there is money to be made from today's relatively affluent youth and so both Silja Line and Viking Line have introduced regular club nights on their ferries sailing on the

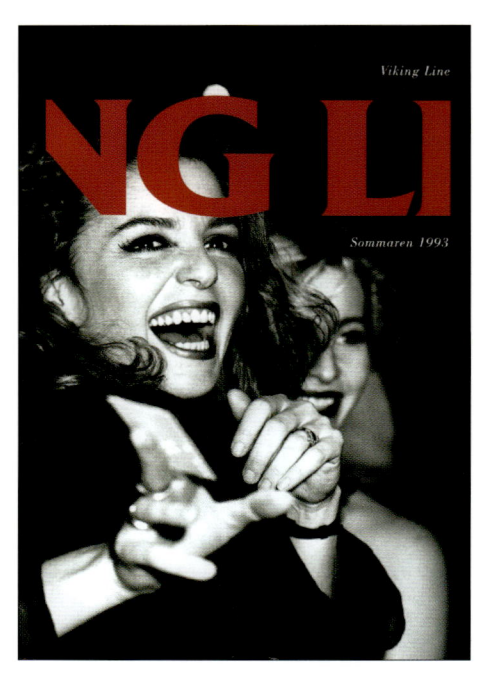

From the latter 1980s until the early 1990s, Viking Line's brochures became ever more noteworthy in terms of graphic design and photography. The 1993 effort was their most remarkable as it contained documentary images of passengers enjoying themselves on board the company's vessels. *(Anders Bergenek collection)*

Stockholm-Turku route, to attract a youthful audience. On the *Amorella*'s Friday evening departures from Stockholm, Viking have promoted 'Club Red' with international DJs flown in to perform on successive weeks. Silja, meanwhile, entered into an agreement with the Liverpool-based dance music promoter Cream to produce a programme of dance-orientated club nights on board the *Silja Festival*. As Cream also operate in Ibiza, presumably Swedish and Finnish club-goers are familiar with the brand from summer package holidays to the Balearics and from their associated record label. Advertising for Cream nights emphasizes that there will be no Finnish tango music played, the implication being that the over-forties would do best to stay well away! At other times, special cruises take place for Swedish heavy metal fans to indulge in mass air-guitar playing to live appearances by their favourite bands and even lesbian and gay cruises have been attempted.

As has already been noted, however, when in everyday service super-ferries have sufficient facilities and attractions to satisfy broad cross-sections of society. While the techno-beats of 'Club Red' are keeping youthful passengers entertained in the disco, one deck below a more traditional dance orchestra will be entertaining a diverse audience in the show lounge while, in the ship's pub, there is singing to guitar and piano music. Indeed, regular appearances on Baltic ferries have made stars out of many Swedish and Finnish show bands and singers, whose appearances are advertised on the ferry companies' web-sites and in special brochures, meaning that mini-cruise passengers can choose particular sailings to catch their favourite musicians. Although the standards of performance usually are high, the music is popular and rather formulaic, mixing pop and rock hits, invariably featuring an Abba medley, a few country and western numbers and, of course, tango music which older Finnish passengers, in particular, adore. Perhaps slow Latin rhythms of this kind help them on their temporal journeys from the cold, dark North to the warm and sunny South? Cabaret performances featuring kitsch impersonations of American musical stars – such as Elvis Presley and Marilyn Monroe – are also popular with older passengers. The genre has successfully transferred to the ferries from Wallman's famous cabaret restaurant in Stockholm.

Mass culture frequently incorporates commodified aspects of the vernacular and so, on Baltic ferries, one also finds oblique references to Swedish and Finnish 'folksiness'. For example, in the ships' pubs, with their contrived 'maritime atmosphere', the entertainment is provided by a troubadour (a solo singer with guitar) leading the drinkers in rousing renditions of pop and folk songs - a genre known to Swedes and Finns as 'Schlager'. In between these 'live' sessions, passengers can perform their own karaoke versions, with the lyrics repeated on flat-screen TVs. Yet, within this generic formula, there is evidence of carefully-targeted niche marketing. For example, Viking Line seek to attract beer connoisseurs by stocking the pubs with micro-brewed beers, not available on rival ferries.

To the visiting observer, gambling appears to be a noticeable part of Swedish and Finnish mass culture – and a reflection of relatively affluent societies with generally comfortable life-styles and leisure time to be filled, preferably indoors during the winter months.

(Even Swedish and Finnish railway stations have casinos!). Roulette, Blackjack and slot machine gaming are lucrative earners for the ferry lines all year round. Photo-murals showing images of the bright lights of Las Vegas provide a backdrop to the activity around the gaming tables and, seemingly, every spare corner in the hallways on board has slot machines available for use. In winter, the flashing lights and 'fairground' sound effects are in stark contrast to the often bleak weather outside – and that is why passengers travel on Baltic super-ferries throughout the year. By building on the popularity of gambling on ferries, an Åland Islands-based company called PAF (Penning Automat Föreningen) has become one of the biggest suppliers of gaming equipment to the cruise industry world-wide.

Elsewhere on board, healthier leisure pursuits are also available. Large complexes of sauna baths are provided, both for single-sex and family groups. On certain ferries, the top-grade suites even have their own private sauna facilities. In addition, most vessels boast swimming pools and Jacuzzis – and Silja Line's *Silja Serenade*, *Silja Symphony* and *Silja Europa* all have spacious spa facilities. With greater health-consciousness evident among wider cross-sections of society, the ferry companies have come to realize that there is money to be made by providing so-called 'wellness' facilities, offering massages and beauty treatments to the work-weary multitudes. Both the *Birka Paradise* and the *Cinderella* offer such facilities on their 22-hour cruises to Mariehamn. (Beyond these revenue-generating health attractions, arguably the greatest pleasure of sailing on a Baltic ferry is sitting outside on a deck chair, gazing at the beautiful archipelago scenery gliding past and breathing in the fresh sea air, scented by the pine forests which spread across the islands.)

The planning of the passenger accommodation on modern ferries and cruise vessels attempts to stimulate onboard revenue flows through the most effective 'adjacencies' of the various public rooms and income-generating attractions. A side-effect of this is that facilities appealing to particular social groups tend to be grouped in fairly close proximity. This, in turn, means that many different activities can take place simultaneously with one group of passengers being largely unaware of the presence of others. For example, a couple taking a romantic short break, booked in one of the more expensive suites, would probably choose to drink in a cocktail bar and dine in a gourmet restaurant. They would, therefore, only have a peripheral awareness of the presence on board of students accommodated in the cheapest cabins beneath the car deck, who would probably eat in the buffet restaurant or cafeteria and drink and dance in the disco. It is only briefly in the hallways and stairwells that the two groups might encounter one another. Consequently, these areas of the ships have a 'high street' atmosphere with lots of passengers milling around and browsing for food, drink and entertainment.

Because ferries also have their transport function, they inevitably carry minorities whose aspirations and life-styles do not meld with those of the indigenous masses, travelling primarily for leisure purposes. Perhaps understandably, therefore, recent émigrés to Scandinavia – often from the Islamic world – appear to prefer to sit in all-male groups in the ships' foyer spaces in order to avoid the sight of alcohol consumption in the bars and lounges. Romany families also tend to occupy foyer spaces, but they usually camp out in large family groups. Baltic ferries are thus amongst the most democratic of passenger ships, able to accommodate broad cross-sections of population – including marginal groups – in relative comfort.

The need to attract wide ranges of passengers to fill their many ships means that the ferry companies' publicity departments have to target their marketing carefully to appeal to as broad a public as possible. Shipping line publicity material is meticulously designed to give distinct (but related) messages to various categories of potential passenger. On the one hand, the qualities of space, comfort and 'exclusivity' are promoted through lavish and glossy brochures similar to those produced by American-based cruise lines. Equally, the ferries are promoted in other types of literature and, more recently, through the internet to specific niche markets – club-goers, pensioners, business conference organizers and so on. Clearly, engagement with the mass media has the potential to reach very large audiences – as Viking Line's participation in the TV series 'Färjan' has demonstrated. Yet, lurid tabloid headlines ensuing from the occasionally libidinous onboard activities equally have the potential to cause more respectable and genteel passengers – who are the vast majority – to stay away. To counter this, Viking Line in particular have a policy of forceful 'reputation management' and the company tends to react quickly and assertively to unflattering reportage. In their defence, journalists argue that, as very large numbers of Swedes and Finns regularly travel on Baltic ferries each year, the industry is inevitably newsworthy and close press scrutiny is in the public interest. Either way, it seems clear that, for better or for worse, Baltic ferries have a media profile – and a mass popular appeal – that is perhaps greater than any other commercial passenger shipping operation in Europe.

The predominant type of passenger carried varies, however, from season to season and from route to route. During the winter when fares are low, the vast majority are 'mini-cruisers', escaping cold, dark bleakness for a short binge of food, drink and entertainment in a colourful and 'luxurious' environment. In summer, fares are much higher and so the super-ferries are filled largely with tourists and holiday-makers, travelling across the Baltic to get from A to B. Moreover, the 'capital cities' route between Stockholm and Helsinki has always been regarded as being somewhat upmarket in comparison with the shorter

Stockholm-Turku crossing which tends to attract a more boisterous clientele due to its shorter duration and hence lower fares. The Helsinki-Tallinn and Stockholm-Mariehamn cruise-ferry operations are the most party-orientated services of all.

Although it is apparent that the culture on board Baltic super-ferries is generally adult-orientated, these ships do have extensive play-rooms with ball pools, chutes and other play equipment. During the summer holidays when a higher proportion of families travel, it is usual for the conference facilities to be converted temporarily for children's entertainment as well. Both Silja Line and Viking Line have promotions orientated towards children and their parents. Silja market themselves as 'the official carrier of the Moomin', Moomins being the fictitious forest-living creatures invented by the Finnish author Tove Jansson. These feature in popular books, television cartoons and at a theme park called 'Moominland', close to Naantali near Turku. On Silja ships, members of the entertainment staff dress up in Moomin costumes to amuse the children. Viking Line, on the other hand, use a large white cat mascot called 'Villi Viking'. Usually, an entertainer in a Villi Viking costume hands out sweets to children in the ferry terminal before embarkation.

Throughout the low season, from September to May, conference traffic is a highly lucrative source of revenue for Baltic super-ferries and all have extensive suites of meeting rooms and even conference auditoria. Outwith Scandinavia, many ferry lines have tried to emulate the success of the Baltic operators in attracting conference traffic, but with limited success. Partly this is due to the egalitarian Scandinavian employment culture in which senior and middle management have a less hierarchical relationship than is typical of many large companies in Britain. In addition, businesses in Scandinavia have tended to have a paternalistic outlook towards their employees. Conferences on Baltic ferries, with dining, entertainment and dancing, can be seen as being part of this corporate culture. At a more practical level, significant proportions of the mid-Baltic ferry services are routed through the relatively sheltered waters of the Swedish and Finnish archipelagos and so ships are less affected by stormy weather (except occasionally during the middle of the night when most passengers are in bed anyway). This means, of course, that conferences can take place in calm and civilized conditions without the worry of seasickness.

For mini-cruisers, tourists and conference delegates alike, dining is a most significant aspect of the Baltic super-ferry experience. Since the Edwardian era, passenger ships have been judged by the quality of their cuisine. For example, great transAtlantic liners such as Germany's 1913 *Imperator* entrusted their First Class onboard services to the Ritz group. (Indeed César Ritz's architect Charles Mèwes was retained to design the interiors.) Such ships offered fine cuisine in the setting of a luxury hotel, and this tradition has continued on passenger ships ever since, with the difference that, nowadays, there is also demand for informal eating and drinking throughout the day – and into the night. A major appeal of cruising – and of taking shorter trips on super-ferries – is that that passengers can rely on having food that is cooked to their taste, as well as being able to sample moderated versions of 'exotic' foreign cuisine, should they choose to do so. Thus, as well as offering traditional Scandinavian cuisine – seafood, hot and cold meats with berry sauce and so on – a choice of dishes from other countries and cultures is also provided on a rolling basis.

Viking Line have even gone to the trouble of promoting gourmet cruises with acclaimed chefs flown in from overseas especially to cook in the galleys of their ships, and the company have published a cookery book called 'Sea & Food' to allow passengers to attempt the most popular recipes at home. 'Sea & Food' is a fully illustrated hard-back volume containing mouth-watering photographs and images of the company's chefs cooking amid archipelago scenery.

Both Stockholm and Helsinki are, of course, known for their many fine restaurants and Sweden, in particular, has a strong gourmet tradition with a distinctly French influence upon its cuisine. Thus, the *à la carte* restaurants on Viking and Silja vessels tend to be decorated either in the Gustavian manner or in an Art Nouveau style (for example, 'La Belle Epoque' on Viking's *Cinderella* and the 'Maxim' restaurants on the *Silja Serenade* and the *Silja Symphony*). Catering to the middle-market are the self-service 'smorgasbord' buffet restaurants where passengers can eat and drink as much as they like for a fixed price – enjoying not only Scandinavian but also oriental dishes. The sheer quantity of food and drink available for a fixed all-inclusive price can be quite overwhelming and the rival ferry operators compete to provide the biggest and best smorgasbord. Not surprisingly, these are the largest and most popular restaurants on board but a number of more intimate options are also available on certain ships – perhaps a steakhouse, a tapas bar or a seafood restaurant. At the lower end, there will be a self-service cafeteria and, on the *Silja Europa*, a burger bar with games machines.

The sheer logistics of catering on a super-ferry are daunting, even more so as a vessel will often turn round within a couple of hours; time in port is money lost. Sophisticated computer programming allows catering staff to predict with amazing accuracy what passengers will order for dinner on each crossing, while cooking and serving facilities on the most modern vessels are state-of-the-art. The intensive usage of modern ferries has brought about the development of efficient shore-based infrastructures. Everything from toilet rolls to caviar must be sourced and supplied with unfailing dependability several times a day. Most ferries bulk-load stores pre-packed in containers at each terminal port. The containers with food are brought by lift direct to the galley and their contents are then cooked on board.

Apart from being vehicles for shopping, entertainment, drinking and dining – and means of transport – super-ferries are also large hotels, each with berths for several thousand passengers. On the Stockholm-Helsinki route, cabins can be prepared during layovers, but on the Stockholm-Turku service the ships are in constant circulation and so the cabins are cleaned and the beds made up during the day. As with the food supplies, all of the linen is brought on board pre-packed in containers. Thousands of sets of bedding – consisting of sheets, duvets, pillows and towels – are delivered from laundries on *terra firma* already made up so that the cabin stewards only have to remove the existing sets from each bunk and lay the new in place. Meanwhile, large shore-based cleaning crews vacuum and polish intensively to return the vessels to as near a pristine state as possible before the next onslaught of passengers arrives.

CHAPTER FIVE

# Destination Tallinn

During the latter 1990s, the European economies picked up and a new boom in consumerism, coupled with a gradual return of public confidence in the ferry industry, brought about a further expansion of passenger leisure travel in the Baltic. The most lucrative area for growth was between Sweden, Finland and Estonia, which had become the fastest-developing of the formerly Soviet Baltic States with a burgeoning banking and financial services industry and a rapidly-expanding economy.

Following the loss of the *Estonia*, Estline had quickly re-established itself on the Stockholm-Tallinn route, using the former *Diana II* of Viking Line as the *Mare Balticum*. Later, in 1996, the company acquired a further vessel which was larger still – the *Regina Baltica*. This was the former *Viking Song* of 1980 which, in the interim, had served Fred. Olsen Lines on the North Sea and Skagerrak as the *Braemar* before switching to the Russian Baltic Line's route between Stockholm and St Petersburg in 1991 as the *Anna Karenina*. Due to political difficulties in St Petersburg at that time, the route was unsuccessful, but finally the vessel found her niche sailing between Stockholm and Tallinn.

Meanwhile, traffic also grew significantly on the four-hour crossing of the Gulf of Finland between Helsinki and Tallinn, where a whole flotilla of second-hand tonnage was introduced by a number of Finnish and Estonian operators. Both Viking and Silja Line established themselves using vessels switched from other routes – the *Cinderella* and the *Wasa Queen*. The latter was originally the *Bore Star* of 1975, which returned to the Silja fleet after a nomadic life in the interim, spent sailing in the Mediterranean between Venice and Istanbul as the *Orient Express*, in the Caribbean as a cruise ship and, latterly, as a ferry across the Gulf of Bothnia between Umeå and Vaasa. In addition, the Åland Islands-based Eckerö Line (a subsidiary of Rederi AB Eckerölinjen) and the Estonian New Line introduced a couple of former Viking Line 'Papenburgers' on the route. While Estonian New Line was short-lived, Eckerö Line found a market niche catering for older Finnish mini-cruise passengers and in 1998 acquired the *Nordlandia* (ex *Nord Gotlandia*, ex *Olau Hollandia*) for this purpose.

Of the Estonian entrants into the Baltic ferry scene, Tallink was the most successful and quickly grew into a serious rival to the Viking

Eckerö Line's **Norlandia** (originally the **Olau Hollandia**) plays a similar role to the **Birger Jarl** but on the Helsinki-Tallinn route. The vessel is a favourite with Finnish pensioners, who prefer her unostentatious onboard style. Here, she is seen returning from Tallinn to Helsinki in evening light in the summer of 2003. *(Bruce Peter)*

Baltic Ferries

The ex-Soviet ferry **Georg Ots**, on her way from Helsinki to Tallinn in 1997. *(Bruce Peter)*

The **Tallink** in Tallinn Harbour in 1992. *(Søren Lund Hviid)*

Tallink's major units on the Helsinki-Tallinn route in the latter 1990s and early 2000s were the **Fantaasia** (left) and the **Vana Tallinn** (right). The former was originally Viking Line's **Turella**, while the latter was once DFDS' **Dana Regina**. Both were replaced by the new cruise-ferry **Romantika**. Note the rather busy stripey livery. *(Bruce Peter)*

A third major Tallink unit was the **Meloodia**, originally Viking Line's **Diana II**. *(Bruce Peter)*

The **Normandy** was taken on charter by Tallink in 1997. *(Søren Lund Hviid)*

The **Fantaasia**, now minus stripes, photographed in summer sunshine. *(William Mayes)*

The **Regina Baltica** passes Oxdjupet in August 2008. *(Bruce Peter)*

and Silja fleets. In 1989, Finnish and Soviet interests had established Tallink as a joint marketing venture to develop ferry traffic across the Gulf of Finland. The founding partners were Palkkiyhtymä Oy, the City of Tallinn, the Port of Tallinn and the State-owned Estonian Shipping Company, Eesti Merelaevandus. Following the Soviet collapse, this firm was privatized and, thereafter, Tallink's growth in the Eastern Baltic was rapid. Initially, the ferries operated under the Tallink brand belonged to a variety of companies.

The pioneering Tallink vessels were the 1980-built ex-Soviet *Georg Ots*, which was joined in 1989 by the *Tallink*, originally Silja Line's *Svea Regina* of 1972. In 1993, the Finnish partners withdrew from the joint venture and, through a number of deals, the ownership of Tallink passed to the private sector through a firm called Eminre. Later, in 1996, the owner was renamed Hansatee, although the Tallink trademark was retained for publicity purposes.

Tallink subsequently absorbed a significant fleet of 1970s-vintage Baltic ferry tonnage, much of which had started out on Silja and Viking Lines' premier routes. By 1999 Hansatee was one of the largest companies in Estonia, carrying 2.6 million passengers to Finland and Sweden as well as cornering the freight market. Next, in 2001, Tallink took over the Estline fleet, giving them a total of five major ferries and two fast craft. Their front-line vessels at this stage were the *Vana Tallinn* (ex *Nord Estonia*, ex *Dana Regina*), the *Meloodia* (ex *Mare Balticum*, ex *Diana II*), the *Fantaasia* (ex *Turella*), the *Baltic Kristina* (ex *Bore I*) and the *Regina Baltica* (ex *Anna Karenina*, ex *Braemar*, ex *Viking Song*). Others were chartered for short periods as traffic built up and, although the ships were profitable, Tallink's parent company, Hansatee, had expanded too quickly in several business areas besides ferry operation, becoming indebted, and by the mid-1990s, appeared

Tallink's first purpose-built ferry was the **Romantika**, which was introduced on the Helsinki-Tallinn 22-hour cruise circuit. The vessel spent only eight hours a day at sea and was berthed in Tallink harbour the rest of the time, acting as a floating hotel. Later, the **Galaxy** replaced her in this role and she was switched to the Stockholm-Tallinn route. *(Bruce Peter)*

The **Cinderella** was painted white and re-flagged in Sweden to carry out daily cruises from Stockholm to Mariehamn. As there was already a 'Cinderella' in the Swedish register, her official name is actually the **Viking Cinderella**, but the 'Viking' prefix is in very small letters. Here, she passes Oxdjupet in August 2008. *(Bruce Peter)*

to be heading for bankruptcy.

In 1997 the Tallink subsidiary was offered for sale – but Neptune Marine, Silja Line's parent company, did not have sufficient funds while Viking Line also decided not to take over Tallink.

Instead, rescue came from within Estonia itself in the form of two ambitious and talented entrepreneurs, Enn Pant and his friend Ain Hanschmidt. Pant was a senior figure in the Estonian Finance Ministry, while Hanschmidt ran the bank, Eesti Uhispankki. As Eesti Uhispankki was one of Hansatee's major creditors, Pant and Hanschmidt decided to take Tallink over, with Pant acquiring 44% of shares and installing himself as CEO, while Hanschmidt owned a smaller percentage of the company. Through this arrangement, Tallink became very successful and soon began to order new tonnage. At the beginning of 2002, the firm changed its name to AS Tallink Grupp, indicating a desire further to expand into other areas. By then, the first purpose-built Tallink super-ferry was under construction at Aker Finnyards at Rauma.

The 39,864 gt *Romantika* was the first Baltic super ferry of a new generation. In common with the earlier 1980s cohort, she had an attractive array of passenger facilities, spread over two decks. Interior design was carried out jointly by Pille Lausmäe from Tallinn and by the Finnish firm Aprocos. Emphasis was placed on entertainment with two large show lounges filling the entire width of the superstructure forward and aft. The 'Starlight Palace', located in the ship's stern section, is particularly impressive with a horse-shoe-shaped balcony surrounding a semi-circular dance floor with bars on each level and linking spiral staircases. Amidships, there are a number of dining options, including a very swish *à la carte* restaurant, a food court, a fast food café and a very spacious buffet restaurant, the forward section of which overlooks the bow.

Cabins with *en suite* facilities are located on the decks above and below with a conference suite and sauna complex filling the aft third of the topmost passenger deck. All of this, and more, was fitted into a ship intended for a crossing of not more than four hours' duration. Initially, the *Romantika* operated on 22-hour mini-cruises, sailing from Helsinki in the evening and arriving in Tallinn around 22.00. There, the ship acted as a floating hotel and entertainment centre for her passengers before returning to Finland the following afternoon. This meant that the vessel could be serviced by shore-based personnel, with musicians and entertainment staff boarding upon arrival in Tallinn and cleaners arriving in the early morning to restore the public rooms and cabin corridors to as near pristine a condition as possible while the passengers were still sleeping.

Back then, the big attraction of Tallink's fleet was that its short cruises were very competitively priced because the company had lower crewing costs than either Viking or Silja, the majority of whose vessels flew the Finnish flag. Furthermore, Tallink ships sold very cheap duty-free drink and cigarettes. The result was that the *Romantika*'s clientele was often somewhat more rumbustious than those on other Baltic ferries – the aim of the predominantly Finnish passengers apparently being to drink and smoke as much as possible during the crossing. For Tallink, this was undoubtedly lucrative, but unfortunate for the officers and crew who had to contend with their drunken antics on a daily basis. As the behaviour of some was quite rowdy, the ship's fixtures and fittings took very considerable punishment.

### Mini-cruise Developments

When the *Romantika* first entered service, her main rival on the Helsinki-Tallinn route was Viking Line's *Cinderella*. Viking Line evidently detected a subtle difference between their Swedish and Finnish passengers as, before the *Cinderella* was switched to the

The 'Yacht Club' on the **Birka Paradise** features a yacht-shaped bar. *(Bruce Peter)*

The **Birka Paradise**'s night club. *(Bruce Peter)*

The **Birka Paradise** catches the sun as she passes Furusund on her way from Mariehamn to Stockholm in August 2008. *(Bruce Peter)*

'Paradise Beach' on the **Birka Paradise** offers year-round tropical sunshine. *(Bruce Peter)*

The observation lounge on the **Birka Paradise** with fake palm trees. *(Bruce Peter)*

Eckerö Linjen's **Eckerö** (ex **Jens Kofoed**) approaches Grisslehamn in August 2008. The ferry provides a short two-hour hop from the Swedish mainland to the Åland Islands, carrying many Swedes on tax-free shopping trips. *(Bruce Peter)*

Helsinki-Tallinn 22-hour cruise trade from the Stockholm-Mariehamn-Turku route, some of the restaurant space was converted into an extra casino.

Competition from the *Romantika* was intense and so, in the autumn of 2003, Viking Line decided to refurbish the *Cinderella* and to place her on cruises from Stockholm to Mariehamn instead, reviving a service suspended since Rederi AB Slite's bankruptcy in 1993. In order to distinguish the ship as a cruise vessel, Viking Line repainted the hull in white with the name in large cursive lettering amidships. In an attempt slightly to widen the customer base, the refurbished *Cinderella* was fitted with a spa and beauty treatment complex and the casino, installed for the Helsinki-Tallinn cruises, was converted back into a French speciality restaurant. At the same time, to reduce crewing costs a little and better to appeal to a Swedish-speaking clientele, the *Cinderella* was re-registered in Stockholm.

On the Stockholm-Mariehamn route, she was now in head-to-head competition with the Birka Line's well-established and popular *Birka Princess*, a purpose-built cruise ship dating from 1986 with no bow-to-stern car and freight deck whatsoever. At that time, purpose-built cruise ships were seen by some as the next logical step forward for the leisure, entertainment and retail element of the Baltic ferry industry.

Silja had entered the fray in 2002 with the *Silja Opera*, which was formerly the *Sally Albatross*. Between this vessel's 1992 total reconstruction from the underwater hull of what had originally been the *Viking Saga* and her return to Baltic cruising a decade later, she had been used by Norwegian Cruise Line in the Caribbean as the *Leeward* and, later, in the Far East as the *Superstar Taurus*. Thus, Silja could claim that their 'new' fleet member had been used internationally and so was somewhat more glamorous than the average Baltic ferry. Whether or not this was actually so was a moot point, but Silja's marketing department understandably made great capital out of the ship's diverse history and spheres of operation to suggest that she was exotic and special.

The *Silja Opera* was first tried on party cruises from Helsinki to Tallinn, Riga and St Petersburg. Later, she was introduced on similar circuits from Stockholm – but with mixed results. Meanwhile, further new vessels were ordered from Aker Finnyards in Rauma. Tallink's new ferry *Victoria 1*, which made her debut in March 2004, was a similar ship to the existing *Romantika*, but for service between Stockholm, Mariehamn and Tallinn.

The new Birka Line flagship *Birka Paradise*, on the other hand, was a proper cruise ship, designed and built to emulate the style of vessels being introduced by the major Caribbean- and Mediterranean-based lines, but compressed to a scale suitable for short cruises from Stockholm to Mariehamn through the archipelago. The big selling point of the new ship was that she would offer Caribbean sunshine in a 'tropical' environment, all year round. Ordered from the Aker Finnyards at Rauma, she was delivered in November 2004. Externally and internally, the vessel was styled jointly by the Norwegian architects Finn Falkum-Hansen and Yran & Storbraaten, working with the German firm Partnership Design. The former was already noted for his designs for the most recent 'Hurtigrute' ships, the *Trollfjord* and the *Midnatsol* of Troms Fylkes Dampskibsselskap and of the Mediterranean high-speed cruise ferries built at Fosen Mekaniske Verksteder in Norway for the Minoan and ANEK Lines – the *Aretousa*, the *Ikarus*, the *Pasiphae*, the *Olympic Champion* and the *Hellenic Spirit*. Partnership Design, on the other hand, are best known for devising the resort-like German-flagged 'Aida' cruise ships.

The design for the *Birka Paradise* resembled many recent

international cruise ships with low-slung lifeboats, porthole-shaped windows, a clipper-shaped bow and a forward-slanted transom stern, giving her relatively short and beamy hull (177m x 28 m) a sleek appearance. These tactics were followed through in the arrangement of the superstructure, the deck-houses and the funnel. Inboard, there were to be two decks of entertainment facilities, including nine small speciality restaurants and a wide selection of bars, lounges, shops and conference facilities. On the topmost deck, between the mast and funnel, there was to be a swimming pool and jacuzzi complex under a retractable glazed 'magradome' roof. Known as the 'Paradise Beach', this was to be decorated with palm trees and equipped with three large sunray lamps, to produce bright Caribbean sunshine (and sun tans) all year round. A retractable dance floor was to be built into the pool surround which, at the touch of a button, could be rolled out to fill the entire lido area, instantly converting the space into a high-capacity night club with a light show and even smoke effects.

Once in service, the *Birka Paradise* immediately attracted a high degree of attention on account of her progressive appearance and her imaginative interior design. In terms of her functionality, she was, however, a 'booze cruiser' like any other large ship in the Stockholm-Mariehamn and Helsinki-Tallinn trades and this was problematic. Very quickly, Birka Line found that operating both the existing *Birka Princess* and the new *Birka Paradise* was unprofitable and so the older ship was sold in 2006 to the Greek-Cypriot Louis Cruise Lines for short Aegean cruises from Piraeus as the *Sea Diamond*. Unfortunately, the *Sea Diamond*'s operation there was brief as she grounded on rocks near to Santorini in April 2007 and later sank.

Meanwhile, Birka Line was bought out by another Åland Islands-based shipping company, Rederi AB Eckerölinjen. Since the early 1960s, this company had run a succession of ferries between Grisslehamn and Eckerö, before also entering the fray between Helsinki and Tallinn in the 1990s. Their Grisslehamn-Eckerö fleet comprised former Viking Line 'Papenburgers', built in the early 1970s – the *Ålandia* (ex *Botnia Express*, ex *Diana*) and the *Roslagen* (ex *Wasa Express*, ex *Viking 3*). These were replaced in 2005 by the *Eckerö*, a second-hand purchase from Bornholmstrafikken in Denmark which had been built in Aalborg in 1979 as the *Jens Kofoed*. Following a substantial renovation, she became a very successful Baltic ferry, attracting coachloads of passengers to enjoy a short day trip to the Åland Islands and back.

### The Advent of the Ro-pax

Not only have purpose-built cruise ships attempted to find a niche on the mid-Baltic routes between Sweden, Finland and Estonia, but also dedicated freight ferries have increasingly made their presence felt since the mid-1990s. Understandably, truck drivers regard having to travel on a cruise ferry, surrounded by party-goers, as undesirable. With improved motorways through the Swedish archipelago to Kapellskär and from Turku, Naantali and Hanko in South-Western Finland, however, these ports grew alongside ro-ro freight traffic, carried on purpose-built ro-ro vessels. Since the 1980s Finnlink, a subsidiary of Finnlines, have steadily increased their market share between Sweden and Finland, initially transporting only trucks and their drivers but, since 2002, carrying passengers as well. Tallink also introduced their own freight and passenger route from Kapellskär to Paldiski in Estonia. Although Silja Line have not run freight ships under their own brand since a curtailed experiment in the early 1970s, in 1989 the parent companies Effoa and Johnson Line set up a ro-ro freight subsidiary called SeaWind Line. A ro-ro truck and rail ferry, the *Sea Wind*, was purchased to provide a daily return trip

The Greek-owned **Superfast IX** approaches Travemünde, in brilliant summer sunshine at the end of her lengthy crossing from Finland. *(Søren Lund Hviid)*

The reception area on the **Finnmaid**. *(Bruce Peter)*

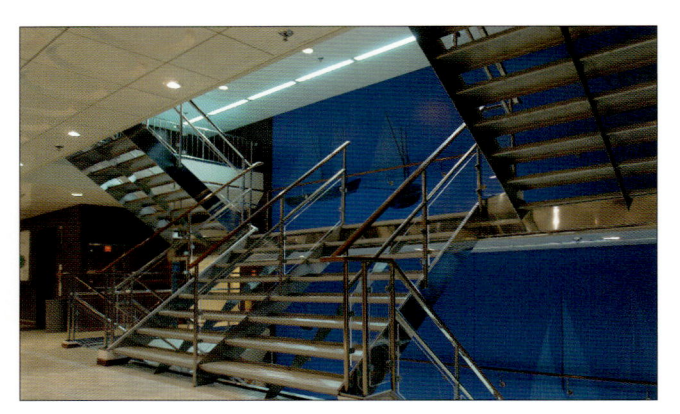

The **Finnmaid**'s main stairwell is boldly designed. *(Bruce Peter)*

The **Finnlady** increases her speed as she enters the Gulf of Finland at the beginning of a voyage to Travemünde in Germany in April 2009. *(Søren Lund Hviid)*

A corner of the **Finnmaid**'s hallway, with a photo-mural on the bulkhead. *(Bruce Peter)*

Looking towards the bar on the **Finnmaid**. *(Bruce Peter)*

The stylish buffet restaurant on the **Finnmaid**. *(Bruce Peter)*

The **Finnmaid**'s Hansa Lounge - a tranquil space in which to relax. *(Bruce Peter)*

from Stockholm to Turku. This vessel had been built in 1972 as the *Svealand* for Rederi AB Svea's Trave Line subsidiary, which operated from Sweden to Germany in the Southern Baltic. By the early 2000s, SeaWind Line were running three freight ferries between Stockholm and Turku although their fleet has since been reduced back to just their original vessel.

Finnlines, meanwhile, grew rapidly to become the dominant operator of ro-ro vessels on the Baltic. Back in the mid-1960s, the company had pioneered a special handling system for reels of paper, shipping these on 20-foot flatbeds to increase efficiency and to reduce the possibility of damage. Marketed as 'Finnflow', this was first installed on the cruise ferries *Finnhansa* and *Finnpartner* between Helsinki and Travemünde in 1966. Three years later, the first of a very advanced trio of dedicated freighters, the Wärtsilä-built *Finncarrier*, was introduced. This vessel was followed by two sisters – the *Finnfellow* and the *Hans Gutzeit* – in 1972-73. Subsequently, Finnlines entered a partnership with the West German Poseidon Lines and it was Poseidon who began carrying passengers as well as freight between Lübeck and Helsinki on their 1976-built *Transgermania*.

During the first half of the 1980s, a second generation of larger ro-ros appeared on routes from Finland to West Germany and also to the United Kingdom. These were shared between Finnlines (the *Finnmerchant*), the Finland Steamship Company (the *Arcturus* and the *Oihonna*), Poseidon Lines (the *Transfinlandia*) and the United Baltic Corporation (the *Baltic Eider*). With up to 2,200 freight lane metres each, this class proved to be very effective and the design was further developed with the Polish-built *Finnsailor* and *Antares* being delivered in 1987 from Gdansk. Poseidon's later *Translubeca* was a ro-pax with comfortable accommodation for 84 passengers, as well as 2,080 lane metres for freight and space for 220 German export cars.

The success of these vessels undoubtedly persuaded Finnlines to dispose of the fuel-hungry and marginally profitable *Finnjet* to the Finland Steamship Company in 1987, after which the company concentrated on expanding their ro-ro freight shipping business between Finland and Germany.

In 1994-95, a third generation of ro-ro freighters was delivered from Gdansk – the *Finnhansa*, the *Finnpartner*, the *Finntrader* and the *Transeuropa* – each with 3,200 lane metres for trucks and capacity for 119 passengers in spacious and luxurious accommodation. While a proportion of berths was sold to truck drivers, the remainder proved popular with travellers seeking a short sea voyage in a tranquil environment – in contrast to the typically rather boisterous 'night club' ambience of the Baltic cruise ferries.

Next, Finnlines developed a second, shorter freight and passenger route from Naantali in Finland to Kapellskär in Sweden, using three Spanish-built ro-pax ferries, the *Finnclipper*, the *Finneagle* and the *Finnfellow*, all of which had been ordered by Stena Line and delivered from Navantia's Puerto Real shipyard in 1999-2000. Supplemented by chartered tonnage, these vessels proved to be an outstanding success. Their capacities of around 3,100 lane metres and 400 passengers each were soon well filled as the late-1990s economic boom gained momentum.

By this point, the advantages for freight hauliers of sailing from Germany to Finland – rather than driving through the Baltic States – were becoming clearer as increasing fuel costs and hefty road tolls, coupled with the enhanced economies of scale of ever-larger ro-pax ships, altered the economic balance between the two options. Thus, Finnlines' routes to Germany continued rapidly to expand and a service to Gdansk in Poland was also introduced.

Next, a further new generation of five very large ro-pax vessels in the 45,000 gt range was ordered, this time from the Italian shipbuilder Fincantieri, for delivery between 2006 and 2008. Named the *Finnstar*, the *Finnlady*, the *Finnmaid*, the *Europalink* and the *Nordlink*, the vessels were built at the Castellamare di Stabia shipyard, close to Naples, and outfitted at a sister Fincantieri-owned yard in Ancona. Each has no less than 4,223 lane metres of freight capacity, as well as space for 500 passengers.

Externally, they are handsome vessels, with an imposing silhouette created by their high topsides and by their towering superstructures, piled up towards the bow and offset by twin funnels some way aft. Their passenger accommodation is very well appointed, being the work of the Finnish interior designers Sistem Oy. Rather than appearing to be floating malls, these vessels are more like stylish boutique hotels with a rather cool and understated ambience. Powered by four Wärtsilä diesels and capable of 25 knots, the new freighters offer unprecedented speed, justified by the savings generated by their large payloads. While the initial trio were employed between Finland and

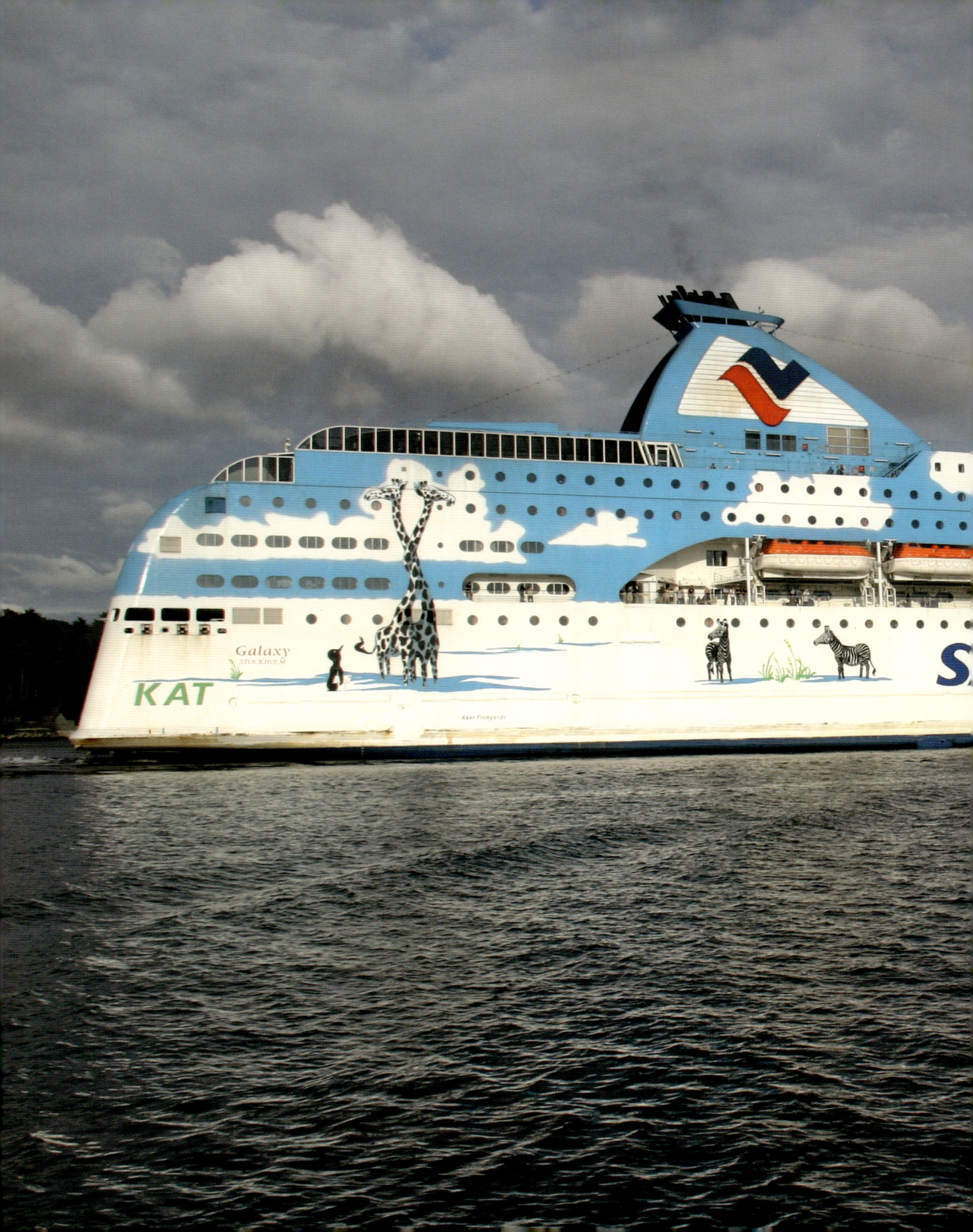
Galaxy
STOCKHOLM
KAT

The **Galaxy** glides past Oxdjupet on her way from Turku and Mariehamn to Stockholm in August 2008. *(Miles Cowsill)*

A game of beach football continues undisturbed as Tallink's Superfast IX glides through the breakwaters on the approach to Travemünde. *(Søren Lund Hviid)*

Germany, the *Europalink* and the *Nordlink* were brought into service on a short hop between Germany and Southern Sweden, linking Travemünde and Malmö.

Finnlines' relationship with Italy has since gone well beyond merely building ships there as, in 2007, the majority of the company's shares were bought by the Grimaldi Group of Naples. Therefore, Finnlines' route network is nowadays part of what is Europe's largest ro-ro freight ship operation, with services not only spanning the Mediterranean but also the North and South Atlantic and, most recently, the Baltic as well.

Another Southern European ro-pax interloper in the latter 1990s was the Greek firm Attica Enterprises, which traded as Superfast Ferries. Taking advantage of European shipping market deregulation, Attica's C.E.O, Pericles Panagopulos, opened routes from Rostock in Germany to Södertälje, just south of Stockholm in Sweden, and to Hanko in Finland using a fleet of purpose-built fast ro-pax ferries, constructed by the HDW shipyard at Kiel in Germany. While the Germany-Finland service was a success, the route to Sweden was a failure and was quickly abandoned. Attica soon discovered that trying to run a Baltic ferry service from a headquarters in an Athens suburb was no easy task and so, after only a few years, both the route and three ships were offered for sale.

### The Rise and Rise of Tallink

By this point, Tallink were expanding at a prodigious rate and so, true to form, in early 2006 the Estonian invaders purchased the Superfast Baltic ferry operation plus its three modern ships, the *Superfast VII*, the *Superfast VIII* and the *Superfast IX*, for 310 million Euro.

Meanwhile, Silja Line was also up for sale following the demise of the parent company, Sea Containers – and here, too, Tallink were keen to make a purchase. Although Viking Line were also attracted (alongside twenty other firms who expressed an interest), the Swedish and Finnish competition authorities warned that they would not be allowed to buy all of Silja without disposing of certain key routes between Sweden and Finland. Tallink, on the other hand, would be required to leave Silja's fast ferry service from Helsinki to Tallinn to another operator, but what Enn Pant's company really wanted was control of Silja's prime Stockholm-Helsinki and Stockholm-Turku routes. Indeed, Tallink had even considered introducing their own ferries between these ports in competition with both Silja and Viking Line. Thus, in early 2006, the deal was completed and shortly thereafter Silja Line's parent company was renamed Tallink Silja.

Although, right from the outset, Silja Line had ultimately been controlled by large conglomerates and banking interests, whereas Viking Line belonged to relatively small family businesses on the Åland Islands and Gotland, some Swedes and Finns apparently were disappointed by the manner in which Silja had been sold, first to Sea Containers, then to Tallink. To these naysayers, the latter appeared to be an upstart company and, alas, the allegedly raucous behaviour of some of the firm's management on board the *Silja Symphony* after a conference in October 2006 did little to calm these concerns. When the *Silja Symphony* docked the next morning, the Swedish and Finnish press and trade unions all but declared war on Tallink. While the ensuing reportage was exaggerated and vindictive, unnecessary short-term damage was done both to Tallink's reputation and to the image of Silja Line. Nonetheless, Tallink were undeterred. By 2007, the entire Silja Board had been replaced and a new Managing Director, Keijo Mehtonen, had successfully taken charge of Silja Line's operations. Mehtonen had been involved with Tallink since their foundation and, in the interim, had gained a great deal of expertise

The Russian à la carte restaurant on the **Galaxy**. *(Bruce Peter)*

The **Galaxy**'s gourmet restaurant. *(Bruce Peter)*

The **Galaxy** shows off Navitrolla's remarkable livery treatment, shortly after her completion in 2006. *(STX Europe)*

The **Galaxy**'s vast show lounge, crowded with dancers on a Friday evening cruise from Helsinki to Tallinn. *(Bruce Peter)*

One of the stairwells on the **Galaxy**, featuring murals by Navitrolla on the bulkhead. Note how the giraffes' necks stretch through foliage between the various decks. *(Bruce Peter)*

in cruise ferry operation. He believed that, to be successful in future, Silja would require to develop a more populist image than in the past and so one of his aims was to bring the Silja operation into line with that of the ferries already trading under the Tallink brand.

Meanwhile, in order to switch the *Romantika* from Helsinki-Tallinn mini-cruises to the Stockholm-Mariehamn-Tallinn ferry route, alongside her near-sister, the *Victoria 1*, Tallink had ordered a considerably larger new cruise ferry as a replacement. Essentially a longer and more glamorously-appointed version of the *Romantika* and the *Victoria I*, the 48,915 gt *Galaxy* was built by Aker Finnyards in Helsinki (formerly the Kværner-Masa shipyard) and delivered in 2006. The usual Baltic cruise ferry ingredients – shops, bars, show lounges, restaurants and saunas – were augmented with a number of new features. For example, as well as offering café, buffet, à la carte and gourmet dining options, the *Galaxy* has a Russian speciality restaurant. Amongst the many bars on board, drinkers can choose between a wine bar, a whisky bar, a pub, a piano bar and a cigar club. Below the vehicle deck, there is a swimming pool and sauna baths while, aft on the topmost deck, there is a substantial and heavily-soundproofed discotheque.

The *Galaxy*'s unmistakable distinguishing feature, however, is her livery. When Tallink ordered the *Victoria I*, it was decided to paint flowers on the bow. With the *Galaxy*, they were much more bold and the entire ship was decorated by the Estonian surrealist artist, Navitrolla. The hull is a white snow-field with penguins, zebras, cows and giraffes plodding through the drifts. The superstructure, however, is sky blue with white clouds spray-painted randomly amongst the windows. The giraffes' necks reach nearly the full height of the superstructure, peering through the clouds. (Navitrolla, apparently, thinks that giraffes and birch trees have some sort of tangential relationship and so they often feature in his work.)

The theme is continued inboard, where Navitrolla has also painted murals in the stairwells and lobby spaces, around which the designers Pille Lausmäe and Aprocos have devised the interiors. The *Galaxy* quickly became popular on the daily Helsinki-Tallinn 22-hour 'booze cruise' circuit. Shortly after she entered service, however, Tallink announced that she would be replaced in 2008 by a new, practically identical sister ship, the *Baltic Princess*. When this new vessel was delivered, painted in a pink and white colour scheme, the *Galaxy* was switched to Silja Line's Stockholm-Mariehamn-Turku route. A third example of the same design was floated out from the Rauma shipyard in December 2008. Named the *Baltic Queen*, upon delivery in April 2009 she was introduced between Stockholm and Tallinn, enabling the *Romantika* to switch to Tallink's Stockholm-Riga route.

As well as offering a daily 22-hour mini-cruise from Helsinki to Tallinn, Tallink planned also to build two large and fast ro-pax ferries to provide a regular two-hourly 'shuttle' service for passengers and freight hauliers wishing to travel quickly between the two ports. Already, Tallink ran two catamaran passenger ferries plus a fast monohull – the *Tallink AutoExpress I*, *Tallink AutoExpress II* and *Tallink AutoExpress III* – but these were greedy on fuel, lacked capacity for freight and were unable to operate either in stormy weather or in winter ice conditions. Looking ahead, Tallink's senior management knew that, before long, Estonia would realize its ambition of becoming a member of an enlarged European Union and would also, most likely, join the Eurozone. With strong economic growth in the latter 1990s and an apparently sustained consumer boom, there would surely be an increased need for freight capacity on ferries crossing the Gulf of Finland. Besides, Tallink's small competitor, Eckerö Line, had already introduced a dedicated freighter, the *Translandia* (ex *Transgermania*), between Helsinki and Tallinn.

Thus, Tallink ordered a 36,250 gt, 27.5-knot ro-pax ferry from Aker Yards for delivery in April 2007. Aker Yards had developed a solid reputation as a builder of ferries of this type. In the latter 1990s, they had built the *Seafrance Rodin* for the Dover Strait and the *Superfast III* and *Superfast IV* for cross-Adriatic routes between Italy and Greece. Tallink's new ferry was to combine their most successful features with many new design ideas.

Named the *Star* and painted in a bright and fresh lime green and white livery, the handsome vessel was every bit as distinctive as her most recent fleet-mate, the *Galaxy*. Perhaps because Tallink's C.E.O, Enn Pant, has a background in finance rather than the ferry industry, the company are practically unique in not having a standard corporate identity for their ships. Pant, however, argues that each Tallink ship should be individually recognizable and this unorthodox approach apparently works very successfully.

The hull design is similar to that of the Superfast ferries, albeit with a more substantial superstructure. Two vehicle decks provide 2,000 lane metres for freight, with three decks of passenger

The spacious forward lounge on the **Star**. *(Bruce Peter)*

The **Star** offers comfortable sofas from which to enjoy the view ahead. *(Bruce Peter)*

The **Star**'s streamlined exterior and bright green livery make her instantly recognizable. Here, she is pictured shortly after completion. *(STX Europe)*

The 'Foodwave' buffet restaurant on the **Star**. *(Bruce Peter)*

The **Star**'s gourmet restaurant has a fresh and bold design. *(Bruce Peter)*

The *Star*'s business lounge, where one can work in tranquil surroundings. *(Bruce Peter)*

The 'Quic&'Easy' cafeteria features vivid graphics on the bulkheads. *(Bruce Peter)*

accommodation above and the officers and crew domiciled mainly on Bridge Deck. Unusually for an Aker-built fast ro-pax, the *Star* is powered by four Caterpillar MaK diesels instead of the more typical Wärtsilä variety, the reason being that Wärtsilä were unable to supply engines in the required time-frame. As Caterpillar were very keen to demonstrate the ability of their 12M43C engine design on a larger Baltic ferry, they made a special effort to squeeze Tallink's order into the production schedule at their Rostock works.

Although the *Star* easily maintains a two-hour crossing schedule, there are somewhat relaxed 90-minute turnarounds at each end because neither port as yet has double-deck loading ramps, meaning that both freight decks must be loaded and unloaded via single sets of bow and stern doors. Thus, there are large internal ramps which can be hoisted between the upper and lower vehicle decks.

The *Star*'s most outstanding feature, however, is her passenger accommodation, designed by Aprocos but in a much brighter and more progressive manner than on the cruise-orientated *Galaxy* and *Baltic Princess*. The lowest of the three passenger decks, Deck 7, contains a large pub and a supermarket, but the most interesting spaces are spread over the two decks above. The aft sections of these both contain cabins, decorated in fresh orange tones, while the forward two-thirds are devoted to cafés, lounges and restaurants. While first and foremost a day ferry, the *Star* also offers short overnight cruises, enabling passengers on the late evening sailing from either Helsinki or Tallinn to remain on board overnight, when the ship is tied up, returning whence they came

The *Star* catches a beam of orange evening light as she begins another fast two-hour crossing of the Gulf of Finland in April 2009. *(Søren Lund Hviid)*

The business lounge on the **Superstar**. *(Bruce Peter)*

The **Superstar**'s 'Fellini' à la carte restaurant. *(Bruce Peter)*

The **Superstar** arrives at Tallinn at the end of her crossing from Helsinki. The livery is certainly eye-catching! *(Bruce Peter)*

The tiered 'La Dolce Vita' lounge on the **Superstar**. *(Bruce Peter)*

The aft 'Leonardo Da Vinci' lounge has the atmosphere of a winter garden. *(Bruce Peter)*

The cocktail bar on the **Baltic Princess**. *(Bruce Peter)*

The **Baltic Princess**' gourmet restaurant. *(Bruce Peter)*

The **Baltic Princess** moves astern leaving Tallinn at the beginning of her afternoon return crossing to Helsinki in May 2009. *(Bruce Peter)*

The forward-facing 'Tango' lounge on the **Baltic Princess**. *(Bruce Peter)*

The disco on the **Baltic Princess**, located aft on the highest passenger deck. *(Bruce Peter)*

*Tallink's latest cruise-ferry, the* **Baltic Queen**, *sails through the archipelago in evening light in May 2009. The vessel is employed on the Stockholm-Tallinn route. (Micke Asklander)*

the next morning. The central section of Deck 8 is filled by the 'Snacktime' cafeteria, again in orange, with the large 'Foodwave' buffet restaurant, forward, in lime green. On the port side amidships, there is a very stylish à la carte restaurant in stark black, grey, beige and white. The forward part of Deck 9 contains a large and very comfortable observation lounge, giving a panoramic view over the Gulf of Finland as the *Star* surges along. Overall, the *Star*'s interiors are very cohesive and singularly devoid of kitsch ornamentation. Indeed, the *Star* is the first ferry in the region to emulate the elegance of Silja Line's 1966 *Fennia* – albeit using fixtures and fittings appropriate for a state-of-the-art ro-pax ship constructed in the early 2000s.

While the *Star* was under construction, Tallink placed an order for a second fast conventional ferry, this time with Fincantieri's Ancona shipyard in Italy. At first, it was unclear where the new vessel, which was code-named 'Tallink Veloce', might serve and it was even speculated that Tallink had plans to introduce a route across the Kattegat, presumably in competition with Stena Line. In the end, the ferry was completed in 2008 as the *Superstar* and placed in service between Helsinki and Tallinn, sailing opposite the *Star*.

Being a Fincantieri design, the *Superstar* is the product of a very different concept from the *Star*. In fact, her origins can be traced back to two ferries designed in Denmark by Knud E. Hansen A/S in the latter 1990s and built in Korea by Daewoo Heavy Industries. Delivered in 2001 as the *Moby Freedom* and the *Moby Wonder* for Moby's routes from Italy to Corsica and Sardinia, the two sisters combined cruise ferry design features – for example, a large tiered show lounge featuring a forward-facing, three-deck-high panoramic window – with a very large freight capacity and also an impressively high speed potential. So successful were they, in fact, that Moby Lines ordered a third example of the type, this time from Fincantieri, and it was this vessel, named the *Moby Aki*, which provided the blueprint for Tallink's *Superstar*.

Although slightly shorter and narrower than the rather sleek ro-pax *Star*, the *Superstar* actually represents more of a return to 1980s jumbo ferry design, with her squared-off aft superstructure built right out to the stern and enabling a larger capacity of 2,020 passengers and 665 cars, as opposed to the 1,900 and 520 of the *Star*. In addition, the *Superstar*'s cabin and public room arrangement has a horizontal layering, with cabins filling the forward section of Deck 6 with shops aft and the entire Deck 7. Thus, the whole of Deck 8 is given over to public rooms – all of which have Italian names and are designed by the same Italian architect, Carlo Ciribi, who drew up the interiors of the three Moby Lines sisters. Forward, La Dolce Vita Gran Teatro, a vast show lounge, gives a spectacular vista ahead. Moving aft from there, the Fellini à la Carte Restaurant is on the port side with Pizza Corner to starboard. Next, a burger café and the Pinnochio ice cream bar are located adjacent to the children's play area, while the Buffet Toscana is towards the stern. Above, the double-height Leonardo Da Vinci Bar, with its glazed walls and deckhead, provides something of the atmosphere of a modern winter garden. Both the *Star* and the *Superstar* have very elegant and comfortable executive lounges and these attract a regular clientele of business travellers, who pay a small premium to use these facilities.

The *Superstar* entered service between Helsinki and Tallinn in April 2008 and, sailing opposite the *Star*, Tallink's high-speed 'Shuttle' service gives departures every two-and-a-half hours from each port. During the winter, a less intensive service is provided. From the passengers' viewpoint, the *Star* and the *Superstar* are most attractive ships – and they have also proven to be outstandingly effective carriers of freight.

The buffet restaurant on the **Viking XPRS**. *(Bruce Peter)*

The **Viking XPRS**' spacious cafeteria servery. *(Bruce Peter)*

The **Viking XPRS** departs from Helsinki on her maiden voyage: the **Gabriella** and the **Rosella** are in the background. *(Viking Line)*

The ferry's forward saloon combines dining with music and dancing. *(Bruce Peter)*

The **Viking XPRS**' pub has a more traditional atmosphere. *(Bruce Peter)*

Tallink's remarkable growth to become the biggest operator of cruise ferries on the Baltic reflects the rapid development of Estonia as one of the region's new 'tiger economies.' As well as developing an enviable fleet of ferries, the parent company, Tallink Grupp, have also built up a chain of hotels in and around Tallinn and – most recently – a taxi business in the city. Thus, Tallink have quickly become a leading transport and leisure conglomerate.

In contrast with Tallink's hectic new-building programme, Viking Line entered the new millennium with a fleet dating mainly from the mid-1980s on the main Stockholm-Helsinki and Stockholm-Turku routes and with only the ageing *Rosella* to link Helsinki and Tallinn, while the even older (but notably well-maintained) *Ålandsfärjan* continued to shuttle regularly between Kapellskär and Mariehamn. Unlike Tallink, however, Viking Line had already paid off a substantial part of their mortgages by this point and so the company had a low level of debt.

The Eklund family, who have been involved with Viking Line practically since its creation, are prudent and canny business strategists. Thus, for CEO Nils-Erik Eklund, and his fellow directors, the challenge was to design a new Helsinki-Tallinn ferry not only to replace the *Rosella* but also to try to emulate the work of the three Tallink vessels – the *Baltic Princess*, the *Star* and the *Superstar*.

In addition, Viking Line believed that any new ferry would be a substantial long-term investment and so it would be necessary to gaze into the future as much as possible to try to work out the kinds of life-style trends which might affect whether passengers would want to book a passage or short cruise to Estonia. Since the early 1990s, the attraction had been principally the lure of cheap alcoholic drinks and cigarettes. Initially making a virtue of lower wage Estonian labour, Tallink had enthusiastically embraced this retail and night club culture when developing their own new cruise ferry tonnage. Viking Line, although traditionally associated with this kind of business model, detected changing trends towards healthier life-styles in Finland, including the imposition of a public smoking ban. Moreover, once Estonia joined the European Union, the cost differentials between buying drink and tobacco in the two countries were lessened and, in addition, Estonia experienced significant wage inflation.

In order to distinguish the new ship from her predecessors, Viking Line adopted a radical new naming policy: the concept name of 'Viking XPRS' was adopted for the completed ferry – the first ship in the world with a name chosen to be text-able by mobile phone! Of course, the 'Viking…' prefix also references the Line's first steamer, the former Southern Railway turbine *Dinard*, and so the *Viking XPRS* looks forward as well as back. Indeed, throughout the passenger accommodation, there are black and white photo-montages showing first-generation Viking Line ferries and passengers enjoying life on board, dressed in the fashions of the 'sixties and 'seventies.

In terms of her design formula, the new ferry is surprisingly similar to the existing *Rosella*, only much bigger, faster, more spacious and sophisticated. While the interior design by Lasse Heikkinen and Tillberg Design is arguably less dramatic than on either Tallink's *Star* or the *Superstar*, it is nonetheless a departure from the onboard concepts on Viking Line's existing fleet.

By day, the *Viking XPRS* can accommodate 2,500 passengers, but there are comfortable and well-appointed cabins for a smaller number who choose to remain on board overnight while the ship is in port. Consequently, as with the *Star* and the *Superstar*, those travelling on her late-evening departure from Helsinki can enjoy an overnight cruise, returning to Finland at a civilized time the following morning. Otherwise, the majority of public rooms are on a single saloon deck, with a combined cafeteria and night club occupying the full width of the forward portion. Viking Line reasoned that, as the area would host these two functions at different times of day, it would be possible to optimize the space utilization by this means.

Moving aft, there is an attractive and comfortable coffee lounge to starboard and a most spacious buffet restaurant to port. All of the dining facilities are serviced from a single galley amidships to port. Viking Line are justifiably proud of their smorgasbord and, on the new ferry, the idea has been to expand choice to include Mediterranean and Asian dishes as well as the usual Scandinavian favourites.

One deck below is the pub, which also features live music, and a large shopping centre, selling a higher proportion of consumer goods and slightly more exclusive drinks but far less cigarettes, crates of beer and vodka than has been traditional on the Helsinki-Tallinn route. In addition, Viking Line have banned smoking on board the *Viking XPRS* – and, indeed, their entire fleet. Whereas in the past it was almost impossible to escape smokers on Baltic ferries, the *Viking XPRS* has a clean and healthy atmosphere which the majority of passengers seem to appreciate. (Tallink were at first less enthusiastic about banishing those who smoke to the outside decks although the *Star* and the *Superstar* are also smoke-free.)

Intriguing too is the fact that only a single freight deck was specified, capable of providing 1,000 freight lane metres, rather than the double-height solution of Tallink's *Star* and *Superstar*. Additionally, there is a separate upper car deck – much as on the *Rosella*.

As delivered, the *Viking XPRS* had magnificent sun decks and also a very pleasant sheltered lido café and bar area, which could equally have been on one of the better Mediterranean ferries. After only a few months in service, however, it was found that there was insufficient space inboard and so the vessel's superstructure was extended aft, enclosing a large section of sun deck to create a new lounge and disco overlooking the stern.

Externally, the *Viking XPRS* is sleek and handsome with striking streamlined lines and interesting design details. The curved treatment of the top deck shelter screens gives the ferry a bold and harmonious external profile. Curiously, although the vessel has a largely Finnish crew she is, in fact, Swedish-flagged and registered in Norrtälje. The reason is that this offers Viking Line certain advantages over the Finnish flag with regard to crew costs. Although the *Viking XPRS*' four Wärtsilä diesels theoretically provide a 25-knot speed, in reality she sails more sedately, taking nearer three hours for each crossing as opposed to the fuel-guzzling two-hour trips offered by Tallink's *Star* and *Superstar*. Nonetheless, with careful timetabling, Viking Line ingeniously offer convenient departures for those travelling from A to B as well as providing an overnight cruise option. As well as sailing more slowly to save fuel, Viking Line, almost uniquely in the ferry

The brand new **Viking XPRS** manoeuvres ahead of the **Gabriella** on the occasion of her maiden voyage from Helsinki to Tallinn. Great care was expended on the ferry's external appearance, which is animated by sleek, curvaceous lines. *(Viking Line)*

industry, have attempted to emphasize their environmental credentials in all aspects of their operations – from recycling waste to burning low sulphur fuel. In the present climate, this may have helped the company to be perceived in a more positive light than Tallink, who have been criticized in the Swedish and Finnish press for using disposable plastic cutlery and paper plates in some of their ferries' cafeterias.

Given that Finnlines freight-orientated ro-ro ferries have become a serious competitor to established operators on the mid-Baltic routes, however, it is also evident that carrying lorries and trailers has become an important potential source of revenue. In that regard, the fact that the *Viking XPRS* has only one vehicle deck capable of transporting freight may prove to have limitations in comparison with the double-decker *Star* and *Superstar*.

Early indications suggest that, in terms of carrying passengers, she is an outstanding success and, being the only ferry to sail to Tallinn from central Helsinki, she is ideally placed to attract those wishing spontaneously to take a mini-cruise or day trip. Indeed, Tallink have therefore responded with a plan to move their Tallinn ferries from Helsinki's Western Harbour to Silja Line's Olympia Terminal in the city centre.

The development of the Baltic ferry industry is a fascinating story of business entrepreneurship and technical ingenuity. Today, nearly 10 million passengers per annum sail between Sweden and Finland on a magnificent array of massive ferries. The voyage through the archipelago is a captivating experience and the atmosphere on board the ferries – the food, drink and entertainment – also remains a big attraction. Yet, with the exception of Tallink's recent vessels and the *Viking XPRS*, the majority of the Baltic super-ferries are now ageing – Viking Line's *Mariella* is 24 years old, for example, and even the *Silja Serenade* is approaching her 18$^{th}$ birthday. The sale of the *Finnjet* for scrap in 2008 was perhaps a sign that these ships have finite lives. Viking Line have already begun work on a new ferry for their Kapellskär-Mariehamn route, which will be built in Spain, and it cannot be long, surely, before a new generation of ferries is ordered for the Stockholm-Helsinki and Stockholm-Turku routes. That depends also on the global financial situation which, at the time of going to press, appears decidedly unstable.

Another potential threat to the cruise ferry business in the Baltic comes – ironically enough – from the international cruise giant Royal Caribbean, who are stationing one of their ships in Stockholm for part of the 2009 summer season, offering a mixture of short two-night and longer five-night itineraries. In public at least, Viking Line's Nils-Erik Eklund is upbeat about the possible consequences of this innovation for his business, arguing that the new entrant will excite larger numbers of Swedes about the idea of cruising as a popular and affordable leisure activity and, thus, expand the market overall. Besides, Royal Caribbean may also attract a slightly different clientele from the predominant demographic who regularly take short cruises on the ferries. (Intriguingly, Eklund's replacement as Viking Line's CEO will be Mikael Backman, previously an executive at Royal Caribbean.)

Whatever happens in the future, the Baltic ferry scene is certain always to be interesting and taking a ferry between Sweden, Finland and Estonia will remain a great pleasure for many years to come.

The **Viking XPRS**'s sun deck after heavy rain. *(Bruce Peter)*

# Appendix 1
# Ship Statistics

## VIKING LINE

T/S VIKING (ex DINARD)
Owner: Rederi AB Vikinglinjen, Mariehamn. Built: 1924 by William Denny & Bros Ltd, Dumbarton, Scotland. Dimensions: 99.05 x 12.53 x 3.80 m. Tonnage:1,765 grt. Engines: Four William Denny & Bros steam turbines. Power output: 3,935 hp. Speed: 19 knots. Passengers: 900. Vehicle capacity: 85 cars, 3 trucks.

M/S SLITE
Owner: Rederi AB Slite, Slite. Built: 1955 by Sölvesborg Varv, Sölvesborg, Sweden. Dimensions: 56.47 x 10.11 x 3.65 m. Tonnage: 499 grt. Engine: One 8-cyl Deutz RV8M545 diesel. Power output: 725 hp. Speed: 11 knots. Passengers: 235. Vehicle capacity: 30 cars, driven on board via a ramp, or lifted on board by crane.

M/S BOGE
Owner: Rederi AB Slite, Slite. Built: 1956 by Sölvesborgs Varv, Sölvesborg, Sweden. Dimensions: 66.35 x 10.04 x 3.76 m. Tonnage: 530 grt. Engine: One 8-cyl Alpha diesel. Power output: 933 kW. Speed: 12 knots. Passengers: 436. Vehicle capacity: 45 cars, driven on board via a ramp, or lifted on board by crane.

M/S PANNY (ex HMS LCF No 3)
Owner: Rederi AB Sally, Mariehamn. Built: 1942 by Teesside Bridge & Engine Co Ltd, Middlesbrough, Scotland. Dimensions: 73.10 x 9,17 x 2,72 m. After rebuilding: 61,87 x 9.17 x 2.72 m. Tonnage: 715 grt. After rebuilding 1949: 761 grt. Engines: Two Davey Paxman diesels. Power output: 920 hp. Speed: 10 knots. Passengers: 200. Vehicle capacity: 70 cars.

S/S ÅLANDSFÄRJAN (ex S/S BRITTANY)
Owner: Rederi AB Ålandsfärjan, Mariehamn. Built: 1933 by William Denny & Bros Ltd, Dumbarton, Scotland. Dimensions: 79.01 x 11.88 x 3.77 m. Tonnage: 1,482 grt. Engines: Four William Denny & Bros steam turbines. Power output: 2,800 hp. Speed: 15.8 knots. Passengers: 800. Vehicle capacity: 40 cars, 2 trucks.

S/S DROTTEN
Owner: Rederi AB Vikinglinjen, Mariehamn. Built: 1928 by Oskarshamns Varv, Oskarshamn, Sweden. Dimensions: 56.53 x 9.34 x 4.60 m. Tonnage: 819 grt. Engine: One 3-cyl steam engine. Power output: 1,000 hp. Speed: 12 knots. Passengers: 480. Cabin berths: 109.

M/S APOLLO
Owner: Rederi AB Slite, Slite. Built: 1964 by Sölvesborgs Varv, Sölvesborg, Sweden. Dimensions: 71.90 x 12.70 x 3.61 m. Tonnage: 1,291 grt. Engines: Two 8-cyl Klöckner-Humboldt-Deutz diesels. Power output: 3,133 kW. Speed: 17.5 knots. Passengers: 1,080. Vehicle capacity: 75 cars, 10 trucks.

M/S VISBY
Owner: Rederi AB Gotland, Visby; chartered to Rederi AB Ålandsfärjan, Mariehamn. Built: 1964 by N.V. Scheepswerf Gebroeders, Bolnes, The Netherlands. Outfitted by N.V. Zaanlandsche Scheepsbouw Maatschappij, Zaandam, The Netherlands. Dimensions: 88.19 x 16.41 x 5.36 m. Tonnage: 2,825 grt. Engines: Two 12-cyl Klöckner-Humboldt-Deutz diesels. Power output: 4,774 kW. Speed: 16.5 knots. Passengers: 1,200. Cabin berths: 245. Vehicle capacity: 120 cars.

M/S KAPELLA
Owner: Rederi AB Ålandsfärjan, Mariehamn. Built: 1967 by Brodogradiliste Titovo, Kraljevica, Yugoslavia. Dimensions: 97.54 x 18.22 x 4.75 m. Tonnage: 3,159 grt. Engines: Two Jugo-Sulzer 8TAD48 diesels. Power output: 5,150 kW. Speed: 19 knots. Passengers: 1,200. Cabin berths: 108. Vehicle capacity: 220 cars, 23 trucks.

M/S VIKING 2 (ex MARSK STIG)
Owner: Rederi AB Sally, Mariehamn. Built: 1940 by Aalborg Værft A/S, Aalborg, Denmark. Dimensions: 70.02 x 11.54 x 4.00 m. Tonnage: 1,217 grt. Engines: Two 8-cyl B&W diesels. Power output: 3,200 hp. Speed: 16 knots. Passengers: 600. Vehicle capacity: 60 cars.

M/S APOLLO
Owner: Rederi AB Slite, Slite. Built: 1970 by Jos L Meyer Werft, Papenburg-Ems, West Germany. Dimensions: 108.70 x 17.20 x 4.60 m. Tonnage: 4,238 grt. Engines: Two Deutz SBV 12M 350 diesels. Power output: 8,000 hp. Speed: 18.8 knots. Passengers: 1,200. Cabin berths: 222. Vehicle capacity: 260 cars, 23 trucks.

M/S VIKING 1
Owner: Rederi AB Sally, Mariehamn. Built: 1970 by Jos L Meyer Werft, Papenburg-Ems, West Germany. Dimensions: 108.70 x 17.20 x 4.60 m. Tonnage: 4,239 grt. Engines: Two Deutz SBV 12M 350 diesels. Power output: 8,000 hp. Speed: 18.5 knots. Passengers: 1,200. Cabin berths: 222. Vehicle capacity: 260 cars, 23 trucks.

M/S MARELLA
Owner: Oy SF Line AB, Mariehamn. Built: 1970 by Brodogradiliste Titovo, Kraljevica, Yugoslavia. Dimensions: 99.15 x 17.20 x 4.90 m. Tonnage: 3,930 grt. Engines: Two Jugo-Sulzer 10TAD48 diesels. Power output: 6,470 kW. Speed: 18.5 knots. Passengers: 1,200. Cabin berths: 176. Vehicle capacity: 225 cars, 24 trucks.

M/S VIKING 3
Owner: Rederi AB Sally, Mariehamn. Built: 1972 by Jos L Meyer Werft, Papenburg-Ems, West Germany. Dimensions: 108.70 x 17.20 x 4.60 m. Tonnage: 4,240 grt. Engines: Two Deutz SBV12M350 diesels. Power output: 5,885 kW. Speed:18.5 knots. Passengers: 1,200. Cabin berths: 222. Vehicle capacity: 265 cars, 23 trucks.

M/S DIANA
Owner: Rederi AB Slite, Slite. Built: 1972 by Jos L Meyer Werft, Papenburg-Ems, West Germany. Dimensions: 108.70 x 17.20 x 4.60 m. Tonnage: 4,152 grt. Engines: Two Klöckner-Humboldt-Deutz SBV 12M 350 diesels. Power output: 5,968 kW. Speed: 18.5 knots. Passengers: 1,200. Cabin berths: 240. Vehicle capacity: 265 cars, 23 trucks.

M/S VIKING 4
Owner: Rederi AB Sally, Mariehamn. Built: 1973 by Jos L Meyer Werft, Papenburg-Ems, West Germany. Dimensions: 109.15 x 17.20 x 4.70 m. Tonnage: 4,477 grt. Engines: Two Smit-Bolnes V314HDK diesels. Power output: 10,200 hp. Speed: 19.7 knots. Passengers: 1,200. Cabin berths: 280. Vehicle capacity: 265 cars, 23 trucks.

M/S AURELLA
Owner: Oy SF Line AB, Mariehamn. Built: 1973 by J.J. Sietas Schiffswerft, Hamburg, West Germany. Dimensions: 125.22 x 21.53 x 5.27 m. Tonnage: 7,210 grt. Engines: Two Stork-Werkspoor 16TM410 diesels. Power output: 15,445 kW. Speed: 21.5 knots. Passengers: 1,500. Cabin berths: 330. Vehicle capacity: 420 cars, 35 trucks.

M/S VIKING 5
Owner: Rederi AB Sally, Mariehamn. Built: 1974 by Jos L Meyer Werft, Papenburg-Ems, West Germany. Dimensions: 117.79 x 17.20 x 4.70 m. Tonnage: 5,280 grt. Engines: Two 14-cyl Smit-Bolnes diesels. Power output: 8,120 kW. Speed: 19.5 knots. Passengers: 1,200. Cabin berths: 410. Vehicle capacity: 285 cars, 23 trucks.

M/S VIKING 6 (ex WICKERSHAM, ex M/S STENA BRITANNICA)
Owner: Rederi AB Sally, Mariehamn. Built: 1967 by A/S Langesund Mekaniske Verksted, Langesund, Norway. Completed by Framnæs Mekaniske Verksted A/S, Framnæs, Norway. Dimensions: 110.80 x 18.04 x 4.82 m. Tonnage: 5,073 grt. Engines: Two 16-cyl MAN diesels. Power output: 12,891 kW. Speed: 23.5 knots. Passengers: 1,170. Cabin berths: 370. Vehicle capacity: 210 cars.

S/S APOLLO III (ex SVEA JARL)
Owner: Rederi AB Slite, Slite. Built: 1962 by Finnboda Varv, Nacka, Sweden. Dimensions: 101.4 x 19.25 x 4.76 m. Tonnage: 4,334 grt. Engine: One 6-cyl A.D.M. Skinner Marine U6 Uniflow SK 6/23/26 steam engine. Power output: 3,603 kW. Speed: 16 knots. After re-engining 1982: Two MAN 18-V-20/27 diesels. Power output: 3,603 kW. Passengers: 1,020. Cabin berths: 339. After rebuilding: 472. Vehicle capacity: 60 cars. After 1976: 20 cars.

M/S TURELLA
Owner: Oy SF Line AB, Mariehamn. Built: 1979 by Oy Wärtsilä AB, Turku, Finland. Dimensions: 136.11 x 24.24 x 5.40 m. Tonnage: 10,604 grt. Engines: Four Wärtsilä-Pielstick 12PC2 2V diesels. Power output: 17,650 kW. Speed: 21.5 knots. Passengers: 1,700. Cabin berths: 740. Vehicle capacity: 554 cars.

M/S DIANA II
Owner: Rederi AB Slite, Slite. Built: 1979 by Jos L Meyer Werft, Papenburg-Ems, West Germany. Dimensions: 137.01 x 24.21 x 5.50 m. Tonnage: 11,671 grt. Engines: Four MAN 8L40/45 diesels. Power output: 17,650 kW. Speed: 21 knots. Passengers: 1,900. Cabin berths: 867. Vehicle capacity: 555 cars, 45 trucks.

M/S ROSELLA
Owner: Oy SF Line AB, Mariehamn. Built: 1980 by Oy Wärtsilä AB, Turku, Finland. Dimensions: 136.11 x 24.24 x 5.40 m. Tonnage: 10,757 grt. Engines: Four Wärtsilä-Pielstick 12PC2 2V diesels. Power output: 17,652 kW. Speed: 21.5 knots. Passengers: 1,700. Cabin berths: 740. Vehicle capacity: 535 cars, 43 trucks.

M/S VIKING SAGA
Owner: Rederi AB Sally, Mariehamn. Built: 1980 by Oy Wärtsilä AB, Turku, Finland. Dimensions: 145.19 x 25.51 x 5.52 m. Tonnage: 14,330 grt. Engines: Four Wärtsilä-Pielstick 12PC2 5V diesels. Power output: 19,480 kW. Speed: 21.3 knots. Passengers: 2,000. Cabin berths: 1,223. Vehicle capacity: 462 cars, 56 trucks.

M/S VIKING SALLY
Owner: Rederi AB Sally, Mariehamn. Built: 1980 by Jos L Meyer Werft, Papenburg-Ems, West Germany. Dimensions: 155.43 x 24.21 x 5.55 m. Tonnage: 15,566 grt. Engines: Four MAN 8L40/45 diesels. Power output: 17,652 kW. Speed: 21 knots. Passengers: 2,000. Cabin berths: 1,190. Vehicle capacity: 460 cars, 52 trucks.

M/S VIKING SONG
Owner: Rederi AB Sally, Mariehamn. Built: 1980 by Oy Wärtsilä AB, Turku, Finland. Dimensions: 145.19 x 25.51 x 5.52 m. Tonnage: 13,878 grt. Engines: Four Wärtsilä-Pielstick 12 PC2 5V diesels. Power output: 19,480 kW. Speed: 21.3 knots. Passengers: 2,000. Cabin berths: 1,250. Vehicle capacity: 462 cars, 56 trucks.

M/S MARIELLA
Owner: Oy SF Line AB, Mariehamn. Built: 1985 by Oy Wärtsilä AB, Turku, Finland. Dimensions: 177.00 x 28.40 x 6.51 m. Tonnage: 37,799 gt. Engines: Four Wärtsilä-SEMT Pielstick 12 PC2 6V diesels. Power output: 23,000 kW. Speed: 22 knots. Passengers: 2,447. Cabin berths: 2,447. Vehicle capacity: 580 cars, 62 trucks.

M/S OLYMPIA
Owner: Rederi AB Slite, Slite. Built: 1986 by Oy Wärtsilä AB, Turku, Finland. Dimensions: 177.10 x 28.40 x 6.51 m. Tonnage: 37,799 gt. Engines: Four Wärtsilä-Pielstick 12PC2 6V diesels. Power output: 23,000 kW. Speed: 22 knots. Passengers: 2,500. Cabin berths: 2,372. Vehicle capacity: 580 cars, 62 trucks.

M/S ÅLANDSFÄRJAN (ex nf TIGER, ex KATTEGAT)
Owner: Rederi AB Viking Line, Norrtälje, a Swedish subsidiary of Oy SF Line AB, Mariehamn. Built: 1972 by Helsingør Skibs & Maskinbyggeri, Helsingør, Denmark. Dimensions: 104.04 x 18.93 x 4.37 m. Tonnage: 3,960 gt. Engines: Two HSM/ B&W 10U45HU diesels. Power output: 8,096 kW. Speed: 17 knots. Passengers: 1,200. Cabin berths: 63. Vehicle capacity: 220 cars.

M/S AMORELLA
Owner: Oy SF Line AB, Mariehamn. Built: 1988 by Brodogradevna Industrija, Split, Yugoslavia. Dimensions: 169.40 x 27.61 x 6.26 m. Tonnage: 34,384 gt. Engines: Four Wärtsilä-Pielstick 12PC2 6V-400E diesels. Power output: 24,000 kW. Speed: 21.5 knots. Passengers: 2,420. Cabin berths: 1,986. Vehicle capacity: 550 cars, 53 trucks.

M/S ATHENA
Owner: Rederi AB Slite, Slite. Built: 1989 by Oy Wärtsilä AB, Turku, Finland. Dimensions: 176.60 x 29.00 x 6.00 m. Tonnage: 40,012 gt. Engines: Four Wärtsilä-Sulzer 9ZAL40S diesels. Power output: 23,760 kW. Speed: 21 knots. Passengers: 2,200. Cabin berths: 2,394. Vehicle capacity: 90 cars as a cruise ship.

M/S ISABELLA
Owner: Oy SF Line AB, Mariehamn. Built: 1989 by Brodogradevna Industrija, Split, Yugoslavia. Dimensions: 169.40 x 27.61 x 6.26 m. Tonnage: 34,386 gt. Engines: Four Wärtsilä-Pielstick 12PC2 6V-400E diesels. Power output: 24,000 kW. Speed: 21.5 knots. Passengers: 2,200. Cabin berths: 1,983. Vehicle capacity: 410 cars, 53 trucks.

### M/S CINDERELLA
Owner: Oy SF Line AB, Mariehamn. Built: 1989 by Oy Wärtsilä AB, Turku, Finland. Dimensions: 191.00 x 29.60 x 6.60 m. Tonnage: 46,398 gt. Engines: Four Wärtsilä-Sulzer 12 ZAV40S diesels. Power output: 28,800 kW. Speed: 22 knots. Passengers: 2,700. Cabin berths: 2,700. Vehicle capacity: 480 cars, 60 trucks.

### M/S KALYPSO
Owner: Rederi AB Slite, Slite. Built: 1990 by Masa Yards Oy, Turku, Finland. Dimensions: 176.60 x 29.61 x 6.20 m. Tonnage: 40,012 gt. Engines: Four Wärtsilä-Sulzer 9ZAL40S diesels. Power output: 17,811 kW. Speed: 21 knots. Passengers: 2,200. Cabin berths:1,950. Vehicle capacity: 490 cars.

### M/S EUROPA
Ordered by: Rederi AB Slite, Slite. Built: 1993 by Jos L Meyer Werft, Papenburg-Ems, West Germany. Dimensions: 201.78 x 32.60 x 6.80 m. Tonnage: 59,912 gt. Engines: Four MAN B&W 6L58/64 diesels. Power output: 31,800 kW. Speed: 21.5 knots. Passengers: 3,123. Cabin berths: 3,746. Vehicle capacity: 400 cars.

### M/S GABRIELLA (ex SILJA SCANDINAVIA, ex FRANS SUELL)
Owner: Oy Viking Line AB, Mariehamn. Built: 1992 by Brodogradiliste Split, Split, Croatia. Dimensions: 169.40 x 27.60 x 6.25 m. After rebuilding: 171.50 x 28.20 x 6.25 m. Tonnage: 35,285 gt. Engines: Four Pielstick 12 PC2 6V-400E diesels. Power output: 23,780 kW. Speed: 21.5 knots. Passengers: 2,400. Cabin berths: 2,170. Vehicle capacity: 480 cars, 53 trucks.

### M/S VIKING XPRS
Owner: Oy Viking Line AB, Mariehamn. Built: 2008 by Aker Finnyards, Helsinki, Finland. Dimensions: 185.00 x 27.70 x 6.55 m. Tonnage: 34,000 gt. Engines: Four Wärtsilä 8L46F diesels. Power output: 40,000 kW. Speed: 25 knots. Passengers: 2,500. Cabin berths: 732. Vehicle capacity: 240 cars.

## SILJA LINE

### S/S SILJA (ex HEIMDALL)
Owner: Oy Silja Line AB (1/3 Rederi AB Svea, Stockholm, 1/3 Finska Ångfartygs Aktiebolaget, Helsinki, 1/3 Bore Ångfartygs Aktiebolaget, Turku). Built: 1915 by Oskarshamns Mekaniska Verksteder, Oskarshamn, Sweden. Dimensions: 67.60 x 10.97 x 4.78 m. After lengthening 1948: 73.77 x 11.01 x 5.30 m. Tonnage: 1,312 grt. After rebuilding: 1,598 grt. Engine: One 3-cyl steam engine. Power output: 1,430 hp. Speed: 12 knots. Passengers: 600. Cabin berths: 108. Vehicle capacity: 47 cars, lifted on board by crane.

### S/S REGIN
Owner: Rederi AB Svea, Stockholm. Built: 1921 by Oskarshamns Varv, Oskarshamn, Sweden. Dimensions: 71.46 x 10.98 m. After rebuilding: 73.0 x 10.98 m. Tonnage: 1,373 grt. After rebuilding 1952: 1,431 grt. Engine: One Alfa Laval steam turbine. Power output: 1,600 hp. Speed: 14 knots. Passengers: 465. Cabin berths: 64.

### M/S SKANDIA
Owner: Oy Silja Line AB (1/3 Rederi AB Svea, Stockholm, 1/3 Finska Ångfartygs Aktiebolaget, Helsinki, 1/3 Bore Ångfartygs Aktiebolaget, Turku). From 1973 Finska Ångfartygs Aktiebolaget, Helsinki. Built: 1961 by Oy Wärtsilä Sandviken AB, Helsinki, Finland. Dimensions: 101.60 x 18.53 x 4.62 m. Tonnage: 3,593 grt. Engines: Two 9-cyl Wärtsilä-Sulzer diesels. Power output: 4,924 kW. Speed: 18 knots. Passengers: 1,200. Cabin berths: 136. Vehicle capacity: 175 cars, 20 trucks.

### M/S NORDIA
Owner: Oy Silja Line AB (1/3 Rederi AB Svea, Stockholm, 1/3 Finska Ångfartygs Aktiebolaget, Helsinki, 1/3 Bore Ångfartygs Aktiebolaget, Turku). From 1973 Rederi AB Svea, Stockholm. Built: 1962 by Oy Wärtsilä Sandviken AB, Helsinki, Finland. Dimensions: 101.60 x 18.53 x 4.62 m. Tonnage: 3,631 grt. Engines: Two 9-cyl Wärtsilä-Sulzer diesels. Power output: 4,924 kW. Speed: 18 knots. Passengers: 1,000. Cabin berths: 124. Vehicle capacity: 175 cars, 20 trucks.

### M/S HOLMIA (ex CALMAR NYCKEL, ex PRINS BERTIL)
Owner: Oy Silja Line AB (1/3 Rederi AB Svea, Stockholm, 1/3 Finska Ångfartygs Aktiebolaget, Helsinki, 1/3 Bore Ångfartygs Aktiebolaget, Turku). Built: 1960 by Århus Flydedok, Århus, Denmark. Dimensions: 88.36 x 15.26 x 4.57 m. Tonnage: 2,196 grt. Engines: Two Nohab M66TS diesels. Power output: 4,235 kW. Speed: 17.5 knots. Passengers: 900. Cabin berths: 44. Vehicle capacity: 80 cars, 10 trucks.

### M/S FENNIA
Owner: Oy Silja Line AB (1/3 Rederi AB Svea, Stockholm, 1/3 Finska Ångfartygs Aktiebolaget, Helsinki, 1/3 Bore Ångfartygs Aktiebolaget, Turku). From 1973 Rederi AB Svea, Stockholm. Built: 1966 by Öresundsvarvet AB, Landskrona, Sweden. Dimensions: 128.40 x 19.63 x 5.00 m. Tonnage: 6,178 grt. Engines: Four 9-cyl, Ruston & Hornsby ATCM diesels. Power output: 8,760 hp. Speed: 18 knots. After re-engining 1975: Four Atlas-MaK 9M453AK diesels. Power output: 8,825 kW. Speed: 18.5 knots. Passengers: 1,200. Cabin berths: 300. Vehicle capacity: 225 cars, 32 trucks.

### M/S BOTNIA
Owner: Oy Silja Line AB (1/3 Rederi AB Svea, Stockholm, 1/3 Finska Ångfartygs Aktiebolaget, Helsinki, 1/3 Bore Ångfartygs Aktiebolaget, Turku). From 1973 Bore Ångfartygs Aktiebolaget, Turku. Built: 1967 by Oy Wärtsilä AB, Helsinki, Finland. Dimensions: 101.60 x 18.53 x 4.90 m. Tonnage: 3,514 grt. Engines: Eight Wärtsilä-Vaasa 814TK diesels. Power output: 6,140 kW. Speed: 19 knots. Passengers: 1,042. Cabin berths: 198. Vehicle capacity: 195 cars, 24 trucks.

### M/S FLORIA
Owner: Finska Ångfartygs Aktiebolaget, Helsinki. Built: 1970 by Oy Wärtsilä AB, Helsinki, Finland. Dimensions: 101.60 x 18.53 x 5.00 m. Tonnage: 4,051 grt. Engines: Eight Wärtsilä-Vaasa 814TK diesels. Power output: 6,140 kW. Speed: 19 knots. Passengers: 1,042. Cabin berths: 198. Vehicle capacity: 195 cars.

## ÅNGFARTYGS AKTIEBOLAGET BORE

### S/S BORE
Built: 1898 by A/S Helsingør Jernskibs og Maskinbyggeri, Helsingør, Denmark. Dimensions: 58.19 x 8.99 x 4.70 m. Tonnage: 820 grt. Engine: One 3-cyl steam engine. Power output: 1,000 hp. Speed: 12 knots. Passengers: 90. Cabin berths: 90.

### S/S BORE II
Built 1900 by A/S Helsingør Jernskibs og Maskinbyggeri, Helsingør, Denmark. Dimensions: 58.10 x 8.90 x 4.70 m. Tonnage: 820 grt. Engine: One 3-cyl steam engine. Power output: 950 hp. Speed: 12 knots. Passengers: 123. Cabin berths: 123.

S/S NORDSTJERNAN
Built: 1871 by Motala Mekaniska Werkstad AB, Norrköping, Sweden. Dimensions: 61.44 x 8.35 x 4.47 m. Tonnage: 788 grt. Engine: One 3-cyl steam engine. Power output: 845 hp. Speed: 13 knots. Passengers:122. Cabin berths: 122.

S/S HALLAND
Built: 1884 by Motala Mekaniska Werkstad AB, Lindholmens Werkstad, Gothenburg, Sweden. Dimensions: 51.50 x 7.80 x 3.20 m. Tonnage: 466 grt. Engines: Two 2-cyl compound steam engines. Power output: 480 hp. Speed: 12 knots. Passengers: 61.

S/S BORE II
Built: 1938 by AB Chricton-Vulcan Oy, Turku, Finland. Dimensions: 77.50 x 12.15 x 4.87 m. Tonnage: 1,965 grt. Engine: One 4-cyl double compound steam engine. Power output: 2,300 hp. Speed: 14 knots. Passengers: 239. Cabin berths: 184.

S/S BORE II (ex DRONNING MAUD)
Built: 1906 by A/S Burmeister & Wain's Maskin og Skibsbyggeri, Copenhagen, Denmark. Dimensions: 87.53 x 11.28 x 5.49 m. Tonnage: 1,761 grt. Engines: Two 3-cyl steam engines. Power output: 2,360 hp. Speed: 14 knots. Passengers: 783.

S/S BORE III
Built: 1952 by Oskarshamns Varv, Oskarshamn, Sweden. Dimensions: 90.77 x 14.26 x 5.00 m. Tonnage: 3,007 grt. Engines: One quadruple expansion steam engine with exhaust steam turbine by Helsingør Skibsværft og Maskinbyggeri, Helsingør, Denmark. Power output: 3,300 hp. Speed: 15 knots. Passengers: 700. Cabin berths: 220.

S/S KASTELHOLM
Built: 1929 by Eriksbergs Mekaniska Verkstad AB, Gothenburg. Dimensions: 55.66 x 9.42 x 3.66 m. Tonnage: 921 grt. Engine: One 3-cyl steam engine. Power output: 1,034 hp. Speed: 12 knots. Passengers: 150. Cabin berths: 150.

S/S BORE
Built: 1960 by Oskarshamns Varv, Oskarshamn, Sweden. Dimensions: 99.38 x 15.28 x 5.26 m. Tonnage: 3,492 grt. Engines: One quadruple expansion steam engine with exhaust steam turbine by Götaverken, Gothenburg, Sweden. Power output: 3,920 hp. Speed: 16 knots. Passengers: 1,028. Cabin berths: 333. Vehicle capacity: 50 cars, 4 buses.

M/S BORE I (ex M/S SANKT IBB)
Built: 1935 by Frederikshavns Værft & Flydedok, Frederikshavn, Denmark. Dimensions: 54.14 x 10.28 x 2.73 m. Tonnage: 527 grt. Engines: Two 6-cyl Klöckner-Humboldt-Deutz diesels. Power output: 1,130 hp. Speed: 14 knots. Passengers: 425.

M/S BORE I
Built: 1973 by Oy Wärtsilä AB, Turku, Finland. Dimensions: 127.80 x 22.05 x 5.92 m. Tonnage: 8,528 grt. Engines: Four Wärtsilä-Sulzer 9ZH40/48 diesels. Power output: 13, 240 kW. Speed: 22 knots. Passengers: 1,200. Cabin berths: 332. Vehicle capacity: 359 cars.

M/S BORE STAR
Built: 1975 by Dubigeon-Normandie S.A. Prairie au doc, Nantes, France. Dimensions: 153.00 x 22.04 x 5.84 m. Tonnage: 12,343 grt. Engines: Four SEMT-Pielstick 12 PC2 2V-400 diesels. Power output: 17,600 kW. Speed: 21 knots. Passengers: 1,200. Cabin berths: 799. Vehicle capacity: 240 cars.

## FINSKA ÅNGFARTYGS AKTIEBOLAGET

S/S NORRA FINLAND
Built: 1885 by Motala Varv, Norrköping, Sweden. Dimensions: 54.20 x 8.07 m. Tonnage: 617 grt. Engine: One steam reciprocating engine. Power output: 480 hp.

S/S FINLAND
Built: 1876 by Wm Chricton-Vulcans Varv, Turku, Finland. Dimensions: 50.08 x 7.80 m. Tonnage: 611 grt. Engine: One steam reciprocating engine. Power output: 600 hp. Passengers: 70. Cabin berths: 70.

S/S WELLAMO
Built: 1898 by Gourlay Brothers & Co, Dundee, Scotland. Dimensions: 64.70 x 9.55 m. Tonnage: 1,043 grt. Engine: One 4-cyl steam engine. Power output: 1,260 hp. Speed: 12.5 knots. Passengers: 300. Cabin berths: 129.

S/S OIHONNA
Built: 1898 by Gourlay Brothers & Co, Dundee, Scotland. Dimensions: 64.69 x 9.55 x 5.49 m. Tonnage: 1,072 grt. Engine: One 4-cyl steam engine. Power output: 1,260 hp. Speed: 12.5 knots. Passengers: 163. Cabin berths: 163.

S/S ARCTURUS
Built: 1898 by Gourlay Brothers & Co, Dundee, Scotland. Dimensions: 85.80 x 11.60 x 6.35 m. Tonnage: 2,017 grt. Engine: One 3-cyl steam engine. Power outpout: 3,500 hp. Speed: 13.5 knots. Passengers: 265. Cabin berths: 265.

S/S ARIADNE
Built: 1914 by Lindholmens Verkstad AB, Gothenburg, Sweden. Dimensions: 83.20 x 13.30 x 5.40 m. After lengthening 1946: 88.00 x 13.30 x 5.40 m. Tonnage: 2,558 grt. After rebuilding 1946: 2,898 grt. Engine: One 3-cyl steam engine. Power output: 2,665 hp. Speed: 14 knots. Passengers: 400. Cabin berths: 246.

S/S OBERON
Built: 1925 by Chantiers et Ateliers de Penhoet, St Nazaire, France. Dimensions: 92.33 x 13.40 x 6.59 m. Tonnage: 3,008 grt. Engine: One 3-cyl steam engine. Power output: 4,500 hp. Speed: 13.5 knots. Passengers: 357. Cabin berths: 357.

S/S WELLAMO
Built: 1927 by A/S Kjøbenhavns Flydedok & Skipsværft, Søndre Værft, Copenhagen, Denmark. Dimensions: 80.01 x 12.23 x 5.24 m. Tonnage: 2,096 grt. Engine: One 3-cyl Burmeister &Wain steam engine. Power output: 2,190 hp. Speed: 13 knots. Passengers: 214. Cabin berths: 177.

S/S ILMATAR
Built: 1929 by A/S Burmeister & Wain's Maskin og Skibsbyggeri, Copenhagen, Denmark. Dimensions: 86.35 x 12.69 x 5.60 m. Tonnage: 2,364 grt. Engine: One 3-cyl Burmeister &Wain steam engine. Power output: 2,190 hp. Speed: 13.5 knots. Passengers: 150. Cabin berths: 150.

S/S AALLOTAR
Built: 1937 by Helsingørs Skibsværft og Maskinbyggeri A/S, Helsingør, Denmark. Dimensions: 90.06 x 13.83 x 5.94 m. Tonnage: 2,916 grt. Engine: 4-cyl Lentz compound steam engine. Power output: 3,600 hp. Speed: 14 knots. Passengers: 181. Cabin berths: 181.

S/S AALLOTAR
Built: 1952 by Helsingørs Skibsværft og Maskinbyggeri A/S, Helsingør, Denmark. Dimensions: 92.44 x 14.26 x 5.00 m.

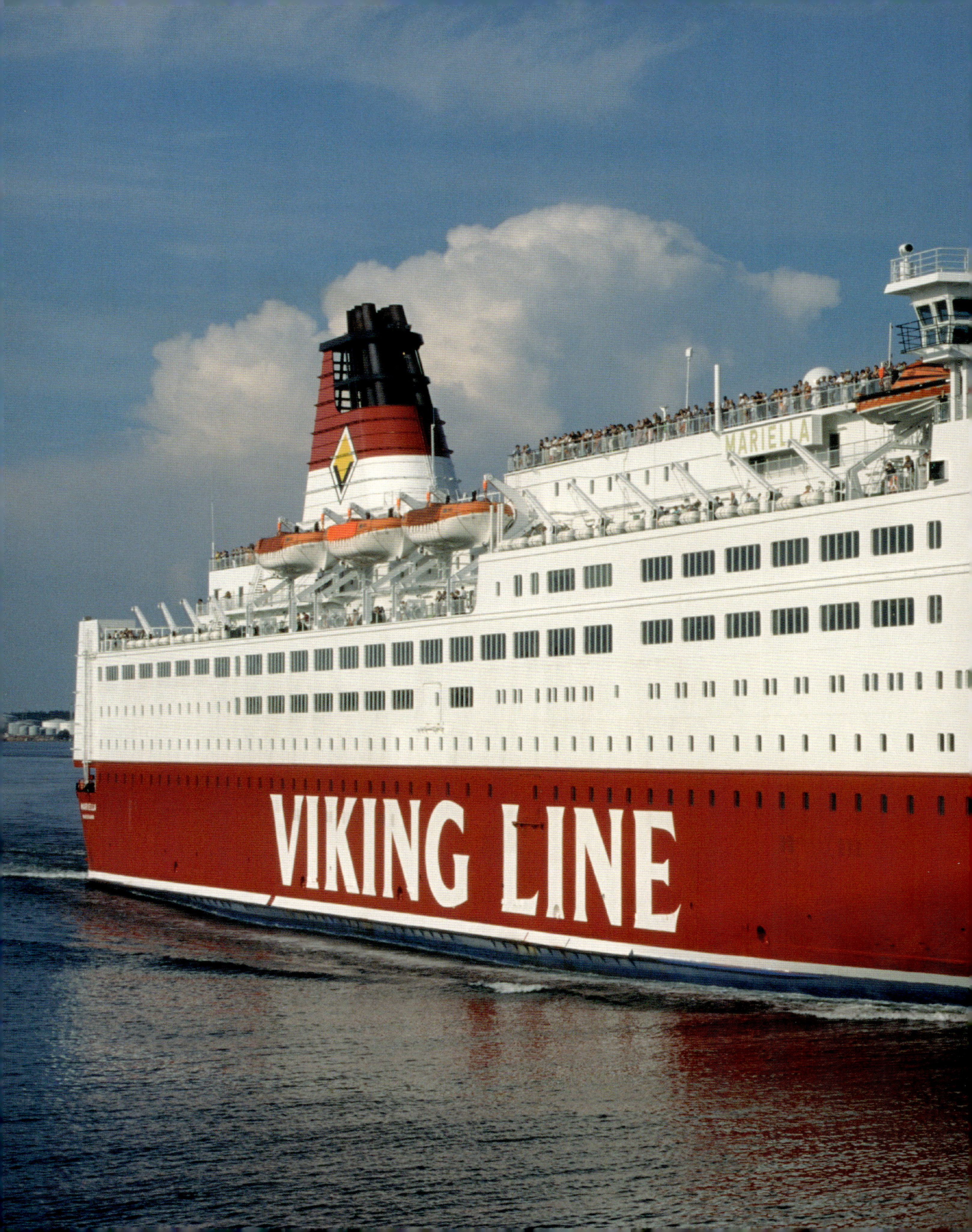
MARIELLA
VIKING LINE

The **Mariella** passes Suomenlinna Island off Helsinki is the summer of 1997. *(Bruce Peter)*

Tonnage: 2,776 grt. Engines: One 4-cyl steam engine with exhaust steam turbine. Power output: 2,430 kW. Speed: 15 knots. Passengers: 1,000. Cabin berths: 230. After rebuilding 1964: 298. Vehicle capacity: 20 cars.

M/S ILMATAR
Built: 1964 by Oy Wärtsilä AB, Helsinki, Finland. Dimensions: 108.27 x 16.40 x 4.50 m. After lengthening 1973: 128.31 x 16.40 x 4.50 m. Tonnage: 5,101 grt. After rebuilding 1973: 7,155 grt. Engine: One Wärtsilä-Sulzer 12MD51 diesel. Power output: 3,300 kW. Speed: 16.5 knots. After rebuilding 1973: Two Nohab SF116VSF diesels supplementing one Wärtsilä-Sulzer 12MD51 diesel. Power output: 7,535 kW. Speed: 19 knots. Passengers: 1,100. After rebuilding 1973: 470. Cabin berths: 450. After rebuilding 1973: 470. Vehicle capacity: 50 cars.

M/S FINLANDIA
Built: 1967 by Oy Wärtsilä AB, Helsinki, Finland. Dimensions: 153.00 x 20.00 x 5.60 m. Tonnage: 8,583 grt. Engines: Four Wärtsilä-Sulzer 9ZH 40/48 diesels. Power output: 12,060 kW. Speed: 22 knots. Passengers: 1,000. Cabin berths: 647. Vehicle capacity: 321 cars, 36 trucks.

M/S AALLOTAR
Built: 1972 by Dubigeon-Normandie S.A, Prairie au doc, Nantes, France. Dimensions: 126.79 x 19.54 x 5.15 m. Tonnage: 7,800. Engines: Four Pielstick 16PC2 V-400 diesels. Power output: 11,936 kW. Speed: 21 knots. Passengers: 1,000. Cabin berths: 439. Vehicle capacity: 170 cars.

M/S WELLAMO
Built: 1975 by Dubigeon-Normandie S.A. Prairie au doc, Nantes, France. Dimensions: 153.12 x 22.04 x 5.80 m. Tonnage: 12,348 grt. Engines: Four SEMT-Pielstick 12 PC2 2V-400 diesels. Power output: 17,660 kW. Speed: 21 knots. Passengers: 1,200. Cabin berths: 799. Vehicle capacity: 240 cars.

M/S FINLANDIA
Built: 1981 by Oy Wärtsilä AB, Perno Varvet (hull). Outfitted by Oy Wärtsilä AB, Turku, Finland. Dimensions: 166.10 x 28.46 x 6.70 m. Tonnage: 25,905 grt. Engines: Four Wärtsilä-Pielstick 12PC2 5V diesels. Power output: 22,948 kW. Speed: 22 knots. Passengers: 1,676. Cabin berths: 1,650. Vehicle capacity: 450 cars, 70 trucks.

M/S WELLAMO
Built: 1986 by Oy Wärtsilä AB, Helsinki, Finland. Dimensions: 168.00 x 27.60 x 6.50 m. Tonnage: 33,818 gt. Engines: Four Wärtsilä-SEMT-Pielstick 12PC2.6V diesels. Power output: 26,200 kW. Speed: 22 knots. Passengers: 2,000. Cabin berths: 1,625. Vehicle capacity: 400 cars, 60 trucks.

GTS/M/S FINNJET
Built: 1977 by Oy Wärtsilä AB, Helsinki, Finland. Dimensions: 212.96 x 24.45 x 6.50 m. Tonnage: 24,605 grt. Engines: Two Pratt & Whitney FT 4C-1 DLF gas turbines. Power output: 55,200 hp. After rebuilding 1981: Two Wärtsilä-Vaasa 18V32 diesels, alternating with two Pratt & Whitney FT 4C-1 DLF gas turbines. Power output of diesels: 23,040 kW. Speed: 30.5 knots with gas turbine propulsion, 18.5 knots with diesel propulsion. Passengers: 1,800. Cabin berths: 1,532. Vehicle capacity: 380 cars, 34 trucks.

## REDERI AB SVEA, STOCKHOLM

S/S HEIMDALL – See SILJA

S/S REGIN
Built: 1921 by Oskarshamns Varv, Oskarshamn, Sweden. Dimensions: 71.46 x 10.98 m. After rebuilding 1952: 73.46 x 10.98 m. Tonnage: 1,373 grt. After rebuilding: 1,431 grt. Engine: One Alfa Laval steam turbine. Power output: 1,600 hp. Speed: 14 knots. Passengers: 465.

S/S BIRGER JARL
Built: 1953 by Finnboda Varv, Nacka, Sweden. Dimensions: 92.50 x 14.28 x 5.50 m. Tonnage: 2,798 grt. Engine: One 4-cyl steam engine. Power output: 3,300 hp. Speed: 15 knots. Passengers: 515. Cabin berths: 515. Vehicle capacity: 30 cars.

S/S SVEA JARL – See APOLLO III

M/S SVEA REGINA
Built: 1972 by Dubigeon-Normandie S.A., Nantes, France. Dimensions: 126.93 x 19.59 x 5.15 m. Tonnage: 8,020 grt. Engines: Two Pielstick 16PC2 V-400 diesels. Power output: 11,770 kW. Speed: 21 knots. Passengers: 1,000. Cabin berths: 412. Vehicle capacity: 170 cars.

M/S SVEA CORONA
Built: 1975 by Dubigeon-Normandie S.A., Nantes, France. Dimensions: 153.00 x 22.04 x 5.80 m. Tonnage: 13,275 grt. Engines: Four SEMT-Pielstick 12 PC2 2V-400 diesels. Power output: 17,904 kW. Speed: 21 knots. Passengers: 1,200. Cabin berths: 674. Vehicle capacity: 240 cars.

M/S SILVIA REGINA
Built: 1981 by Oy Wärtsilä AB, Perno Varvet (hull). Outfitted by Oy Wärtsilä AB, City Varvet, Turku, Finland. Dimensions: 166.10 x 28.46 x 6.70 m. Tonnage: 25,905 grt. Engines: Four Wärtsilä-Pielstick 12PC2 5V diesels. Power output: 22,948 kW. Speed: 22 knots. Passengers: 2,000. Cabin berths: 1,601. Vehicle capacity: 450 cars, 70 trucks.

M/S SVEA
Ordered by Rederi AB Svea, but delivered to Rederi AB Nordstjernan. Built: 1985 by Oy Wärtsilä AB, Helsinki, Finland. Dimensions: 168.03 x 27.60 x 6.70 m. Tonnage: 33,829 gt. Engines: Four Wärtsilä-Pielstick 12PC 6V diesels. Power output: 26,200 kW. Speed: 22 knots. Passengers: 1,803. Cabin berths: 1,625. Vehicle capacity: 400 cars, 60 trucks.

## EFFJOHN

M/S SILJA SERENADE
Built: 1990 by Masa-Yards Oy, Turku, Finland. Dimensions: 203.03 x 31.93 x 7.12 m. Tonnage: 58,376 gt. Engines: Four Wärtsilä-Vaasa 9R46 diesels. Power output: 32,560 kW. Speed: 21.5 knots. Passengers: 2,626. Cabin berths: 2,626. Vehicle capacity: 450 cars, 60 trucks.

M/S SILJA SYMPHONY
Built: 1991 by Masa-Yards Oy, Turku, Finland. Dimensions: 203.00 x 31.50 x 7.10 m. Tonnage: 58,376 gt. Engines: Four Wärtsilä-Vaasa 9R46 diesels. Power output: 32,560 kW. Speed: 21.5 knots. Passengers: 2,626. Cabin berths: 2,626. Vehicle capacity: 450 cars, 60 trucks.

M/S SILJA EUROPA – See EUROPA
M/S SILJA SCANDINAVIA – See GABRIELLA

## FINNLINES Oy

### M/S HANSA EXPRESS
Built: 1962 by Hanseatiche Werft GmbH, Hamburg, West Germany. Dimensions: 88.20 x 15.85 x 4.40 m. After rebuilding: 95.99 x 15.88 x 4.47 m. Tonnage: 2,268 grt. After rebuilding 1963: 2,977 grt. Engines: Two Nohab-Polar M66TS diesels. Power output: 4,297 kW. Speed: 16 knots. Passengers: 419. After rebuilding 1963: 680. Cabin berths: 173. After rebuilding 1963: 259. Vehicle capacity after rebuilding 1963: 125 cars.

### M/S FINNHANSA
Built: 1966 by Oy Wärtsilä AB, Helsinki, Finland. Dimensions: 134.40 x 20.10 x 5.70 m. Tonnage: 7,820 grt. Engines: Two Wärtsilä-Sulzer 8RD56 diesels. Power output: 10,300 kW. Speed: 20 knots. Passengers: 1,424. Cabin berths: 350. Vehicle capacity: 308 cars.

### M/S FINNPARTNER
Built: 1966 by Oy Wärtsilä AB, Helsinki, Finland. Dimensions: 134.40 x 19.90 x 5.20 m. Tonnage: 7,458 grt. Engines: Two Wärtsilä-Sulzer 8RD56 diesels. Power output: 10,300 kW. Speed: 21 knots. Passengers: 1,400. Cabin berths: 612. Vehicle capacity: 241 cars, 18 trucks.

### M/S FINNPARTNER (ex SAGA, ex STENA ATLANTICA)
Built: 1966 by Lindholmens Varv, Gothenburg, Sweden. Dimensions: 141.20 x 20.96 x 5.34 m. Tonnage: 8,869 grt. Engines: Four 6-cyl 6PC2 2L400 Lindholmens-Pielstick diesels. Power output: 10,000 hp. Speed: 20 knots. Passengers: 408. Cabin berths: 408. Vehicle capacity: 300 cars.

### GTS/M/S FINNJET
See under Silja Line/Finska Ångfartygs Aktiebolaget.

## BIRKA LINE

### M/S PRINSESSAN (ex PRINSESSEN, ex PRINSESSE MARGRETHE)
Built: 1957 by Helsingør Skibs & Maskinbyggeri A/S, Helsingør, Denmark. Dimensions: 121.03 x 16.18 x 4.87 m. Tonnage: 5,061 grt. Engines: Two B&W 850-VBF-90 diesels. Power output: 7,300 hp. Speed: 20.5 knots. Passengers: 1,200. Cabin berths: 395. Vehicle capacity: 35 cars.

### M/S BARONESSAN (ex KONG OLAV V)
Built: 1961 by Aalborg Værft A/S, Aalborg, Denmark. Dimensions: 121.01 x 16.18 x 5.10 m. Tonnage: 4,555 grt. Engines: Two B&W 850-VBF-90 diesels. Power output: 5,595 kW. Speed: 20.5 knots. Passengers: 977. Cabin berths: 220. Vehicle capacity: 18 cars.

### M/S FREEPORT
Built: 1968 by Orenstein-Koppel und Lübecker Machinenbau, Lübeck, West Germany. Dimensions: 134.42 x 21.50 x 5.50 m. Tonnage: 10,448 grt. Engines: Two Pielstick 16PC2 V diesels. Power output: 11,768 kW. Speed: 19 knots. Passengers: 812. Cabin berths: 690. Vehicle capacity: 220 cars.

### M/S DROTTNINGEN
Built: 1968 by Uddevallavarvet AB, Uddevalla, Sweden. Dimensions: 115.70 x 18.02 x 4.75 m. Tonnage: 5,625 grt. Engines: Four Pielstick 12PV-400 diesels. Power output: 8,210 kW. Speed: 18 knots. Passengers: 1,000. Cabin berths: 347. Vehicle capacity: 175 cars, 3 railway tracks capable of holding 23 wagons.

### M/S PRINSESSAN – See FINNHANSA

### M/S BIRKA PRINCESS
Built: 1986 by Oy Valmet AB, Helsinki, Finland. Dimensions: 142.9 x 24.7 x 5.75 m. Tonnage: 21,484 gt. Engines: Four Wärtsilä-Vaasa 12V32 diesels. Power output: 17,652 kW. Speed: 20 knots. Passengers: 1,500. After rebuilding 1999: 1,537. Cabin berths: 1,394. After rebuilding 1999: 1,537. Vehicle capacity: 80 cars (no vehicle capacity after rebuilding as the car deck was converted to cabins).

### M/S BIRKA PARADISE
Built: 2004 by Aker Finnyards Oy, Rauma, Finland. Dimensions: 177.00 x 28.00 x 6.50 m. Tonnage: 34,728 gt. Engines: Four Wärtsilä 6L46 diesels. Power output: 23,400 kW. Speed: 21 knots. Passengers: 1,800. Cabin berths: 1,800.

## TALLINK

### M/S TALLINK – See SVEA REGINA
### M/S SAINT PATRICK II – See AURELLA
### M/S GEORG OTS
Built: 1980 by Stocnia Szczecinska im A Warskiego, Szczecin, Poland. Dimensions: 125.00 x 21.00 x 5.70 m. Tonnage: 9,841 grt. Engines: Four Sulzer-Zgoda 6 LZ40/48 diesels. Power output: 12,800 kW. Speed: 18 knots. Passengers: 600. Cabin berths: 340. Vehicle capacity: 150 cars.

### M/S VANA TALLINN (ex NORD ESTONIA, ex DANA REGINA)
Built: 1974 by Aalborg Værft A/S, Aalborg, Denmark. Dimensions: 153.70 x 22.31 x 6.00 m. Tonnage: 10,002 grt. Engines: Four B&W DM845HU diesels. Power output: 12,945 kW. Speed: 21.5 knots. After 1996 re-engining: Two Zgoda Sulzer 6ZAL 40 S diesels plus two B&W DM845HU diesels. After 2001 re-engining: Two Två Zgoda Sulzer 6ZAL 40 S diesels plus two Zgoda Sulzer 8ZL 40/48 diesels. Power output: 12,250 kW. Speed: 18 knots. Passengers: 1,500. Cabin berths: 861. Vehicle capacity: 370 cars.

### M/S CORBIERE – See APOLLO (1970)
### M/S BALANGA QUEEN – See FREEPORT
### M/S MELOODIA – See DIANA II
### M/S NORMANDY (ex PRINSESSAN BIRGITTA)
Built: 1981 by Götaverken Arendal AB, Gothenburg, Sweden. Dimensions: 149.03 x 26.01 x 6.10 m. Tonnage: 14,368 grt. Engines: Four Nohab-Wärtsilä Vaasa 12V32A diesels. Power output: 15,360 kW. Speed: 19.5 knots. Passengers: 2,060. Cabin berths: 1,156. Vehicle capacity: 450 cars, 50 trucks.

### M/S FANTAASIA – See TURELLA
### M/S BALTIC KRISTINA – See BORE I
### M/S REGINA BALTICA – See VIKING SONG
### M/S ROMANTIKA
Built: 2002 by Aker Finnyards, Rauma, Finland. Dimensions: 193.80 x 29.00 x 6.50 m. Tonnage: 39,864 gt. Engines: Four Wärtsilä 16V32 diesels. Power output: 26,240 kW. Speed: 22 knots. Passengers: 2,500. Cabin berths: 2,172. Vehicle capacity: 300 cars.

### M/S VICTORIA I
Built: 2004 by Aker Finnyards, Rauma, Finland. Dimensions: 193.80 x 29.00 x 6.50 m. Tonnage: 40,975 gt. Engines: Four Wärtsilä 16V32 diesels. Power output: 26,240 kW. Speed: 22 knots. Passengers: 2,500. Cabin berths: 2,252. Vehicle capacity: 400 cars.

M/S *SUPERFAST VII*, M/S *SUPERFAST VIII* and M/S *SUPERFAST IX*
Built: 2001 by Howaldtswerke-Deutsche Werft AG, Kiel, Germany. Dimensions: 203.90 x 25.00 x 6.60 m. Tonnage: 30,285 gt. Engines: Four Wärtsilä-Sulzer 12ZAV40S diesels. Power output: 46,000 kW. Speed: 28.9 knots. Passengers: 626. Cabin berths: 626. Vehicle capacity: 661 cars.

M/S *GALAXY*
Built: 2006 by Aker Finnyards, Rauma, Finland. Dimensions: 212.10 x 29.00 x 6.40 m. Tonnage: 48,915 gt. Engines: Four Wärtsilä 16V32 diesels. Power output: 26,240 kW. Speed: 22 knots. Passengers: 2,800. Cabin berths: 2,500. Vehicle capacity: 420 cars.

M/S *STAR*
Built: 2007 by Aker Finnyards, Helsinki, Finland. Dimensions: 186.00 x 27.70 x 6.50 m. Tonnage: 36,250 gt. Engines: Four Caterpillar-MaK 12M43C diesels. Power output: 48,000 kW. Speed: 27.5 knots. Passengers: 1,900. Cabin berths: 520. Vehicle capacity: 450 cars.

M/S *SUPERSTAR*
Built: 2008 by Fincantieri Cantieri Navali Italiani SpA Stabilimento di Ancona, Ancona, Italy. Dimensions: 176.95 x 27.60 x 7.10 m. Tonnage: 36,277 gt. Engines: Four 12-cyl Wärtsilä diesels. Power output: 50,400 kW. Speed: 27 knots. Passengers: 2,020. Cabin berths: 1,256. Vehicle capacity: 665 cars.

M/S *BALTIC PRINCESS*
Built: 2008 by Aker Yards, Helsinki, Finland. Forward section of hull fabricated by Aker Yards, Saint Nazaire, France and towed to Finland. Dimensions: 212.10 x 29.00 x 6.40 m. Tonnage: 48,915 gt. Engines: Four Wärtsilä 16V32 diesels. Power output: 32,000 kW. Speed: 24.5 knots. Passengers: 2,800. Cabin berths: 2,500. Vehicle capacity: 600 cars.

## Appendix 2
## Names in Swedish and Finnish

Bolaget: Company
AB, or Aktiebolaget: Company Limited (literally 'Shareholder Company')
Rederi: Shipping company
Rederi AB: Shipping Company Limited
In Finland, both Finnish and Swedish are official languages. Thus, most large towns and cities have both Finnish and Swedish names. In this book, the Finnish version has been used wherever possible:
Finnish: Swedish
Helsinki: Helsingfors
Turku: Åbo
Naantali: Nådendal
Vaasa: Vasa

## Appendix 3
## Short Company Histories

Viking Line and its constituents
The origins of Viking Line go back to 1959, but the name was used as a joint marketing brand identity from 1966 onwards.

Rederi AB Vikinglinjen/Rederi AB Solstad/Rederi AB Sally (Mariehamn)
Founded in 1959 by Gunnar Eklund and Henning Rundberg with financial backing from Algot Johansson, the owner of Rederi AB Sally. Renamed Rederi AB Solstad in 1966 when Viking Line became the brand name for all ferries belonging to the firm, as well as those of Rederi AB Slite and Rederi AB Ålandsfärjan. When Algot Johansson became the majority shareholder in Rederi AB Solstad shortly thereafter, the company was absorbed into Rederi AB Sally. Johansson retired in 1976 and Rederi AB Sally subsequently over-invested in a number of shipping enterprises. The major creditor, Föreningsbanken, took control and in 1987 and sold 66% of the shares to Effoa and Johnson Line, the parent companies of Silja Line. At this point, Rederi AB Sally ceased to be involved in Viking Line's operations. Later, in 1990, the two formed a joint company, Effjohn, to buy the remaining shares. Rederi AB Sally's operations were subsequently fully absorbed into Silja Line.

Rederi AB Slite (Slite)
Founded in 1959 by Carl Bertil Myrsten, a shipowner whose family lived in Slite, a village on the island of Gotland. Declared bankrupt in 1993 and assets liquidated.

Rederi AB Ålandsfärjan/Oy SF Line AB/Viking Line (Mariehamn)
After Gunnar Eklund withdrew from the Board of Rederi AB Vikinglinjen, he founded Rederi AB Ålandsfärjan in 1963. This was renamed SF Line in 1969. Following first the sale of Rederi AB Sally to Silja Line's parent companies and then the bankruptcy of Rederi AB Slite, SF Line became the sole surviving Viking Line company and so the name was changed to Viking Line.

Silja Line and its constituents
Silja Line was formed in 1957 as a jointly-owned subsidiary of three established Swedish and Finnish shipping companies: Rederi AB Svea, headquartered in Stockholm, Finska Ångfartygs Aktiebolaget, based in Helsinki, and Ångfartygs Aktiebolaget Bore of Turku. In 1970, Silja Line became a marketing brand name and the ownership and operation of the ships was split between the three owning companies. In 1976, Finska Ångfartygs Aktiebolaget was renamed Effoa, the phonetic pronunciation of the initials 'FÅA'.

In 1980, Ångfartygs Aktiebolaget Bore withdrew from the Silja Line consortium, concentrating instead on the operation of freight ro-ro ferries. In 1981, Rederi AB Svea withdrew from shipping operations and became a property development company. Rederi AB Svea's ships were taken over by Rederi AB Nordstjernan, which traded as Johnson Line. In 1990, Effoa and Johnson Line formed a joint company, Effjohn, to buy the remaining shares in Rederi AB Sally and, in 1992, the two companies merged fully as Effjohn International. In 1995, the firm was renamed Silja Oy AB. In 1997, it became Neptune Marine. In 1999, Sea Containers bought 50% of the capital in Neptune Marine, increasing their shareholding to 92% by 2002. The company was renamed Silja Oy AB. When Sea Containers went bankrupt in 2006, Silja was sold to Tallink. It is presently a subsidiary of Tallink Grupp.

## Appendix 4
## Translations of Ship Names

Viking Line
Rederi AB Vikinglinjen/Rederi AB Solstad/Rederi AB Sally:
All ships had 'Viking' names with a numerical suffix until the early 1980s, when the *Viking Song*, the *Viking Saga* and the *Viking Sally* were introduced.
Rederi AB Slite:
Apart from the initial ferries converted from coasters, all Rederi AB Slite ships, except the *Kalypso,* were named after gods in Greek and Roman mythology:
*Apollo*: Ancient Greek God of Light and Sun.
*Diana*: Roman Goddess of the Moon.
*Olympia*: Site of Ancient Greek Olympic Games.
*Athena*: Ancient Greek Goddess who was Patron of Athens.
*Europa*: Phoenician Princess in Greek mythology after whom the continent of Europe was named.
Rederi AB Ålandsfärjan/SF Line/Viking Line:
The first and second generations of ships belonging to this company took their names from the first syllable of towns and regions to which they operated, with the suffix 'ella' being derived from 'Ellen', the wife of the shipowner Gunnar Eklund:
*Kapella*: Kapellskär, a Swedish ferry port to the east of Stockholm, plus 'ella'.
*Marella/Mariella*: Mariehamn, the main port town on the Åland Islands where the company is headquartered, plus 'ella'.
*Aurella*: The River Aura, which flows through Turku, plus 'ella'.
*Turella*: Turku, a Finnish port and shipbuilding city, plus 'ella'.
*Rosella*: Roslagen, the region to the north and east of Stockholm, plus 'ella'.

Subsequent vessels were given supposedly romantic names, such as the *Amorella* and the *Cinderella*.
Silja Line
Initial Silja Line ships were given the Latin names of areas around the Baltic:
*Skandia*: Latin for the Scandinavian Peninsula.
*Nordia*: Latin for 'The North'.
*Holmia*: Derived from 'Stockholm'
*Fennia*: Latin for Finland.
*Bothnia*: The Latin name of the northern part of the Baltic Sea (ie the Gulf of Bothnia).
*Floria*: Derived from 'Flower', as reflected in the slightly psychedelic theme of the ship's interior design.
Following a reorganization in 1970, the ships were split between the three owning companies and Silja Line became only a marketing brand name. All subsequent new-buildings perpetuated the traditional naming policies of each of the owning companies:
Finska Ångfartygs Aktiebolaget/Effoa
Ships of the FÅA/Effoa fleet generally were named after figures in Finnish folk mythology, particularly female characters associated with water in the Kalevala:
*Aallotar*: A water nymph whose presence calms the sea and, therefore, she is revered by seasick travellers.
*Ilmatar*: Daughter of the wind.
*Wellamo*: Lady of the lakes.
*Oihonna*: The girl from the waves.
*Finlandia*: Named after the famous suite by the composer Sibelius.
Other FÅA/Effoa vessels had names derived from Greek mythology:

The **Silja Festival** approaches Oxdjupet in August 2008. She has recently been swtiched from the Silja Line fleet to that of Tallink and introduced on the route from Stockholm to Riga. Now, she is 24 years old and, therefore, probably approaching the end of her career on the Baltic. *(Bruce Peter)*

*Ariadne*: Daughter of King Minos and Queen Pasiphae of Crete; helped Theseus to overcome the Minotaur and became consort of Dionysus.

*Arcturus*: The fourth brightest star in the sky (from the Greek 'Great Bear').

Ångfartygs Aktiebolaget Bore

Ships of the Bore Line were named *Bore*, followed by a numerical suffix. King Bore was the Nordic God of Winter.

Rederi AB Svea

Post-war passenger ships of Rederi AB Svea usually used the prefix 'Svea', the Latin name for Sweden, followed by a suffix. The *Birger Jarl* and the *Silvia Regina* were exceptions:

*Birger Jarl*: Earl Birger, 13th century Swedish aristocrat who consolidated Sweden and reputedly founded Stockholm around 1250.

*Svea Jarl*: Swedish Earl.

*Svea Regina*: Swedish Queen.

*Svea Corona*: Swedish Crown.

*Silvia Regina*: HM Queen Silvia of Sweden, consort to King Carl Gustav XVI.

## BIBLIOGRAPHY

Ahlerup, Anders Apollo III: Ett fartyg och dess rederi (Mar Production, Solna, 1988).

Bergenek, Anders and Brogren, Klas Passagerare till Sjöss: Den svenska färjesjöfartens historia (Shippax, Halmstad, 2006).

Björk, Hans-Göran Den Ene Den Var Vit…Om konsten at sänka skepp (HGB Media, Stockholm, 2006).

Blomgren, Riitta, Malmberg, Thure and Raudsepp, Paul Ett Skepp Anlöpte Helsingfors (Oy Raud Publishing Oy, Helsinki, 1996).

Breeze, Geoffrey H. The Papenburg Sisters (Kingfisher Railway Productions, Southampton, 1988).

Burgess, Jacqueline and Gold, John R. Geography, The Media and Popular Culture (Croom Helm, London,1985).

Chaney, D. Public Drama in Late Modern Culture (Routledge, London, 1993).

Cunningham, H. Leisure in the Industrial Revolution (Croom Helm, London, 1980).

Dawson, Philip Cruise Ships: An Evolution in Design (Conway Maritime Press, London, 2000).

Dumell, Matts Sjövägen till Sverige (Schildts Forlag, Helsinki, 2007).

Eliasson, Thor-Alf Med Carl Bertil Myrsten från Ö til Ö: En envisgottlänning och färjetrafiken Sverige-Åland-Finland (Viking Line, Stockholm, 1990).

Jackson, Peter Maps of Meaning: An Introduction to Cultural Geography (Unwin Hyman, London, 1989).

Jansson, Gösta Fartyg jag skådat – en hamnroddare I Stockholm mins sitt 1690-tal (Trafik-Nostalgiska förlaget, Stockholm, 2004).

Kendrew, W.G. The Climates of the Continents (Oxford University Press, 1941).

Malmberg, Thure and Stampehl, Marko Femtio år med Silja ((Tallink Silja OY, Helsinki, 2007).

Mead, W.R. and Smeds, H. Winter in Finland (Allen and Unwin, London, 1967).

Peter, Bruce Knud E. Hansen A/S: Ship Design through Seven Decades (Forlaget Nautilus, Copenhagen, 2007).

Plummer, Russell Superferries of Britain, Europe and Scandinavia (Patrick Stephens Ltd,Wellingborough, 1988).

Quartermaine, Peter Building on the Sea: Form and Meaning in Ship Architecture (Academy Editions, London, 1996).

Stenros, Manne and Hornmalm, Erik (eds) Sea & Food (Studio Avec Audiovisual Ky, Lahti and Stockholm, 2003).

Urry, John The Tourist Gaze: Leisure and Travel in Contemporary Societies (Nottingham Trent University TCS series, Nottingham, 1990).

Venturi, Robert, Scott-Brown, Denise and Izenour, Stephen Learning from Las Vegas: The Forgotten Symbolism of Architectural Form (MIT Press, Cambridge, Mass., 1972).

Viking Line 25 (Viking Line, Mariehamn, 1984).

En man och hans linje: Gunnar Eklund och färjetrafiken Sverige-Åland-Finland (Viking Line, Mariehamn, 1986)

Witthöft, Hans Jürgen Meyer Werft: Innivativer Schiffbau aus Papenburg (Koehlers Verlagsgesellschaft, Hamburg, 2005)

European Ferry Scene

Cruise & Ferry Info

Designs

European Ferry Scene

Guide

Hansa

The Motor Ship

The Scandinavian Shipping Gazette

Sea Breezes

Shipbuilder and Shipping record

Shipping World and Shipbuilder

Ships Monthly

The Shipping Record

Svenska Sjöfarts Tidning

## ACKNOWLEDGEMENTS

My especial thanks to Miles Cowsill and to John Hendy for their enthusiasm and kind assistance with this publication, to Klas Brogren for reading the manuscript, to David Parsons for editing the manuscript and to John Peter for preparing the illustrations.

My thanks to:

Peter Albrecht; Micke Asklander; Anders Bergenek; Stephen Berry; Jonathan Boonzaier; Klas Brogren; David Buri; Anthony Cooke; Philip Dawson; Nils-Erik Eklund; Ambrose Greenway; Dr. Ann Glen; Knud E. Hansen A/S; Søren Lund Hviid; Per Jensen; Peter Knego; Tarja Koskinen; Srecko Kurtovic; Mick Lindsay; Glenn Mattas; William Mayes; Keijo Mehtonen; Clare Price; René Taudal Poulsen; Mate Renic; Henrik Segercrantz; Tony Smith; Johan Snellman; Tage Wandborg; Thomas Wigforss.